Create Your Own Desktop Publishing System

Other books by Harley Bjelland

How to Sell Your Own House Without a Broker

How to Buy the Right Home

Writing Better Technical Articles

The Write Stuff

Business Writing—The Modular Way

Using Online Scientific and Engineering Databases

Online Systems: How to Access and Use Computer Data Bases:
A Guide to Electronic Information Sources for Health Care
Professionals

Outrageous DR DOS Batch File Programming (coauthored with Dan
Gookin)

Free and Low-Cost Software for Scientists and Engineers

Other books in the Create Your Own Series

Configuring a Customized Engineering Workstation
by *Harley Bjelland*

Create Your Own Graphics Workstation by *Horace W. LaBadie, Jr.*

Create Your Own Virtual Reality System by *Joseph R. Levy* and
Harley Bjelland

Create Your Own Multimedia System by *John A. McCormick*

Create Your Own Desktop Publishing System

Harley Bjelland

Windcrest®/ McGraw-Hill

New York   San Francisco   Washington, D.C.   Auckland   Bogotá
Caracas   Lisbon   London   Madrid   Mexico City   Milan
Montreal   New Delhi   San Juan   Singapore
Sydney   Tokyo   Toronto

1 2 3 4 5 6 7 8 9 0   DOH/DOH   9 9 8 7 6 5 4

Library of Congress Cataloging-in-Publication Data

Bjelland, Harley.
   Create your own desktop publishing system / by Harley Bjelland.
     p.   cm.
   Includes bibliographical references and index.
   ISBN 0-07-005923-3 (pbk.)
    1. Desktop publishing—Equipment and supplies.   I. Title.
Z253.53.B59 1994
686.2'2544536'028—dc20   94-5619
                                                       CIP

Acquisitions editor: Brad J. Shepp
Editorial team: Robert Ostrander, Executive Editor
                Aaron Bittner, Book Editor
Production team: Katherine G. Brown, Director
                  Ollie Harmon, Coding
                  Susan Hansford, Coding
                  Rose McFarland, Desktop operator
                  Linda L. King, Proofreading
                  Stephanie Myers, Computer Illustrator
                  Jodi L. Tyler, Indexer
Design team: Jaclyn J. Boone, Designer
             Brian Allison, Associate Designer
Cover design: Stickles Associates, Bath, PA.
Cover photograph © L. Bertrand/Superstock Inc.   0059233
Cover copy writer: Cathy Mentzer   WK2

Dedication

To my beloved and ever patient wife:

Dorrie, a.k.a Tokiko

Acknowledgments

My sincere thanks to my agent, Magnanimous Matt Wagner, of Waterside Productions, and to Benevolent Brad Schepp, of Windcrest/McGraw-Hill, both of whom conspired to induce me to write this book.

Special thanks to editor Aaron Bittner who turned my rough draft into near perfect prose, and to all the other talented people who contributed to this book.

Uffdah! It was great fun.

Contents

Part 3
Peripheral upgrades

Introduction

Until recently, creating high-quality documents having text integrated with graphics and photographs was the restricted province of graphics specialists, artists, and layout designers. In 1975, Aldus Corporation created PageMaker for the Macintosh and the revolution known as desktop publishing began. At last DTP professionals were freed from the frustration and expense of tortuous typesetting and pragmatic pasteup. For the first time an entire page of text and graphics could be blended and concocted quickly, economically, and viewed on an interactive display screen.

Modern computer software and hardware developments have now obsoleted the T-square, rubber cement, pasteup, and the laborious and onerous tasks of making changes. Omphaloskepsis has been supplemented by a multi-color display, a mouse, and a keyboard.

Replacing these manual tools are high-speed hardware and easy-to-use software which have automated these tasks, a serendipity making it possible for virtually anyone to be able to create and publish all types of quality publications, ranging from black-and-white, single page announcements, to multi-color newsletters, luminous ads, sage periodicals, and brilliant books. The modern era of desktop publications has revolutionized the world of publishing and provided

the tools to create new and revolutionary methods of sharing knowledge.

 # What this book can do for you

This book is written so that people entirely new to the DTP profession, as well as experienced DTP virtuosos, can learn more about the hardware and software elements which respond to one's mind, eyes, and hands. The synergism of mind and body has empowered those of us who could not draw a straight line with a ruler (that includes me) to be able to create art and graphics that were far beyond our ken a few years ago.

Emphasis in this instructive manual is on learning how to choose the proper empowerment hardware and software to accomplish all varieties of DTP tasks from gorgeous graphics, to heady headlines, to towering titles, to kaleidoscopic colors.

With these new tools, you can unleash your imagination, liberate the thoughts which have lain imprisoned in your mind, ideas that have flourished in your intellect, but which you did not know how to bring to fruition.

Desktop publishing is not just putting words on paper and adding a few graphics. It is a highly creative task, probably one of the most imaginative of all professions associated with the teaching, seduction, enticement, and captivation of your audience to not only see your message, but also to be influenced, entertained, educated, and excited by it.

But hardware and software are only tools, the nuts and bolts, the wood and nails, the bricks and mortar. It is the truly creative mind that is needed to combine these primary elements in such a manner that they produce documents, brochures, and advertisements which literally shout to be heard. Ideas are fine fodder, but unless you do something worthwhile with them, they remain only insignificant specks of neurons locked inside your brain.

 # Who can profit from this book?

Readers can use this book to upgrade their existing PC, to procure a new or used PC and upgrade it, or to build their own DTP system from scratch. Most of the chapters are modular in that one does not have to read every chapter to accomplish the tasks described in a given chapter.

Although the primary emphasis in this text is hardware, several DTP software programs are also reviewed with respect to the impact they have on the hardware. In this sense, the software drives the hardware, because if the hardware is inadequate, the software is unproductive.

Emphasis is on the ability to upgrade gradually, one step at a time. Not only is this wise from an economic standpoint, it is also sagacious in that you need to thoroughly evaluate any new components you add to your DTP system to make sure that both the hardware and software are compatible for all their modes of operation. If you add several improvements at once and discover incompatibilities, you'd be at a loss to determine the culprit.

The same is true of software. Add only a single program at a time and thoroughly exercise it before you install additional software.

So, enjoy. The journey you are about to embark on can be an exciting one and rewarding in many ways, in outcomes you never dreamed possible. This book will only give you a start, provide the key tools you need. How you fare on this journey is up to you.

Good luck. And may the wind always be at your back.

1

Welcome to desktop publishing

DESKTOP publishing (DTP) is the process of combining text and graphics to create documents. DTP is a rapidly expanding and fascinating field of endeavor. It's growing faster than a teenager's ravenous appetite. More and more the personal computer (PC) is being called upon to produce a wider and more diverse variety of publications, ranging from single-page flyers to newsletters to fully-illustrated, multivolume, full-color documents. And never before has the demand for image manipulation been greater, or more important to one's success.

Over the past few years, most of the onerous and arduous DTP tasks have been computerized. No longer do you have to contend with limited capabilities, lack of time, and trial-and-error pasteups where a minor change throws your schedule off like the arrival of a new baby in a family. Now you can throw away your T-square, your X-acto knife, and your rubber cement. With modern DTP hardware and software you can easily and quickly envision, implement, improvise, experiment with, and finalize all of your pasteups on a fast-reacting and accurate computer screen. Converting your innovations to a practical design has never been easier.

There are no special educational or technical requirements to use this book. It doesn't matter whether you are a neophyte or a pro in the art and science of desktop publishing. You need not be a computer expert, either, to profit from this book. Computer jargon is minimized; considerable use is made of photos. Explanations emphasize the how-to-do-it aspect, rather than detailing how the computer hardware and software accomplish their functions. You don't even have to know how to spell DOS or Windows to benefit from this handbook.

You will learn how to create a desktop publishing system that will open totally new horizons for you, horizons limited not by technology, but only by your own creativity and your own imagination. The technical shackles which previously had been imposed on you have been broken by modern advancements in DTP technology.

Progress is inevitable

Even when you do create what you consider to be an ideal DTP system for your use, you will never be finished with it. As sure as the coming of a tiny toddler's tottering first steps, the creative and highly motivated individuals working in the computer profession are going to continue to develop advanced hardware and software that will improve and often revolutionize DTP and related applications: multimedia, virtual reality, faster and faster hardware, wider buses, pen and voice input . . . So, no matter what kind of PC you purchase, assemble, or upgrade, it will be outdated as soon as you plug it in.

But don't let the inevitability of progress discourage you. Consider these innovations as positive developments for you and take advantage of these enhancements. Using the methods covered in this book, you don't have to keep discarding your existing computer whenever some new and exciting hardware or software becomes available. You can accommodate the continual improvements by learning as much as possible about the hardware and software that your computer uses so you can make the proper decisions with respect to incorporating the new developments. That is the goal of this book.

Modern computers are designed to be easily upgraded, so you can keep your computer "tintinnabulating" for many years to come if you follow the procedures I describe. You can continually upgrade it at a pace determined by your needs and your budget. This book shows you how to maintain pace with all new software and hardware developments for a minimum cost, without puzzlement, and with maximum effectiveness.

 # According to the IRS

Here's another excellent and pragmatic reason for upgrading your computer rather than buying a new model: If you claim your computer as a tax deduction, the Internal Revenue Service insists that

your PC has a life of five years, so they won't allow you to discard your old Model-T PC until you have fully amortized it. Unable to take advantage of the rapid developments in technology, according to the IRS you'll have to chug along with your low-mileage system, your inadequate disk drive, your small screen display, and your slow CPU.

But there is a way out of this dilemma. You can upgrade your computer, improvement by improvement, module by module. Add more RAM, a bigger disk, a CD-ROM drive. Your upgrade modules can probably be expensed immediately as replacement parts or components, rather than as a capital expenditure that must be depreciated over a period of five years. In this way you can incorporate all of the modern developments and deduct their cost.

Accommodating continued hardware improvements, the personal computer has been designed with inherent upgrade potential. Spare plug-in card slots, spare bays, and standard, interchangeable component sizes for increasing capacity and speed make upgrading easy and economical. Just keep your old case and keep adding improvements, upgrade the insides with the latest low-cost high-capacity disk drive, more RAM, a faster CPU or motherboard, a new display driver and so on; take advantage of the latest developments.

You can always have a "new" computer and deduct it, too.

Possible paths

Four possible paths for achieving a given level of proficiency in creating DTP documents are covered in this book.

Path 1—Upgrade your computer's DTP capability

The approach illustrated in Fig. 1-1 assumes that you already have a clone computer you wish to upgrade to provide more desktop publishing power.

Figure 1-1

Upgrade path No. 1.

Upgrades can include adding more RAM, a larger hard disk, a modem/fax board, a scanner, a higher resolution and larger monitor, a removable backup media, and so on.

Using this path you don't need to discard your old computer that the IRS has assigned the long life of five years. You're simply going to perform some easy-to-accomplish transplants that will modernize your computer as your budget and needs dictate, and as new hardware and software developments become available. Path 1 provides you with a custom DTP system that continues to grow with your needs and lets you add new capabilities as they are developed to considerably enhance your desktop publishing capabilities. Sooner or later the other three paths merge into this one, because all of the other paths are amenable to upgrading.

⇨ Path 2—Buy a custom DTP computer

Path 2 lets you specify and purchase precisely what you want in a clone computer. You list the specific components you want in your DTP system and a component vendor assembles and tests the computer for you. Path 2 is illustrated in Fig. 1-2.

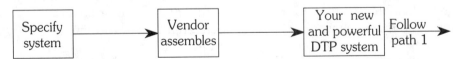

Figure 1-2

Upgrade path No. 2.

One important advantage of this approach is that you obtain a system in which all of the components will work together, because the vendor who assembles your custom clone per your specifications

assumes the responsibility that everything will function as a unit. This is an excellent approach if you have any qualms about building your first one from scratch. Once you use this approach, open the case and look inside; you'll see how easy it is going to be to accomplish further upgrades.

This path may be a little more expensive than Path 1 because you have to purchase all of the components from a single vendor and will have little bargaining power. You may opt to purchase a very basic DTP system and upgrade by adding new components later, following Path 1.

⇨ Path 3—Build it yourself

If you're considering assembling your own computer from scratch by procuring the individual components, this book shows you what to purchase and how to assemble the components. This path, illustrated in Fig. 1-3, is similar to Path 2 except that you design your own system, then purchase the DTP components from one or several different vendors.

Figure 1-3

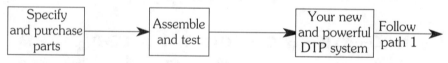

Upgrade path No. 3.

In this way you can shop for the best competitive prices and save some money in the process. Not only is this approach economical, this is also an excellent path from an educational standpoint. You will get unbeatable on-the-job training regarding which components go into a computer, how they interconnect, what functions they accomplish, and how to optimize them for your requirements. This path also prepares you for further upgrading as your DTP needs change.

 # Path 4—For tight budgets

To use Path 4, the low budget approach illustrated in Fig. 1-4, you purchase a used (but still functioning) clone computer at a low cost. If your budget is extremely tight, you'll learn how to periodically upgrade it as your finances and needs dictate.

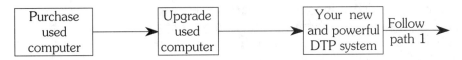

Figure 1-4

Upgrade path No. 4.

Because many versions of clone computers are no longer being manufactured, they are available from users, computer stores, ads, and computer swap meets. They can usually be purchased for around a couple of hundred dollars. This gives you an excellent foundation to begin with.

If your budget is very tight, you can use this bootstrap approach; you begin with a minimal, low-cost hardware and software system configuration and build up your clone as your budget and earnings allow. (You don't need to do Windows for a low-budget DTP system.) For starters, you don't need a color monitor; a CGA monochrome monitor will suffice. For a printed output you can utilize a low-cost (even a "previously owned") 9-pin dot matrix printer. Shareware software programs (see appendix C) can control the dot matrix printer so it makes multiple passes. This significantly improves the 9-pin printing quality, providing an output that is acceptable for many DTP applications. If you need a much higher resolution for your output, you can store your document on a disk and bring it to a print shop, where they can provide a high-quality print output.

Free and low-cost software programs are available for use in desktop publishing. One excellent, full-featured, WYSIWYG desktop publishing program available in the shareware market is Envision Publisher. Several other software DTP and word processing programs are available that can function in an elemental DTP mode of

combining text and graphics. A huge volume of free and low-cost clip art is also available in the shareware market.

This path is a good one to follow if your budget is minimal and you're anxious to get started in DTP. Your clone can be modernized later as your budget allows and your needs develop.

So, if you're weary of creating "plain vanilla" documents, flyers, pamphlets, advertising circulars, brochures, reports, and newsletters that are as insipid, as uninspiring, and as cold as a December day in Siberia, then travel down one of these paths and get ready for the fascinating realm of desktop publishing.

⇨ On the levels

Covered in this text is the entire spectrum of desktop publishing power for programs ranging from producing a single-page flyer or brochure to a 1,000-page book with full-color illustrations, and all of the steps in between. Using this book, you can start out at or upgrade to any or all of these DTP operating levels illustrated in Fig. 1-5.

Figure 1-5

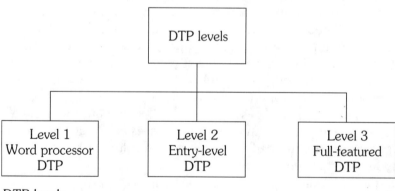

DTP levels.

Upgrades and custom designs covered show you how to incorporate additional RAM, larger capacity floppy and hard-disk drives, high-resolution monitors, CD-ROM drives, scanners, modems and fax/modems, and removable media backup systems, as well as several additional peripherals that can significantly augment DTP capabilities.

 Many applications for DTP

Desktop publishing is utilized in a wide range of applications, including, but not limited to:

> Business communications: Annual reports, letters, forms, pamphlets, product-specs, reports, product labels, memos, overheads, slides, handouts . . .

> News reporting: Leaflets, notices, newsletters, tabloids, journals, news articles . . .

> Publicity: Posters, advertising circulars, flyers, press-releases, brochures, mailings, directories, catalogs . . .

> Education, research, and government reports: Proposals, forms, presentations, lesson assignments, tables, textbooks, diagrams, training guides . . .

> Documentation: Manuals, technical articles, engineering guides, reports, technical books, catalogs, engineering and scientific proposals . . .

Some DTP software is limited in scope and can accomplish only a few of these functions. Full-featured DTP accommodates all of them, and much more.

It's easy to upgrade

You need not be a technician nor even be mechanically inclined to upgrade a PC. Detailed step-by-step guidelines, instructions, checklists, photographs, and illustrations included in this book simplify these upgrades, making it easy for virtually anyone to accomplish, regardless of their skill level. When you accomplish these upgrades yourself:

> You'll save hundreds of dollars, from 20 to 50 percent or more of the cost of a technician's upgrade charges.

> With the money saved, you can invest some of it in procuring quality components that will ensure a long and active life for your system.

- You won't have to pay for features you neither want nor need.
- You can tailor your system to meet your specific needs, your budget, and your schedule.
- It's easy to accomplish. Upgrading is basically the assembly and plug-in of components and cables. No special tools or knowledge are required. The only tools you need are a screwdriver and small pliers.
- Most upgrading takes only a hour or two.
- You can upgrade your design one major component at a time as your needs and finances dictate.
- By performing the upgrades yourself, you'll learn what the basic components look like and understand how they function. Thus you'll be better equipped to troubleshoot and determine what is wrong with your computer if it malfunctions.
- You can take justifiable pride in your accomplishments.
- It's educational and fun.

⇨ A plethora of parts

One of the problems of upgrading your own computer is that there are so many different component manufacturers that it's difficult to decide which specific part to purchase, or which vendor to purchase from. I've helped solve this dilemma by providing detailed tradeoffs, specifications, and questions to ask vendors so you can make sure you're obtaining the proper components for your needs.

When you buy a new house, you decide on the basis of what you can afford to spend. You'd probably like a 4,000-square-foot, 6-bedroom, 6-bathroom (if you have teenagers) house with a jacuzzi (for parties), a separate cottage (for your in-laws), and a heated swimming pool (for the neighbors) on an acre of ground (and a riding mower) in the country . . . but it's a trifle over your budget.

The same is true of computers. Of course you'd like to get the biggest, best, fastest, and most powerful machine possible. But it's

also a trifle over your budget (like about 10 times your budget). Besides, you might be wasting your money for accomplishing the specific tasks you have in mind. You could be financing an eight-cylinder gas guzzler when all you need is a two-cylinder engine. When you buy a computer, you have to decide how much you can afford to spend and then make tradeoffs, just as you do when you buy a house. To help you with these tradeoffs, I've listed the approximate costs involved in the upgrades and listed the basic factors to trade off when weighing the alternatives.

Next, let's get into the exploding profession of desktop publishing and find out what it is and what it can do for you.

⇨ DTP for everyone

Documents created with desktop publishing software differ considerably from what I call "plain vanilla" documents. Plain vanilla refers to the output of staid word processors; that is, drab documents, banal bulletins, colorless creations designed with little or no embellishments, little or no graphics or fancy borders, text printed in a single, solid column, the same font used throughout, etc. . . . boring, insipid, dull.

DTP, however, converts a blasé-looking vanilla document into an exciting work of art that begs to be read. Multiple columns, beautiful borders and banners, fanciful fonts, gorgeous graphics, and resplendent rosiness reach out and grab readers' attention and seduce them into perusing your document. Because isn't that why a document is created and printed, to be read?

And what I consider to be one of the most significant advantages of modern DTP hardware and software is that they also bring out the inherent creativity in people who are skilled in imagining concepts but who are not as skilled as graphics artists in being able to transfer their ideas onto display screens and the printed page.

Modern hardware and software provide multi-talented people with the easy-to-use tools needed to design the pages of documents as they

envision them and to create documents as they imagine them to look, documents which shout to be studied. Because of the incredible advances in PC hardware and DTP software, desktop publishing is no longer the exclusive province of graphics artists. No more rubber cement, no more manual cut-and-paste; now it's all done electronically by your PC. People not skilled in graphics, typesetting or layout, virtually anyone, can now create all types of documents that not only look appealing, but are also informative and easy to read. Figure 1-6 shows the basic steps involved in upgrading.

How to use this book

First read chapters 1, 2 and 3 in their entirety. They will help you decide what type of desktop publishing software to invest in and how to perform basic upgrading functions. Later chapters show you what hardware upgrades you need to accomplish to be able to utilize this software on your PC. These later chapters address specific upgrades and are pretty much stand-alone chapters. For example, if you need to add a higher capacity hard drive, read chapter 5.

Before you start any specific upgrades, review in detail the appropriate chapter(s) that deal with that specific upgrade. Also review the Buying Guide in appendix A before you purchase any components. Be sure to review the tradeoffs covering the specific component you are about to purchase in the applicable chapters to make sure you are obtaining the best component for the job.

Book summary

The following section provides a summarized overview of the text.

Part 1: The basics

Part one of this book explains elementary upgrade principles and procedures, how to use them, and why they are necessary.

Figure 1-6

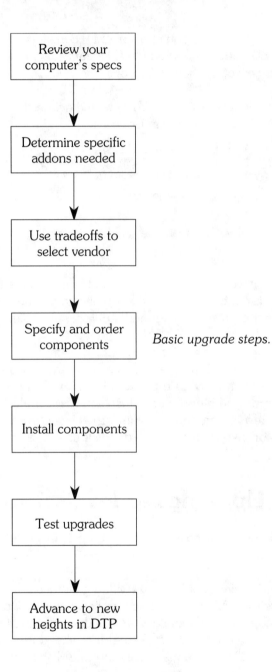

Basic upgrade steps.

* **Chapter 1** The introduction explains DTP concepts and discusses strategies for planning the upgrade to DTP capability. It also provides a summary overview of the book's sections.

* **Chapter 2** "Software selection" covers and defines the three different levels of DTP upgrades covered in this book:

> ➤ Level 1—Word Processing DTP

> ➤ Level 2—Entry-Level DTP

> ➤ Level 3—Full-Featured DTP

Specs for a baseline design to be used as a starting or reference point for upgrading are also covered.

* **Chapter 3** "It's easy to upgrade" covers the mechanics of upgrading. Included are a list of guidelines to follow while upgrading, as well as the basic tools required: a screwdriver and a pair of small pliers.

For most of the upgrades, it's necessary to remove the cover or "skin" from the case. Because this is a basic task for most upgrades, the procedure for removing the cover is covered in this chapter, along with illustrations and step-by-step instructions. Similarly, illustrations and step-by-step instructions explain other basic procedures: how to remove and/or install plug-in boards, disk drives, and other components.

Part 2: Upgrades to levels 1–3

This is the section that covers basic equipment upgrades for your CPU itself.

* **Chapter 4** "Adding RAM" begins with a general discussion of RAM, the types available (SIMM, SIP, etc.), their applications, sizes, performance, and comparative costs. Next the discussion gets down to specifics: how much RAM is required to add Windows (2 to 4MB), what do several entry-level and full-featured DTP programs require (up to 8MB), how to use cache effectively, etc.

✳ **Chapter 5** "Added hard drive capacity" first covers the various types of major hard drives available (IDE, SCSI, ESDI, etc.), their relative storage capacities, advantages and disadvantages, applications, and comparative costs. Next, this chapter covers how the various software programs impact on establishing hard drive capacity. For example, incorporating Windows alone requires from 6–10MB of hard drive storage. Some of the more costly, full-featured DTPs require upwards of 10–20MB or more to store their program, the accompanying clip art, etc.

Four basic methods for adding more hard disk capacity are:

> ➤ Use a disk-compression program.

> ➤ Add a second hard disk (internally or externally).

> ➤ Replace an existing hard disk with one of greater storage capacity.

> ➤ Add a hard disk card.

All four methods are discussed in this chapter and tradeoffs are provided to help readers select the optimum configuration for their applications.

✳ **Chapter 6** "Adding or replacing a removable media drive": For some applications a second disk drive (5¼-inch, high-density drive) may be required because considerable software is only available on 5¼-inch disks. Also, a second disk drive is convenient because readers can store data or software on either size for exchange or delivery to a printing shop, a customer, etc. It can also serve as a backup to a 3½-inch drive.

The features, advantages, and disadvantages of various types of 5¼-inch drives are compared and covered. If mounting space is at a premium, another possibility is to mount a 3½- and 5¼-inch drive combined in a single chassis. The combination drive mounts in a single drive bay and has the advantage that only a single drive card is required because only one drive will be used at a time.

Another possibility covered is the addition of an external floppy drive if the space inside the PC case is not adequate for an internal mount, a not too uncommon occurrence.

Other types of removable media provide significantly more storage capacity than floppies. Among these other removable media covered in this chapter are floptical drives (21MB), Bernoulli drives (90–150MB), and magneto-optical drives (up to 1.3Gb).

✳ **Chapter 7** "High resolution display and display driver": The baseline system of chapter 2 specified a modest resolution VGA color monitor (640 × 480 pixels) and a compatible monitor drive card. For DTP Level 1, this resolution may be adequate. For entry level DTP, Level 2, a 14–17-inch Super VGA (1,024 × 768 pixels) color monitor with a 0.32 mm (0.013 in.) spot size should be adequate. Tradeoffs in making this decision are covered.

For full-featured DTP, however, monitor requirements are more stringent. A noninterlaced 1,280 × 1,024 pixel, flat-faced, color monitor with a 0.28 mm (0.011 in.) or less spot size is required. Some advanced monitors offer as high as a 1,600 × 1,280 pixel resolution. The monitor for a full-featured DTP should also be 17 to 21 inches in size. Because this is a significant expenditure, a detailed list of tradeoffs is covered to help make these purchasing decisions.

Another alternative for high resolution DTP is the use of "paper-white" monitors. These monitors have resolutions as high as 1,664 × 1,200, screens as large as 20 inches, and can display two pages of a DTP document side-by-side. This is also a considerable investment. Tradeoffs are provided to help select the proper monitor resolution, refresh rate, spot size, etc.

✳ **Chapter 8** "CPU/motherboard transplant": The motherboard is truly the heart of the PC, so, if the PC's heart does not beat fast enough, you have to perform a transplant. This chapter guides you through this vital operation.

For Levels 1 and 2, a 386 motherboard (or one easily upgradeable to a 486) should be adequate. For Level 3, a 486 or Pentium (a.k.a. 586) motherboard is probably needed, depending on the type of documents to be created, the types and quantity of graphics, the use of color, and so on. Guidelines for selecting a motherboard and detailed tradeoffs are provided to help the reader make the optimum selection for a given type of DTP.

There are also several attractive alternatives to a motherboard transplant, such as installing a plug-in module to replace the CPU and allied circuitry. This and other alternatives are covered to help you make this selection.

⇨ Part 3: Peripheral upgrades

You may have the most powerful CPU in town, but it can't do much without its peripherals. This section covers:

✳ **Chapter 9** "Printers": Basic types of printers covered are:

> ➢ Dot matrix
> ➢ Inkjet
> ➢ Laser
> ➢ PostScript Laser

The relative advantages and disadvantages (as well as the application and costs of all the printer types) are covered in this chapter, along with discussion of tradeoffs to aid the reader in selecting a specific model and type of printer.

Enhancement boards are available to plug into a computer and enhance the performance of laser printers. The new features and capabilities they add, along with cost and performance tradeoffs and installation, are also covered in this chapter.

✳ **Chapter 10** "CD-ROM drivers" are the library of the future (and the future is almost here). Capable of enormous storage (640MB), they provide an enormous amount of software, clip art, dictionaries, thesauri, reference material, encyclopedias, etc. in a very small space. A single, 5-inch CD-ROM disk, for example, can store 14,000 clip art images for use in DTP, and each image can be rapidly located and accessed by the sophisticated "search-engine" software provided. If you rely heavily on clip art and require access to many large volumes, a CD-ROM drive becomes a necessity. How to choose a CD-ROM drive and the installation procedure are also covered in this chapter.

❋ **Chapter 11** "Scanners and screen capture": Another excellent source of inputting both graphics and text into DTP is the optical scanner. Scanners convert black-and-white, gray scale, and color images into a digital form that can be incorporated into DTP, then manipulated, cropped, sized, etc. Photographs, drawings, text from documents, etc. can be digitized and saved for use in DTP.

OCR (Optical Character Recognition) software can convert bit map text, such as from a facsimile or scanned image into digital codes that can be edited by a word processor.

Another method of importing graphics into DTP is with screen capture software, such as PizzazPlus and HiJaak Pro. Specialty software allows you to select a specific portion of a DOS or Windows screen, then capture and save it in memory. Windows also has a similar but more limited capability. Captured images can then be incorporated into DTP documents. Black-and-white, gray scale, and color images can be captured in this manner.

❋ **Chapter 12** "Modems facsimile, and FAX/modems" transmit and receive information, including images and text, to and from remotelocations. The modem also provides access to enormous databases—telelibraries such as CompuServe and Dialog. Telelibraries store copies of up-to-date, as well as back issues of many periodicals that can be accessed and downloaded into your computer for review or printout. They also have considerable free software available. There are also DTP working groups which DTP users can communicate with and have their questions answered. In addition, these databases provide up-to-date upgrades of software changes that have evolved since the program has been installed.

A combination FAX/Modem board provides not only the modem capabilities discussed above, but also the ability to transmit facsimile documents directly from a PC. Tradeoffs involved, comparative specs, and performance are also covered in this chapter.

❋ **Chapter 13** "Removable backup media": When considerable vital data exists (illustrations, text, documents, etc.) and this data must be preserved to protect against loss, a removable media backup system should be installed. It's very difficult and time-consuming to frequently back up a 100–200MB hard disk using floppy disks. A removable media backup

18

system can store up to 250 megs or more on a single tape or disk in a relatively short time, without user intervention. Removable backup media covered in this chapter are tape, floptical drives, Bernoulli drives, magneto-optical drives, DAT, and optical drives.

✳ **Chapter 14** "Special upgrades": This chapter covers a number of additional potential hardware upgrades. For example, a faster CPU can increase the overall speed of operation and generate graphic displays quicker. A higher resolution mouse can improve the accuracy and speed of operation for certain DTP operations.

Alternative input media also considered in this chapter include the use of a track ball and a graphic tablet for inputting and manipulating information. Printer switch boxes, manual or automatic, to enable a number of PC stations to share a high-cost printer are other options.

Adding a fan and using other methods to cool the interior are also covered, along with adding more serial and parallel ports, installing a larger power supply, incorporating surge suppressors and upgrading to a UPS (Uninterruptible Power System).

⇨ Additional sections

The Bibliography lists several reference texts that help the reader learn more about specific components that can provide additional capabilities to a PC. The comprehensive Glossary defines most of the unusual (and usual) terms you'll encounter in this book and in related publications.

Appendix A is a buyer's guide which details how to procure components, what to check for in a vendor, and what recourses are available if the components obtained are not satisfactory. Appendix B lists the names, addresses, and telephone contact numbers of representative vendors who market computer components, along with other pertinent information, such as if they charge restocking fees, their warranty policies, etc.

Appendix C lists free and low-cost software that is useful for various levels of desktop publishing, as well as utility software programs that

are helpful in DTP. Appendix D covers preventive maintenance and describes a number of techniques that are easy to accomplish and will help your electronics and electro-mechanical components live a long, healthy, and productive life.

⇨ To continue

One personal comment: I hope you'll never be finished with upgrading your PC; I hope that you will continue adding components, installing advanced designs, incorporating new media, installing new and exciting software, and adding new developments so that your PC can serve you for many years (hopefully 10 or so) to come. Fortunately most PCs are easy to upgrade, unlike most home appliances and automobiles, which are dead-end designs.

So continue to upgrade your existing PC as new components, new software become available and you can accomplish these upgrades without having to discard your PC. You may even be able to recover some of your expenditures by selling the used components you replace. Next, let's take a look at the software programs that make DTP happen; that's in chapter 2.

Software selection

INITIALLY, hardware is the driving force which dictates software design. If a computer programmer designs software for which no hardware exists, it's an exercise in futility. For the user, however, once the software is designed, the reverse situation exists: software drives the hardware. Once a specific software program is chosen, the user must make sure that the proper hardware is available to take full advantage of the software.

To help you select the proper hardware for your specific application(s), this chapter classifies DTP software into three basic levels of capabilities. Each level requires a different complement of hardware. These basic levels are defined and covered in this chapter, along with their hardware impact.

As far as choosing software to use for DTP, the decision should be made on the basis of the cost of both the hardware and software you wish to invest in, the ease and convenience of use, the DTP tasks you require the software to accomplish, and the "growth potential." And you're going to hear a lot about growth potential in this book, because it's a vital concept in planning for your computer's hardware and software future. It helps to make sure that your PC is not rendered obsolete after only a short period of time.

To begin, let's establish some basic definitions for the three levels that we can use for our comparisons. These are not limiting definitions because some of the programs overlap from one level to another. Some specific programs may not have all of the capabilities; some may have more than are listed. Consider these to be a set of average specifications for the three levels.

⇨ Definitions of the levels

Here are the definitions of the three levels of DTP that will be covered in this book:

⇨ Level 1

Level 1 word processing DTP includes the hardware and software required to:

➢ Create columns

➢ Incorporate graphics

➢ Provide limited graphic creation, importing, and editing

⇨ Level 2

Level 2 DTP includes the hardware and software required to:

➢ Create columns

➢ Insert and position graphics

➢ Create limited graphics

➢ Accomplish limited word processing

➢ Create variable width columns on the same page

➢ Link columns, flow text to discontinuous pages

➢ Flow text around rectangular graphics

➢ Accommodate documents of up to 120 pages

➢ Incorporate black-and-white graphics

➢ Import documents from several word processors

⇨ Level 3

Level 3 (full-featured) DTP includes the hardware and software required to:

➢ Create columns

➢ Insert, crop, edit, and position B&W and color graphics

➢ Create graphics, tables

➤ Link columns, flow text to discontinuous pages

➤ Automatic text flow

➤ Flow text around all shapes of graphics

➤ Provide precision control of all elements

➤ Kern to adjust the spaces between letters

➤ Create documents of more than 100 pages

➤ Accommodate four-color creation and printing

➤ Automatically create indexes and TOCs

➤ Import documents from most word processors

➤ Input filters for color images

Types of layout mechanics

Two basic types of layout formats currently used in DTP are illustrated in Fig. 2-1. Listed below them are representative commercial programs using them.

Figure 2-1

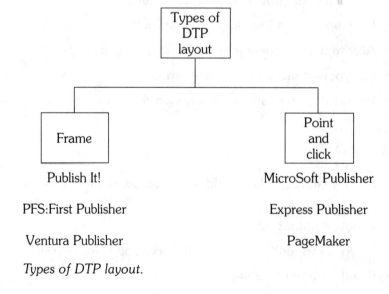

Types of DTP layout.

⇨ Frames

For the frame type of layout format, you first draw frames (which are displayed on the screen but are not printed; they are only used as guidelines) into which you later import your text and graphics. You can link frames when you want text to flow from one frame into the next, and you can change the size of the frames when you decide to experiment with a different layout.

Most DTP programs also provide standard frame layouts (called "templates") for standard types of documents, such as frames for a one-page flyer or a multipage newsletter. You can call up these templates and use them for your document, or modify them for your specific applications.

⇨ Point and click

"Point and click" refers to the type of layout mechanics in which text and graphics are pulled into a document even before a layout has been created. Then, by using a mouse, the cursor keys, or other input device, you point at the area you want to modify, click on it, then perform the tasks you need to accomplish. Such tasks might be moving a section of text from one column or page to another, or sizing or cropping graphics, for example.

As far as which to choose, it depends on the type of DTP you are going to accomplish. The frame type is easier to use and is used for the more routine document formats such as periodicals, books, and manuals where consistency and planning are important. Point and click is more complex to learn and use, but provides a wider range of creative formats, layouts, and text and manipulation of graphics.

⇨ Cost ranges

Cost ranges for the three levels are roughly as depicted in Fig. 2-2. Typical software programs are listed below each type. Level 1

Figure 2-2

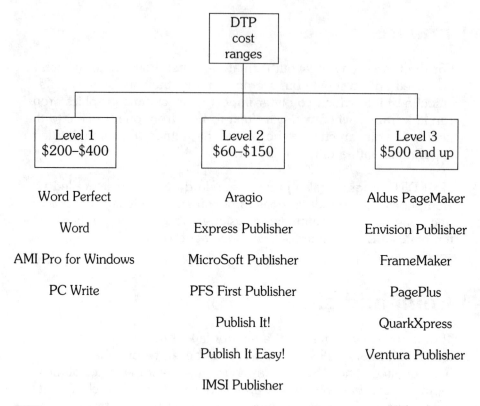

DTP cost ranges.

software is more expensive than Level 2, because Level 1's primary function is word processing, with desktop publishing being pretty much added on by word processor programmers as a plus feature.

The primary reason for working at Level 1 DTP would be that the user already has a word processor capable of limited DTP, or if the user is primarily interested in word processing and has only modest DTP requirements. Level 3 programs, with the most capabilities and the greatest versatility, are the most expensive.

In the following sections the basic capabilities of these three levels will be compared. Their impact on hardware will be delineated in later chapters.

⇨ Operating systems

Basic operating systems included in this book are DOS, Windows, OS/2, and NT as illustrated in Fig. 2-3. (To find out what version of DOS you're using, input VER/R at the C prompt.) DOS, of course, was one of the original operating systems and continues to be used today. Windows is the highly touted GUI (Graphical User Interface) system that is growing rapidly in its usage and its multimillion dollar promotions.

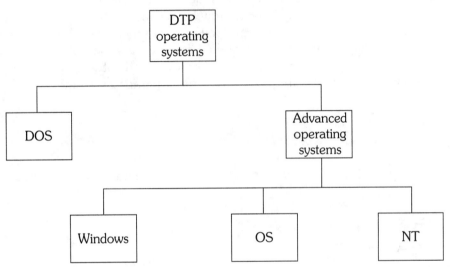

Figure 2-3

DTP operating systems used.

OS/2 is an operating system developed by IBM and which is a considerable advance over Windows. The fourth system, NT, is another Microsoft operating system which is an interim system that will be replaced by an advanced version of Windows. The arrival of the next generation of Windows may well be the death knell for DOS.

I'm not about to get into the relative merits of which system is the best one. Each system has its adherents, and they can be obdurate in their various justifications for the system they have chosen. I'm willing to let the marketplace and the users determine which will survive. For the purposes of this book, I'll use Windows as a generic

term to cover all present and future GUI operating systems, because Windows is most likely to persist.

As for which system to choose for your applications, note that DOS uses the least RAM and hard disk storage. DOS is an excellent starting point if you're limited by budget. It is, however, only a temporary solution, because programmers and software vendors will undoubtedly be concentrating most of their efforts on advanced DTP software for Windows.

Advanced operating systems require much more RAM and hard disk space. This, again, is why I stress growth potential in designing, buying, or building your own DTP system. However, no matter which operating system you begin with, if you have the proper growth potential built into your DTP, you can upgrade your hardware and software to accommodate virtually any current or future operating systems.

Types of data input

Desktop publishing software functions with three basic types of data:

➤ Alphanumeric

➤ Bit map

➤ Vector

Alphanumeric includes the alphabet, numerics, basically any symbol you can input from upper- or lowercase on your keyboard. This category also includes the control codes such as Alt, Ctrl, and Esc, plus special symbols that the combination of the Alt key plus a code (such as Alt 21 produces the § symbol). Also included are the box drawing symbols such as ⌐ and ⊤ that are used to draw boxes and lines. The alphanumeric characters and special symbols can be described by a few bits, so they require very little storage.

Bit map or "paint" data incorporates symbols, characters, drawings, and basically any object that is constructed of dots or individual bits. Each individual dot must be stored, so the requirements for large bit maps can be quite immense.

Vector or "drawing" data is graphics that are specified by mathematical formulas and can be used to draw lines of virtually any shape. Because vectors are created by formulas and the data which specifies the values, vector storage requirements are much lower than for bit map data.

Inexpensive software

The high cost of software programs can often deter you from taking full advantage of the capabilities of the more feature-rich DTP programs and related software. And sometimes after you invest in a specific program and use it for a while, you slowly begin to be aware of its limitations and would like to discontinue using the program. You may choose to move up to higher level software, but the high costs of the more full-featured programs is prohibitive. Not to be discouraged. There are several sources for low-cost software:

➢ Shareware

➢ Surplus software and hardware

➢ Software promotions

Shareware

Shareware is a special class of software that is marketed by individual entrepreneurs under a "try before you buy" concept. You can obtain a copy of this full-featured program for evaluation from a shareware distributor for a few dollars from one of the following vendors:

PC-SIG
1030-D East Duane Avenue
Sunnyvale, CA 94086
Orders 800-245-6717, ask for Operator 2228
Information: 408-730-9291
FAX Orders: 408-730-2107

PSL (PUBLIC SOFTWARE LAB)
P.O. Box 35705
Houston, TX 77235-5705
Orders: 800-2424-PSL
Info/Help: 713-524-6394
FAX Orders: 713-524-6398

REASONABLE SOLUTIONS
1221 Disk Drive
Medford, OR 97501
Orders: 800-876-3475
Info/Help: 503-776-5777
FAX Orders: 503-773-7803

Under the Shareware concept, you can evaluate the program for your applications for a period of about 30 days. If at the end of this period you decide you want to continue to use the software, you send in a nominal registration fee which entitles you to a more advanced version of the program, a printed manual, and consultation with the shareware author(s).

Shareware catalogs are available from the above listed vendors and many other vendors. A few shareware programs are listed in appendix C.

 # Surplus software

When software marketeers unveil a new and updated version of their software programs, they usually have many copies of the older version that they have been unable to sell. They often dispose of these outdated surplus versions by selling them to various companies who specialize in handling this type of material. The companies receiving this surplus software market them for a much reduced price, often one-fourth (or even less) of the original selling price. Often these surplus programs differ little from the newer, full-priced versions, so you may lose little by taking advantage of this approach.

Not only is the low cost an inducement to purchasing surplus programs, there is also another advantage. When you send in the registration card that you obtain with the surplus software, you become a fully registered owner of that specific program and are often entitled to contact the company for help. This registration also makes you eligible to "trade up" or upgrade to a more advanced version of the program at a special reduced price, often one-third or less of the cost of the version being offered to first-time customers.

In this way you can keep up with the latest software versions for a fraction of the going market price. Here are a couple of companies that regularly market surplus computer programs:

Surplus Software Incorporated
489 North Street
Hood River, OR 97031
1-800-753-7877
Fax (503) 386-4227
Customer Service (503) 386-5215
International Orders (503) 386-1375

Damark
7101 Winnetka Avenue N.
P.O. Box 29900
Minneapolis, MN 55429-0900
1-800-729-9000
Customer Service (612) 535-8880

Surplus Software Inc. has an outstanding variety of surplus software at bargain prices. Their surplus stocks are usually limited so get your name on their mailing list and respond quickly to their flyers.

Damark offers a limited selection of surplus software; however, they also have surplus computer hardware (plug-in boards, monitors, printers, computers, etc.) for sale, as well as reconditioned computers and related hardware.

Software promotions

Because of fierce competition, software companies frequently offer the latest version of their software at much reduced prices to promote a specific program and register a large number of users. In one type of promotion they slash their prices to a fraction of its market price for a limited time. Some of the larger software companies have been giving away full software programs for only the price of shipping.

Another source of low-cost programs is when software companies "bundle" their software, offering several programs (e.g., separate word processor, database, and telecomm programs) at a very low price.

31

Another avenue of saving money is through a "competitive upgrade." To demonstrate to you that their software is superior to the brand you're currently using, they offer their brand of software to you at a significantly reduced price, often about one-third of the market price. To take advantage of this offer, you usually have to show a "proof of purchase," that you have actually purchased the competitor's software.

So, watch for these avenues and other methods of minimizing your software investments. They often provide not only a means of initially obtaining a specific program, but also a path you can follow in upgrading (I love that word!) your software and hardware.

Level 1 word processing DTP software

Level 1 DTP software programs (such as WordPerfect and Microsoft Word, for both DOS and Windows) have a limited DTP capability because they were primarily designed for word processing, with DTP capability only considered as an added feature. They do not provide the ease of use and the versatility available from true DTP software.

In addition to basic word processing capabilities, word processors also spell-check, supply a thesaurus, run a grammar-check, create limited graphics, and provide mailing list capabilities. They can create columns and incorporate graphics; however, very little precision page design can be accomplished with Level 1 DTP software.

One significant limitation that Level 1 DTP programs also have is that they cannot automatically link text from one column to nonadjacent columns on the same or succeeding pages. If you want to accomplish this with word processing software, you have to cut and paste, a very laborious, inexact trial-and-error process. This severely limits their application principally to DTP documents that cover only a single, continuous topic. However, for simpler documents, such as an ad, a brochure, or a multipage report with limited graphics, Level 1 DTP may meet your requirements.

Thus, Level 1 DTP is adequate if you:

> ➤ Already have a Level 1 word processor capable of limited DTP, or

> ➤ Are going to purchase a program, your principal interest is in word processing, and your DTP requirements are modest.

As far as the cost differential between Level 1 DOS- and Windows-based software, there is no significant difference. The major variations among them are in the amount and cost of hardware required to fully utilize the software. DOS DTP requires much less RAM and hard disk storage capacity (see chapters 4 and 5). Although some DOS Level 1 DTP programs (notably WordPerfect 6 and Word 6) are attempting to emulate Windows and other GUIs in ease of operation and features, these efforts are only stopgap. The future is in Windows, and eventually DOS will only be listed in computer history books. If you decide to upgrade your system to Level 1 DOS DTP, consider it as only a temporary solution, a beginning system. Eventually you'll have to upgrade to Windows.

Among Level 1 Windows programs, there is also no significant difference in either cost or hardware requirements among the major competitors: WordPerfect, Word, and Ami Pro. Any differences that do exist among the three are merely transitory, because fierce competition fortunately forces each vendor to continually strive to improve their products.

So, it's best to consider your own tradeoffs for Level 1 DTP. Check the comparisons published in current computer periodicals to see how the different programs suit your specific needs. Watch for special promotional events where word processor software is offered at special low prices. Compare the software from the standpoints of its usability (easy to learn and easy to use), performance, ease of integration (with other software programs, e.g., spreadsheets and databases), customization capabilities (for your specific purposes), and, (a very important consideration) documentation and support. Without these last two, your software programs will end up in your closet.

33

⇨ Level 2 DTP software

Level 2 (entry-level) DTP software covers low-cost, special-purpose programs that are a step up in DTP capability from word processing programs which can be used for DTP but are specifically designed for word processing.

Level 2 programs usually have a very limited word processing ability, so many depend on using a separate word processing program to perform the bulk of creating, editing, and spell-checking their text. Level 2 programs also have only a limited graphic creation capability, so they also rely heavily on importing artwork from clip-art collections and from other specialty drawing programs (e.g., Corel Draw, WordPerfect Presentations, PC Paintbrush, etc.). The basic function of Level 2 then is to configure and compose documents; that is, they are used to:

> ➤ Import and arrange text and graphics obtained from external sources.

> ➤ Provide limited text and graphics editing.

> ➤ Arrange text and graphics on the pages.

One of the most significant advantages that Level 2 has over Level 1 is that most Level 2 software can link text from one column to nonadjacent columns, either on the same or succeeding pages. Thus, Level 2 can handle documents covering multiple linked topics, such as in a newsletter, and is not limited to the single topic.

Another feature of Level 2 DTP programs is that they are usually easy to learn and easy to use because they were specifically designed and programmed to function only as DTP software. Many software companies claim you can create your first document in less than an hour. Level 2 is also easier to configure when placing graphics in the precise position you desire. And, of course, another important advantage is that because they're designed as a single-purpose program, a fairly good Level 2 DTP program can be obtained for a low cost of about a hundred dollars.

DTP software programs in this category are cost and feature competitive with each other and provide a wide range of capabilities. The choice of which program to use is an individual one and should be based on comparing your requirements with the comparison listings in current computer periodicals. These periodicals often evaluate several competitive programs and compare their features. You can find these evaluations and comparisons in back issues of the periodicals available at your local library, or by querying online databases such as CompuServe, Dialog, GEnie, etc.

⇨ Level 3 DTP software

The top level of DTP (in performance, as well as cost) not only accomplishes most of what Levels 1 and 2 do, but provides much more capability, including the ability to accommodate color, process long documents, automatically create an index and a table of contents, and more. With all of this capability, these programs are also considerably more complex to learn as well as to use.

Because of the high cost and the difficulty of learning and using the software, Level 3 is not for the casual user. If you don't have complex requirements and do not create a wide variety of types of documents, you're probably better off with the simpler and less costly Level 2 DTP. Another important, but often overlooked, factor is that unless you utilize your Level 3 software frequently (such as at least once a week), you're liable to forget many of the numerous nuances of the program and may have to relearn them each time you attempt to accomplish something different with the software.

In summary, if the cost of the software and the required hardware fit your budget, and if you're going to use the program often for complex and large documents, you should invest in Level 3 DTP. As far as the cost differences between Level 3 DOS and Windows programs, they are comparable, with two notable exceptions: Envision Publisher and PagePlus.

Envision Publisher is an excellent, easy to use, full-featured WYSIWYG desktop publishing program available via the shareware

market. It works under DOS, so its RAM (450K) and disk storage (2.5MB) requirements are modest. An advanced version of the program, EnVision Publisher Pro, is also available from the software authors.

PagePlus is another excellent and full-featured commercial DTP program from England. It sells for about $60 and has an estimated 80 percent of the capabilities of the more costly Level 3 programs for about one-eighth the price. PagePlus requires Windows to operate (2- to 3MB RAM and 4MB hard disk storage) so it requires a more costly PC to function than does Envision Publisher.

If you're considering DOS Level 3 programs, I contend that DOS is slowly going to ride off into the sunset and be replaced by Windows in the next few years. Level 3 DOS software should only be considered as a temporary solution. The future is in Windows. Most software development efforts are going to be invested in the Windows software applications.

⇨ Word processing capabilities of DTP

DTP software treats text and graphics as individual elements. The body of the text is an element, each graphic is an element, a headline is an element, etc. How the various software programs process and handle these elements is another way that separates them into the three levels.

True to their major calling, Level 1 DTP software is the program best suited for word processing all types of text. They also have the ability to use various fonts, bold text, spell-check, and provide thesauri for reference. Even after you have composed the text, it's a relatively simple matter to convert word processing text directly to a columnar format, and to accomplish such functions as search and replace, change fonts, and add other embellishments, such as incorporating graphics, boxing text, and headlining.

Level 2 DTP software programs, however, are usually limited in their word processing and editing capabilities. They are best suited for importing processed text from a limited number of word processors (or text in a simple format, such as ASCII) then performing a final polish by operating on that text, adding borders, arranging the text in columns, changing fonts, headlining and so forth. Level 2 can link different stories on the same or succeeding pages.

Full-featured DTP software programs live up to their calling by being able to accomplish considerable editing, spell-checking, searching and replacing, bolding and, very importantly, the ability to automatically flow text from one column to another column, either on the same or succeeding pages.

 Text import capabilities of DTP

Although all three levels of DTP accomplish word processing, they are also required to import, convert, and edit text, spreadsheet data, etc. from external programs. This ability varies considerably among the three levels. And, in this conversion, some of the formatting (bolding, special fonts, etc.) is often lost in the translation.

Level 1 word processors, when utilized for DTP, usually have excellent text import capabilities. Some can import a wide variety of foreign text formats easily; others have to go through a rather convoluted and agonizingly slow process to import. Generally, however, they can import text from a diverse variety of software, including spreadsheets and databases. And they import this text without much loss of text attributes, such as bolding, italicizing, etc.

Level 2 DTP software usually has limited text import capabilities. Some can only import ASCII; others can import text from only two or three brands of word processors. And in importing, they often lose some of the attributes of the text. Usually it's best to accomplish most of the text processing in a word processor, plus performing spell-check and other operations, and save the text in ASCII. Then use the Level 2 DTP program to finish the fonts, headlines, and text attributes.

Level 3 DTP software programs can usually import text from a wide variety of word processors, and they retain most of the processed text's attributes in the translation. Importing ASCII text plus text from spreadsheets and databases is also common in this level of DTP.

Graphic imports of DTP

Another factor that separates the various levels of DTP into the can do's and the wannabe's is their ability to not only import a wide variety of graphics, but also in their capability of editing graphics from within the DTP program. Conversion from one graphics format to another is often required before graphics can be used in a specific DTP program.

In general, Level 1 can only import a limited set of graphics and has very limited capability for editing graphics. Level 2 also usually handles only a limited type of graphics. For example, the lightweight program, Publish It Lite!, can import only GEM Paint and PC Paintbrush formats. The program PFS:First Publisher imports MAC, PCX, MSP, TIF, and PIC formats. Level 3 usually has much better filters for importing graphics from various sources including the above, plus CGM, DRW, EPS, IFF, WMF, WPT, DCS, Photo CD, GIF, etc.

⇨ Graphics creation and editing in DTP

If the required graphics are not readily available, it's desirable to be able to create them within the DTP program, and to be able to edit both internally created and imported graphics. Level 1 DTP generally has very limited graphics creation and editing capabilities. Level 2 DTP has considerably more. Not only can Level 2 software create the basic geometric figures such as rectangles, circles, etc., they also can size, crop, erase, cut, copy, duplicate, fill, move, rotate, and flip; in short, they can perform many of the basic graphics editing tasks that are required. Level 3 accomplishes all of the above and much, much more.

Another significant difference among the three levels is the resolution capabilities of graphics that can be accommodated. Level 1 can usually handle up to about 300 dpi (dots per inch) graphics. Level 2 can utilize graphics having resolutions up to about 300 dpi; however, art with a resolution greater than 72 dpi often cannot be edited with Level 2 software. Level 3 accommodates extremely high resolution graphics, up to as high as 3,000 dpi; 3,000 dpi is an astronomical level generally only needed for professional publications.

⇨ Clip art

Another aspect of graphics that must be considered in selecting software is how they import and are able to edit the two basic types of clip art:

- ➤ Bit map
- ➤ Vector

Bit-map clip art is comprised of individual dots stored to form an image. Vector clip art is stored as mathematical equations, which are then reconstructed into images when accessed. A large variety of bit-map clip art is available; however, this type of art can have huge storage requirements. Often they require up to 1-or 2MB for a single image.

Because of this huge storage requirement, redraw of bit-map images when editing and manipulating them on a screen is often agonizingly slow. The disadvantage of vector clip art is that most of the images exist in an EPS (Encapsulated Post Script) format which has to be printed on a PostScript printer.

⇨ Color in documents

It's no secret that color used in DTP grabs a reader's attention, but the cost of printing full-color documents is often prohibitive. However, there is an effective and economical way to "colorize" a document; it is referred to as "spot color." Full-color printing uses

four colors to print the full range of colors required for continuous-tone images, such as color photographs. Those four colors are cyan (blue), magenta (red), yellow, and black. Spot color requires only two color inks: one to print most of a document and a second to highlight items, such as page borders, rules, and boxes. You can even add the effect of a third color by using a tint of the spot color.

The color capabilities of the three levels varies drastically. In general, Levels 1 and 2 can accommodate color only to a limited degree. Level 3 DTP usually has full-color and high-color-resolution capability.

LAN operation

A LAN (Local Area Network) is an installation where a group of PCs are interconnected so they can communicate with each other, exchange information from one computer to one or more other computers, and share costly peripherals such as huge hard disks, laser and color printers, modems, and fax machines. DTP software programs can be used in a LAN; documents of all types can be quickly passed back and forth for comments, editing, review, and approval.

However, when DTP is used in a LAN, certain precautions must be observed. Each document created should have a log attached to it which records the names (or initials) of all the individuals who accessed the document, whether they created, edited, or reviewed it. This log should record the date and time they reviewed it, plus comments to summarize what the user did with the document.

Security is also vital in a LAN to prevent unauthorized and accidental access. Passwords should be used to restrict access to certain documents. In addition, a level of access should be assigned to each document, restricting access to "review only," "edit," "print," etc.

My recommendations

The upgrades I'm recommending here should be accomplished one at a time. It is unwise to attempt to accomplish several upgrades at the

same time for a number of reasons. First of all, if the upgrades don't work, it will be difficult to determine which new accessory is malfunctioning. You would have to remove the upgrades, one by one, to troubleshoot the problem.

You should also accomplish only one upgrade at a time so you have an opportunity to put each new hardware upgrade through its paces, thoroughly evaluate it, make sure it accomplishes all it is intended to do, make sure that you know how to use it, and make sure that it does not interfere with any other functions. Occasionally you find that one software program you have loaded will interfere with another program, even to the extent of totally making the program and even your computer completely inoperative. Besides, of course, it's much easier on the budget to avoid simultaneous multiple upgrades. So, upgrade one major feature at a time.

Software

As to the choice between DOS or Windows, it is pretty much a compromise between economics and the need to work with the latest programs. DOS functions with much less RAM and less hard disk storage. There are several suitable DOS programs for all levels; the net result in DOS is a much less expensive system. For a limited budget, you can function quite well in DOS. You don't need to do Windows to accomplish some desktop publishing ventures. DOS is also a good starting point; you can upgrade later when your requirements and budget hopefully both increase at the same time.

However, you should consider DOS as only a temporary operating system. Sure, it will be around for a few years, but most of the new developments will be in the Windows area. If you expect to grow with these new developments, sooner or later you're going to have to decide to upgrade to Windows.

When most of your work is going to be word processing and you're going to output mostly text with only occasional graphics, purchase a high-end word processor with graphics and columnar capability. If

your budget is tight, opt for PC Write, an excellent shareware word processor.

If you're going to provide mostly short documents with considerable graphics and a variety of text fonts, such as flyers, brochures, newsletters with one or multiple stories, pamphlets, circulars, advertising circulars, etc., opt for a low-end, Level 2 DTP program. They're inexpensive, easy to learn and use, and they'll give you some excellent on-the-job training on creating DTP documents and prepare you for the high-end DTP programs.

To produce large documents, books, catalogs, color documents, and manuals with considerable, precision graphics, opt for high-end desktop publishing software. Two very low-cost programs are Envision Publisher (which works in DOS, so your RAM and hard disk requirements and hardware costs are minimized) and PagePlus (for Windows) which requires more RAM and a larger hard disk, like all Windows-based programs. PagePlus can also produce color documents. High-end DTP software is harder to learn than the other two levels because of its many capabilities, but can meet virtually any challenge.

⇨ In general

One of the most needed upgrades for all levels is a larger hard disk (see chapter 5). Even though DTP software may only require a few megabytes of disk storage, documents gobble up megabytes of storage. Utility programs consume many more megabytes. Add to this graphic images, which can take up to a megabyte or even more for a single complex image, and you'll soon be out of storage. And it's simply not convenient to have to continually load and unload material to and from your hard disks to make room for other material. So, you should invest in as much hard disk capacity as you can.

Another specific upgrade I highly recommend for all PCs is the addition of a modem/fax board (slower versions are quite inexpensive; see chapter 12). This important upgrade opens the door to the fantastic electronic libraries of the future: CompuServe, GEnie,

Dialog, America Online . . . You can obtain free and low-cost software, plus free and expert technical advice on virtually any topic. You can access and obtain copies of old and newly published periodical articles, and obtain copies of a huge variety of clip art for your documents. And these online vendors are continually improving the features they offer.

If you are going to operate in the Windows environment (and you will, sooner or later), this further increases your need for disk storage. Windows programs also require more RAM (chapter 4), so if you are going to operate with Windows software, you should eventually upgrade to 4-or 8MB (even 16MB) of RAM. Planned properly, RAM upgrades can be accomplished a megabyte or so at a time.

 CD-ROM

Another eventual upgrade I recommend for all PCs is adding a CD-ROM (Compact Disk-Read Only Memory) drive (prices continue to plummet; see chapter 10). A single, 5-inch-diameter compact disk can store about 680 megabytes of information. Storing that same amount of information on high-density (1.44MB) 3½-inch disks requires over 450 floppy disks! The 640MB is equivalent to storing about 500 books of 500 pages each, or a quarter of a million pages of text on a single disk! You don't have to get the fastest, most expensive model in creation; the slow ones make you wait a trifle longer, but they are quite inexpensive.

For graphics, a single CD-ROM can store up to 4,000 color photographs, 1,000 typefaces, or 3,000 illustrations. You can have a gigantic DTP library with thousands of clip-art images and millions of pages of text occupying only a few inches of storage space! Some of the more complex software programs (e.g., Corel Draw) are also being offered on CD-ROM disks, so you may eventually need a CD-ROM drive to load software programs.

A number of other upgrades should be on your wish list. For high-resolution imagery and graphics, you need to add a high-resolution monitor and a compatible graphics card (chapter 7). A scanner

(chapter 11) is also a very useful upgrade because it allows you to scan images from newspapers or other publications, convert and store them for use in your DTP documents. Some scanners also have an OCR (Optical Character Recognition) capability allowing you to scan text from printed sources, convert and import this text into your document, then edit the text.

If you are processing considerable data and images, a removable media backup system such as a tape system (chapter 13) should also be on your upgrade wish list. Backing up your data periodically is essential because computers and hard disks have been known to malfunction by garbling and losing data, sometimes even dying in agony in the process (you will also die in agony). Removable media backup systems can give you this needed security and back up your entire hard disk with very little effort.

And if you're the owner of an older and slower PC, then motherboard or CPU transplant (chapter 8) may be in your future. This gives you a faster and more easily upgradable PC. When you're dealing with considerable graphics, you're going to need this extra speed and capability.

It's easy to upgrade

[C][H][A][P][T][E][R] [3]

THIS chapter covers several basic procedures for hardware upgrading, procedures that are used repetitively. Also included is a list of guidelines to follow while upgrading (i.e., touch the metal case occasionally to prevent any static electricity from harming the components), as well as some of the basic tools required, such as a screwdriver and a pair of small needlenose pliers.

Illustrations and step-by-step instructions show how to remove the case, remove and install plug-in boards, and other components. But before we consider any purchases, let's establish a baseline PC design to use as a reference set of specifications for upgrading.

Basic components

Figure 3-1 diagrams the basic hardware components of a typical PC and how they interconnect.

The computer case may be either a desktop (horizontal) configuration (Fig. 3-2) or a tower (vertical) configuration (Fig. 3-3). The power supply is usually considered to be an integral part of the case. All of the components depicted in Fig. 3-1 are usually mounted inside the case, except for the keyboard and display.

The motherboard, the heart of the system, contains the CPU (Central Processing Unit), memory controllers, timing crystals, ROM-BIOS (Basic Input/Output System), etc. In addition, the motherboard is the home for several slots or sockets which accommodate plug-in modules (a.k.a. option or add-on boards). The motherboard may also contain some I/O ports for controlling the hard and floppy drives.

The keyboard is the major alphanumeric input component for the system. The display driver converts the output of the motherboard to the proper signal format for driving the display. The I/O Interface converts the signals to and from the output ports to the

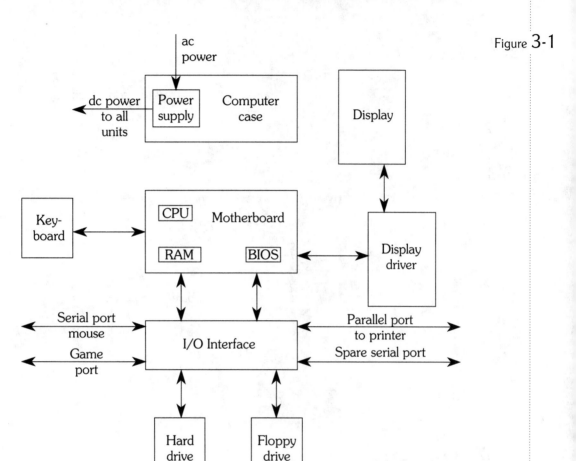

Figure 3-1

Block diagram of basic hardware components.

proper format to converse with the motherboard and may also contain interface circuitry for the hard and floppy drives if the motherboard does not provide this capability. In addition, the I/O Interface outputs to a parallel port for driving a printer, and has two serial ports for controlling such peripherals as an external modem/fax unit and a serial mouse. A game port is usually provided on the I/O Interface also, and is used not only for games, but for some advanced applications like virtual reality programming, for example.

Figure 3-2

Desktop computer.

Figure 3-3

Tower computer.

⇨ Baseline design

Now that you have a general idea of the components that comprise the basic system, let's establish the detail specifications for a baseline design to use as our reference point. Table 3-1 details the specs for the baseline design we'll use as a reference for upgrading:

Table 3-1

Baseline design

386-SX-20 MHz computer

1 megabyte of RAM

40-megabyte hard disk

3½-inch floppy disk

I/O Interface card with 2HD/2FD/1P

DOS installed

Keyboard

Mouse

14-inch VGA color display, 0.39 spot size

Compatible display driver—256K RAM

Resolution 640 × 480

Dot matrix printer

No major word processing software installed

No Windows installed

3–4 spare plug-in slots

2–3 spare drive bay slots

PC case with 230-watt power supply

To be more specific

The first item, 386SX-20, specifies a 386-class computer functioning at 20 MHz, one of the slower configurations. If you have a faster system, you're a leap ahead of the baseline design. If yours is slower than 20 MHz, you may eventually have to upgrade it for faster speed, but this upgrade probably doesn't have to be accomplished until you aspire to Level 3 DTP. However, no matter which system you have, or elect to procure, most of the basic components are interchangeable, so you can retain and utilize many of your existing components on the upgrade route.

As far as RAM is concerned, one megabyte is adequate for DOS for a starter system and for many DTP functions. Only when you add a RAM-hungry program such as Windows, or one of the more complex software programs (e.g., Word, WordPerfect For Windows, and PageMaker) will you need to upgrade your RAM storage capacity. However, adding RAM is one of the least expensive and easiest upgrades to accomplish to enhance your system's capabilities. How much to upgrade, choosing the right type of memory, and how to accomplish the installation are covered in chapter 4.

A 40MB hard disk is a bare minimum storage capacity, especially when you install the memory-hogging Windows programs and other

higher level software. Chapter 5 shows you how to select and install a higher capacity hard disk when you are ready to upgrade.

For most applications, a high-density, 3½-inch floppy disk drive is adequate. The 3½-inch floppy (floppy is a misnomer for this rugged disk) has an excellent storage capacity (1.44MB). If you find that some of the software you wish to install comes only on 5¼-inch disks (1.2MB), or if your customers use this media, you can add this inexpensive drive to your system at any time. Or you can use this extra drive for backup in case the 3½-inch drive fails. Chapter 6 covers the tradeoffs needed to make when selecting a second floppy and details the step-by-step installation required.

DOS (install the latest version of this operating system—or you might consider using one of its able competitors, DRDOS or PCDOS), a keyboard (most keyboards have 101 or 102 keys), and a mouse (also an inexpensive and key peripheral) are essentials for every system, no matter what level.

The I/O Interface listed (2H/2F/2S/1P/1G) provides the proper interface to drive several peripherals: 2H (2 hard drives), 2F (2 floppy drives) plus interfaces for 2S (2 serial ports for a mouse, modem, etc.), 1P (1 parallel port for a printer) and 1G (1 game port). This card is very inexpensive and provides excellent growth potential.

A 14-inch VGA color display with a 0.39 mm (0.015 inches, 67 dots per inch) or smaller spot size and a compatible display driver are assumed for the basic system with a resolution of 640 × 480. This is adequate for Level 1 DTP software. If you require higher resolution, as may be needed for Level 2 and 3, chapter 7 covers the selection of high-resolution and large screen displays. In addition, the selection and installation of a compatible display driver and accelerator are also covered in this chapter.

The motherboard is the basic component which determines the speed, class, and general operation of your PC. It is truly the heart of your computer. So, if your PC's heart does not beat fast enough, you may have to perform a transplant by upgrading to a faster and more modern motherboard. Alternatively you may opt to replace your existing CPU with a faster operating plug-in CPU to accelerate its

heartbeat. Chapter 8 shows you how to select a suitable motherboard or a replacement CPU plug-in and how to perform this transplant or replacement by providing detailed, step-by-step instructions.

A 9- or 24-pin dot-matrix printer provides an acceptable low-cost output for the lower levels of DTP, not only for rough drafts, but also for some limited final copy applications. For the 9-pin, print enhancement software (e.g., Image Print, LQ Print, etc.; see appendix C) provides the multiple passes needed for increased resolution. The 24-pin can also provide excellent print quality with the wide variety of fonts available in most DTP software by making multiple passes. However, if you need a higher print resolution, chapter 9 covers high-quality ink-jet and laser printers, as well as their costs, tradeoffs, and installation considerations. In addition, installing an enhancement board to improve the output of a laser printer is also covered.

The basic design detailed above assumes that neither a major word processing program (e.g., WordPerfect, Word, etc.) nor Windows is installed. If you have such a program, its impact on hardware is covered in the applicable chapters. Chapter 2 covered the characteristics of a number of word processing and DTP software programs, as well as the hardware required to fully utilize them.

To accommodate hardware additions, the basic system assumes that several (3 or 4) spare plug-in slots are available for adding plug-in boards and that a few spare drive bay slots (2 or 3) are available for adding more components (a second hard drive, CD-ROM drive, etc.). A 230-watt power supply is assumed to be mounted in the case.

⇨ CPU smorgasbord

To continue with the analogy of the motherboard being the heart of the PC, the CPU (Central Processing Unit) becomes the lively daughter who takes up residence on the motherboard and controls the main valves of your computer's heart. The CPU is the device that establishes the beat to which the computer's heart will pulsate. A wide variety of CPUs are available; this section lists some of the typical ones and their characteristics.

From the Intel 4004, history's first commercially sold microprocessor—the one that started it all—to the slowly emerging and very expensive Pentium (a.k.a. 586), the race has been devoted to the swift. Faster and faster the beat goes on as each vendor tries to seduce buyers by offering more and more speed, lightning-fast processing power, and more microcircuitry per chip. All at a higher cost, of course. And this higher cost is not only for the CPU itself, but also for more and faster RAM, a larger hard disk, and increased performance from other chips and peripherals.

But you do not need the fastest (and most expensive) chips to accomplish most DTP tasks. If your principal efforts center around inputting words into a computer, as long as your PC can keep ahead of your rapidly flying fingers, you have all the speed you need. And if your graphic requirements are not too demanding, you don't have to try to keep up with the Jones' clones. Even if you are into high-tech graphics, there are several solutions beyond a high-priced CPU to quicken your tasks, such as a graphics co-processor and a graphics accelerator.

So, don't worry about trying to keep pace with the fastest of the fast. Concern yourself principally with trying to obtain the best equipment for the best price to accomplish the specific tasks you plan to specialize in. And don't worry about your computer being "out-of-date." Just as you don't have to purchase a new car every year, you need not trade your PC in for the latest (and very expensive) model that has just been developed. (Besides, the IRS doesn't encourage it either.) A basic, well-designed computer with built-in growth potential can undergo constant makeovers and last from 6 to 10 years.

⇨ CPU jungle

There is justifiably a great deal of confusion among the various CPUs used in different PC models. Table 3-2 is a listing which should help straighten out some of this puzzlement.

CPU specifications Table 3-2

Designation	Class	Clock spd in MHz	Number of transistors	Maximum memory
8086	XT	4.77–10	29,000	1MB
8088	XT	4.77,8	29,000	1MB
80286	AT	8–12	130,000	16MB
386SX	AT	16–33	275,000	16MB
386DX	AT	16–33	275,000	4GB
486SX	AT	16–33	900,000	4GB
486DLC	AT	25–40	600,000	4GB
486DX	AT	25–50	1,200,000	4GB
486DX2	AT	25/50,33/66	1,200,000	4GB
586 a.k.a Pentium	AT	60, 66, 100	NA	4GB

In Table 3-2, column 1 lists the designation for the CPU, the second column the class it belongs to, the third column lists available speeds in megahertz. The Max Memory column lists the maximum memory the system is capable of addressing in MB (megabytes) or GB (gigabytes).

When purchasing components, there are a number of possible sources:

> ➤ From a computer component supplier near you, one who can answer your questions, help and support your decisions. You will probably pay the computer supplier about 60–80 percent higher than you would for mail-order purchases.

> ➤ Mail Order. This one is my favorite. It has the greatest variety, lots of healthy competition, and is the second lowest in cost, about 10 to 20 percent higher than available at computer swap meets. But you can purchase virtually anything by mail order.

> ➤ Computer swap meets near larger cities. Some are held every weekend. Make sure you're buying known manufacturer's parts from a reliable source. Use the tradeoffs in making your decisions. You can usually save about 10 to 20 percent over

mail order when you buy at a computer swap meet, used components can often be obtained very inexpensively. Unfortunately computer swap meets are seldom available to many users such as myself who live in a remote country area and they have little variety available.

Before beginning any of the specific physical upgrades described in the later chapters, review in detail the entire chapter covering the specific upgrade. Always have a pad and pencil nearby for making notes. Review the tradeoffs and consult them when you converse with your vendor, either in person or by phone.

Before you make any changes

With your computer up and running, there are some important preparatory steps you need to take before you begin any upgrades. They are:

1. Back up your hard disk.

2. Prepare recovery information.

3. Record pertinent information about your system.

The first two steps will be covered next. Recording of the pertinent information will be covered later in this chapter.

Back up your hard disk

There are several software programs available for backing up your hard disk. One of the least costly (almost free) comes with your DOS program. It's also one of the worst to use: it's time-consuming and inflexible. But it's something you should do at least once to make you appreciate the need for good backup software.

Several excellent commercial programs are available: Norton Backup, Fastback Plus, and PC Tools. Shareware programs, BackRem and BAKtrack (appendix C) are also available. When you tire of the floppy disk shuffle that's needed for the software backup programs listed

above, consider a tape drive or other removable media for backing up
(chapter 13).

⇨ Prepare recovery information

In accordance with Murphy's Law, "If something can go wrong, it
will," it's a wise preventive idea to prepare recovery information and
a "Recovery Disk" in case Murphy rears his unwelcome head.

First of all, print out your CONFIG.SYS and AUTOEXEC.BAT files
so you can have them on paper for ready reference in case they're
needed. It also helps if you can note on the printout what each line
accomplishes, which peripheral it manages, and the resources it uses.
If you have the time, it's also a good idea to include this data in each
of these files on your hard disk. There is plenty of room in the
CONFIG.SYS and AUTOEXEC.BAT files for these comments. Insert
a REM (REMark) before each command that explains what each line
does. Often when new software is loaded new commands inexplicably
appear in these files without you even knowing about it, so it's a
good idea to monitor and record these changes as they occur. You
may want to purge or modify them later.

To prepare a "Recovery Disk," remember that DOS reacts to the
instructions contained in your CONFIG.SYS and AUTOEXEC.BAT
files before anything can happen. Because these two files are
automatically accessed whenever you boot up, to prepare for the
onslaught of Murphy's Law, first format a disk in your A drive (it has
to be in the A drive) with this command:

```
Format A:/S
```

The /S switch makes it into a "system disk" by copying the needed
DOS files on the disk after the format is completed.

Next, copy the CONFIG.SYS and AUTOEXEC.BAT files on to this
disk in Drive A, then copy the DOS EDIT and FDISK files to the
floppy so you can view and edit your files if needed.

To test your recovery disk, place it in Drive A and boot up your computer. Check to make sure that you can access all of your drives and that your EDIT program runs on Drive A.

Next, rename the CONFIG.SYS and AUTOEXEC.BAT files on Drive A with different file extensions, such as CONFIG.BKP and AUTOEXEC.BKP. In this way the files won't run automatically when you boot up with the disk in Drive A, but they are available if needed. All you have to do is rename them with their original extensions and copy them to your hard disk if something goes awry.

Finally, label your disk "Recovery Disk," store it in a safe place, and hope you'll never need it. This may seem like overkill just to accomplish an upgrade, but you'll soon discover that it's best to err on the side of caution.

Record other information

Here's a simple command that gives you a lot of information about your PC:

CHKDSK /F

The /F switch fixes errors on the disk. To obtain a record of this data, hit your Print Screen key and you'll get a printout something like Fig. 3-4.

Figure 3-4

```
Volume UFFDA    created 08-19-1994
Volume Serial Number is 1B13-7CCA


170450944 bytes total disk space
    81920 bytes in 2 hidden files
   192512 bytes in 45 directories
 98248960 bytes in 2076 user files
 75927552 bytes available on disk

     4096 bytes in each allocation unit
    41614 total allocation units on disk
    18537 available allocation units on disk
   655360 total bytes memory
   631344 bytes free
```

Screen display of CHKDSK command.

Another very useful command is the excellent but little known MSD, which stands for MicroSoft Diagnostics. This useful program was provided beginning with DOS 6. Just input MSD at your C prompt and you receive access to a world of information about your computer. When you display the individual screens (their titles are in caps), hit your Print Screen key each time to obtain a printout of the screens displaying this vital information explained below.

✳ **COMPUTER**   This screen tells you what type of computer you have, the BIOS manufacturer, category and date, the CPU type, whether you have a math coprocessor, the type of keyboard and bus that are installed, and other pertinent information.

✳ **MEMORY**   On this next screen you receive a plot of how your memory is allocated, the amount of conventional and extended memories, MS-DOS upper memory blocks, and XMS information.

✳ **VIDEO**   The VIDEO screen displays the type of video adapter you have installed, the type of display, the columns and rows displayed, and other pertinent information.

✳ **NETWORK**   Here you are informed if you're on a network, and if so, what type.

✳ **OS VERSION**   The operating system version you are using is displayed, along with whether or not it is located in HMA. It also lists your boot drive and other data.

✳ **MOUSE**   This screen lists the mouse hardware type and manufacturer, the mouse COM port, number of mouse buttons, plus other pertinent information.

✳ **OTHER ADAPTERS**   This screen lists the game adapter information.

✳ **DISK DRIVES**   Figure 3-5 is a typical listing for the disk drives:

Figure 3-5

```
Drive type                              Free space    Total size

A:   Floppy drive, 5.25" 1.2M
               80 cylinders, 2 heads
               512 bytes/sector, 15 sectors/track

B:   Floppy drive, 3.5" 1.44M
               80 cylinders, 2 heads
               512 bytes/sector, 36 sectors/track

C:   Fixed disk, CMOS type 47            72M           162M
               1010 cylinders, 15 heads
               512 bytes/sector, 22 sectors/track

SHARE installed
Last drive=E:
```

MSD display of disk drive listing.

To continue with the rest of the information available from the MSD command:

✳ **LPT PORTS**   This display lists your LPT (parallel) ports, the port address, and whether they are on line, etc.

✳ **COM PORTS**   This screen displays your COM (serial) ports, their addresses, baud rate, parity, and other pertinent information.

✳ **IRQ STATUS**   Here your IRQ statuses are displayed, along with the addresses, a description of each IRQ unit, and a listing of how each of the IRQs are handled.

✳ **TSR PROGRAMS**   In this display the allocated memory blocks for TSR programs are listed, along with their size.

✳ **DEVICE DRIVERS**   On this screen you'll see the installable device driver information, including the Device, its Filename, its Header and Attributes.

Uffdah! Now don't tell me you can't find out anything about your computer without opening it up. But there's still more. Here's another command that tells you all about your memory. Just input at the C prompt:

```
MEM/C/P
```

This gives you considerable detail about your memory, how much each unit is using, etc. The /P switch pauses the display because you are probably going to receive more than one screenful of information. Again, hit your Print Screen key to receive a printout of this information for your records.

At this point, if you are becoming intrigued and would like to know what is actually inside your PC chassis, there is a way you can do this without requiring any hardware. Get a copy of the Shareware program, "What's In That Box," (appendix C) and run it. It's an excellent preview of what you're going to see once you open your own case.

⇨ Types of cases

Several different types of PC cases are used in PCs. Some typical ones are listed in Table 3-3.

PC case configurations   Table 3-3

Designation	Height	Width	Depth	Drive bays	Expansion slots
XT	6.5	21.3	18.5	4	8
AT	4.25	17.75	13	4	8
Desktop	6	21	16.5	3–5	5–6
Small footprint	6	16	16	3	5
Slimline	4	16	16	2–3	3
Mini-tower	17	6	17	4–5	6–8
Tower	25	8	17	6 or more	8 or more

The dimensions listed here are only approximate. Individual manufacturers vary the external dimensions; however, the internal mounting dimensions for the disk drives, the plug-in cards, and the mounting provisions for the motherboards are standard, so most components will fit in virtually all of the cases.

When you consider the fact that you may want to have 2 floppy disk drives, a hard drive, a CD-ROM drive, and a tape backup unit, you can see that the drive bays are quickly used up. And when you also need to add a modem card, a CD-ROM card, a scanner, and additional plug-in cards, the expansion slots are also quickly populated. So, carefully consider and provide for growth potential in your purchases.

The XT and AT cases are no longer being manufactured and are listed here for reference in case you begin your journey into DTP with a used XT or AT. (Uffdah! We're getting deeper and deeper into alphabet soup.) The XT was designed for an 8088 motherboard. A Baby AT motherboard will fit in the XT case. The AT case is large and was designed for an AT size motherboard.

As noted in Table 3-3, the desktop case has excellent growth possibilities, but does take up about five inches more width than the small footprint. The small footprint model sacrifices expansion capability for a smaller area being required on your desktop. The slimline is 2 inches less in height, but height is usually not a space problem, so the slimline is limited to applications where little expansion capability is required.

Note that all of the cases have roughly the same depth. This dimension is usually not an important one unless your desk or counter space is limited.

Both the mini- and the standard-tower, because of their height, are best suited to situations where desk space is critical and where the PC can be located on the floor near, or under a desk, or on a counter or shelf with plenty of height space available. If you have an older PC which has little or no expansion potential, you may want to consider buying a PC case (they're reasonably priced) with better growth possibilities and transfer all of your old PC hardware into a new, expandable case with lots of spare bays and plug-in slots. If you can accommodate the physical configuration, the tower cases have the best growth potential. Most modern motherboards will fit in almost any case, so you can use just about any case size you choose.

⇨ Internal vs. external

For several of the upgrades, a decision has to be made as to whether to use an internal or external mounting. Because this applies to the disk drives, CD-ROM drives, removable media drives, modems, facsimile and tape backup, the internal vs. external tradeoff is conducted in this chapter to avoid having to repeat it in several other chapters.

Size of the individual units usually isn't a problem because many of the internals and externals have been designed to conserve space. An internal is mounted on an add-on card or occupies a space in a drive bay. Both the internal and external function identically, so performance is not an issue.

An internal mount uses up a plug-in slot or a space in a drive bay, drains a little power from your PC power supply, and is less costly. It requires no shelf or desk space to mount on and has either no cables or only a single external cable to be connected. There is also an excellent variety of internal mounts to choose from, as compared to the externals.

The external costs a little more than the internal because it has its own chassis. A mounting shelf or space is required, along with cables to connect your PC, plus a power cord. It has its own power supply and may have some indicators on the front panel which, if you can interpret the flashing lights, tell you what the unit is doing. The lights can be an aid in troubleshooting. However, if you don't need the indicators, you can mount the external almost any place its cord and cables allow. The external has another advantage in that it may also be able to be used as a portable and moved from one computer to another, as long as both computers have compatible software and compatible internal controllers if needed.

My recommendation is to mount everything you can internally if you have the space. Internal mounts are usually trouble-free and there are no external cables that inevitably entangle with each other and with external units. Once an internal unit is installed, you can forget it's there.

 # Screws

One important component you will continuously encounter is the screws that hold much of your removable and installable components in place. Store all of your screws in a plastic or other container so they don't get lost. Be careful that they don't fall inside your computer; they can be hard to find and are a good conductor of electricity, and can cause havoc (smoke) with your circuitry.

Most PCs use only three screw sizes. The screws that secure your outer case to the main chassis are usually 8/32. Removable drives are usually anchored to the chassis frame with 6/32. The screws that secure the motherboard are usually 6/32 or 4/40.

One caution about screws: be sure you don't use screws that are too long for their intended purpose. An extra length screw could damage the innards of the component it is securing.

 # Tools required

Although I mentioned earlier that all you need to accomplish most of the upgrades is a screwdriver and a pair of needlenose pliers, a small investment in a special PC tool kit is a wise one. There are several varieties of inexpensive tool kits designed especially for computer upgrading. I purchased the PC tool kit depicted in Fig. 3-6 for about $10 at WalMart.

This kit contains just about everything you need, except for the needlenose pliers. However, it has tools that take the place of the needlenose. All of the tools are mounted in an attractive leatherette padded and zippered case. The kit has 5 screwdrivers of various types and sizes, 2 nut drivers, a tweezers, a small parts-retriever tool (a very handy tool for picking up errant nuts and bolts), a chip remover, and a plastic tube for storing the small parts you remove during disassembly. All of the parts have been demagnetized.

Figure 3-6

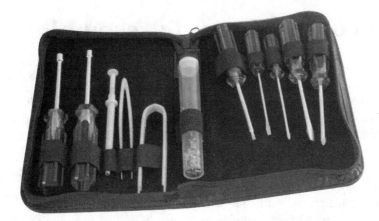

PC tool kit.

 # Case access

For most of the upgrades you'll be making, you'll have to remove the cover or "skin" from your PC to obtain access to its innards. This chapter provides step-by-step instructions, along with drawings and photographs to accomplish this basic task.

The XT and AT cases usually provide two different types of access: slide or hinge. The slide type is where you remove 4–6 screws (usually at the rear) and slide the cover off toward the rear of the chassis. The less common hinge type is hinged near the middle or rear. It has a top (two hinges on either side, located near the rear) which lifts up like the hood of your car. The hinges usually consist of nothing more than a self-locking nut and a bolt. The hinge configuration has the advantage of providing better access because it's easier to get inside, add boards, set switches, etc.

Two types of access are usually provided for the tower cases. With one type you remove about six or so screws from the back, just as you do with the desktop type cases. A more desirable type of tower case has removable side panels that allow access to all the innards with the turning of two large screws.

 # Before you begin to disassemble

Before you remove the cover, disconnect all power and move your computer to a nonmetallic table or bench that has been cleared so you'll have plenty of area to spread out and work with. Keep a small plastic bottle or container (very important so you don't lose anything) nearby to store the screws and any small parts you'll be removing and needing later.

Removing the case is not difficult. Just take your time, unscrew the five or so indicated screws, and slide the cover away from the front panel, slowly and carefully until, voila! You have exposed the inner workings of your magical machine. Here is the detailed procedure:

For desktop cases (Fig. 3-7), there are usually screws (five in the photo) in the four corners at the back and one or two halfway between the two top corner screws. You may also find some desktop cases with screws on the side. A few cases may have to be placed on their backs to access the screws.

Figure 3-7

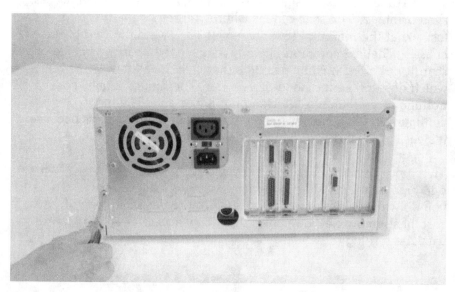

Rear view of PC showing screws at back for removing cover.

Remove the 4–6 screws, place them in a container for safekeeping, then pull back on the cover. It may be firmly attached to the front panel, so it may take a good tug to break it loose, but don't try to yank it all the way back with one motion; you could pull loose or damage the internal cables. Once the cover is loose from the front panel, pull the cover back slowly and observe carefully to make sure that no cables are scraping or being pulled away by the cover (Fig.3-8).

Figure 3-8

Cover partially slid off.

For cases with screws in the rear, pull the cover completely off to the rear to expose the chassis and set the cover to one side. If it's fastened by screws on the sides and back, pull the sides apart and lift the cover off carefully. The inner chassis should now be visible (Fig. 3-9).

Record all pertinent information about your system

Now that you have your cover off, it's a good idea to pause and record all the pertinent information about your PC, especially if this is the first time you've looked inside.

Make a sketch and a list of the plug-in boards you have and the slots they're plugged into. Also record the positions of any switches or

Figure 3-9

View inside of PC.

jumpers on the boards. You may have to loosen or even partially remove the plug-in boards to obtain this information, but it will come in handy sooner or later. It would also be a good idea to make a rough sketch of the location and shape of all the components inside your PC for future reference. You might also supplement this with a few Polaroid pictures.

⇨ Replacing the cover

To replace the cover, carefully fit the case on the rear (or top) of the chassis and slowly push the cover forward. At the same time, be careful that no cables or components obstruct the forward motion. Continue to push the cover forward until it engages the front panel. It may take a little extra push at this point to make sure it is fully seated. Then replace the 4–6 screws you removed earlier, and you're ready to try out your new upgrade.

 # PC sex education

Before you get too entangled with cables and connectors, it's time for a little PC sex education. Just as you may have learned in your earlier years, there are male and female connectors. Each serves a unique function.

Male connectors in electrical units are usually installed on the fixed or stationary components, such as the disk drives or plug-in cards. Female connectors are usually installed on the interconnecting cables. There is a very logical and good reason for this standard arrangement.

Spare cables are often included in a personal computer so they can be used for easy upgrading. These cables are often left loose and dangle within a PC case. They are free to move around when the case is jarred or the computer is moved.

If male connectors with their protruding copper pins are used on cables and the cables are loose, the pins are apt to cause electrical shorts to the computer chassis or other components, damaging or perhaps even ruining the computer.

However, female connectors with their recessed metal contacts are protected by a plastic, insulating shell. Even if they are loose and accidentally contact the chassis, they will not short to a metal object.

 # Cables and connectors

Whenever you disconnect a connector, be sure to label it with a piece of tape attached to it to designate where each cable was connected and how it was oriented. If you're worried about making a mistake, take some shots with a Polaroid camera to document where everything was before you started. And when you disconnect a connector, note that some are seated firmly and may require a slight back-and-forth rocking and rolling motion to remove them.

 # Inserting plug-in modules

This section covers the option or add-on boards that plug in to the existing slots on the motherboard.

When you have a module to plug in, there are certain techniques to observe which simplify the procedure and establish reliable connections. First of all: Plan ahead. If you intend to make future upgrades (and who doesn't?), try to keep as much room free inside your chassis as possible. Beware of long cable runs that might get in the way of your cards or components later. With a display driver card, take special care and mount it as far away from the power supply as possible to avoid pickup from the power supply.

Also, if you have to set any switches or jumpers on the plug-in card (check the documentation that came with your card), do this before you install the card. Unless you have small fingers, use a tweezers or needlenose pliers to move or remove jumpers. For the DIP switches, use a small screwdriver (don't use a pencil, the lead may break off and cause trouble later) to set the DIP switches. After the card is plugged in, the switches and jumpers may be difficult to access.

Once you've selected a vacant slot, remove its slot cover on the back of the case by removing the Phillips head screw (see Fig. 3-10) and the slot cover. Place the screw and the slot cover in a dish or jar for safekeeping. The slot cover is no longer needed, but keep it in your spare parts box. (I never throw any computer parts away in spite of my wife's protestations.) Next, discharge any static electricity that may be in your body by touching the metal part of the chassis.

Pick up the plug-in card by grabbing hold of the opposite ends of the top of the card and hold it by the edges with your fingers (Fig. 3-11), away from the chips, components, or the copper strips at the bottom of the card.

Align the card with the slot as illustrated in Fig. 3-12 and place the bottom of the card (the section with the short, multiple copper conducting strips all lined up in a row—a.k.a. a card-edge connector) into the designated slot.

Figure 3-10

Removal of metal brackets.

Figure 3-11

Hold plug-in card by the edges.

Figure 3-12

Align card with plug-in slot.

Push the card down with your thumbs and index fingers (Fig. 3-13). You should feel a "click" when the card is properly seated and the hole in the angle bracket lines up with the mounting holes in the chassis. If it resists, gently rock and roll the card back and forth, but don't force it. If the card won't go all the way in, pull the card out and try again. Be sure not to force it. The card and the slot are designed for each other, so their union should be a natural one to accomplish.

Finally, secure the angle bracket on the back of the plug-in card to the back of the case with the screw you removed from the slot cover to make sure of continued good contact. Tighten the screw.

If an external cable(s) is to be connected, check the keying or orientation (the connectors are usually marked with a number, but you might need a magnifying glass or a pair of young eyes to see them).

The flat gray cables usually have a red or black stripe running down one side which indicates pin 1. Line pin 1 on the cable up with pin 1 on the connector and plug the cable in, gently. Again, it should slip into place. Don't force it; use a gentle rocking motion to ensure good

Figure 3-13

Push card in and hear click.

contact. Some of the larger external cables have plastic snap locks to hold the cable securely to the card. Snap these closed if they're used.

Some cables are keyed so they only fit one way. If used, check the keying before you make your connections. That completes the installation of a plug-in card.

⇨ Installing/removing chips

You may have to insert or remove a chip (such as a numeric coprocessor or RAM) as part of your upgrade. If you do, there are special precautions to observe.

Chips are susceptible to damage from static discharge (the static charge you can pick up from walking on a carpet), so the chips are stored in protective packages (usually a plastic bag). Before handling any chip, discharge yourself by touching the metal chassis of your computer. Alternatively a grounding strap (available from your local electronics store or mail-order outlet) as illustrated in Figs. 3-14 and 3-15 can be used as an extra safety measure. The strap is connected

Figure 3-14

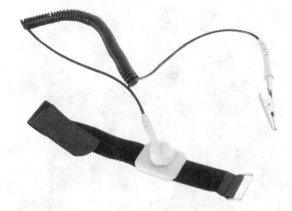

Grounding strap.

Figure 3-15

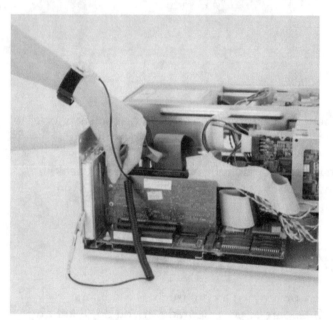

Grounding strap in use.

to your wrist and to the computer chassis and is recommended if you are going to work on your PC for a long period of time. When handling the chips, don't scuffle your feet on the carpet or you'll build up a static charge. If possible, accomplish these upgrades sitting down and avoid shuffling your feet.

Pin 1 of a chip is usually indicated by a painted dot, a notch, a diagonally cut corner, or an arrow. The socket on the board (also

called the "carrier") has pin 1 indicated in a similar manner. Often it has pin 1 designated by the number 1 on the printed circuit board. If you can't find pin 1, look for pin 2. Pin 1 will be opposite or adjacent to pin 2.

Align the chip with the socket and slowly press it down until the body of the chip is flush with the surface of the socket. It should go in easily; they, too, were made for each other. If you suspect that the chip is not properly inserted, carefully pull it up with a chip extractor (also available at your local electronic store, from your mail-order outlet, or your PC Tool Kit), and pry it up a little on one corner at a time until it's free. If you feel the chip may be damaged, re-inspect it and correct any problems. Repeat the insertion as described above.

⇨ Burn-in

Although most computer electronic components are long-lived, a very small percentage of them can fail in a relatively short time, as in hours. This is called "infant mortality." These failures result mostly from poor quality control, inadequate internal connections, and inferior components.

To weed out any components that may be so afflicted, you should put your major components (motherboard, RAMs, plug-in cards, etc.) through a burn-in period of anywhere between eight and twenty-four hours. Some manufacturers do their own burn-in; many do not.

To burn them in properly, operate them for this period accomplishing some function for which they were designed. For example, simply having your display continually present a picture is a good way to test out one of your weakest links. For electro-mechanical components, such as a disk drive, you have to exercise them yourself, command it to write and read data numerous times to make sure it's functioning properly. Alternatively, you could write a short batch file that accomplishes it automatically for you. There are also software burn-in programs that will do this for you. One program, aptly titled Burn-In, (appendix C) for example, is available from most shareware vendors.

Once your components have survived their infancy and enter their teen years, they should be as frisky as a teenager at a dance and be looking forward to their geriatric years with eager anticipation. Infant mortality is an excellent reason why you should only procure components that have at least a 30-day money back guarantee. If your components are going to fail, they will most likely fail during their infancy.

Adding RAM

FIRST, a few clarifications about memory terms. PC memory storage capacity is usually specified in "bytes." A byte is the smallest addressable unit of memory, usually eight bits long. It is the fundamental unit of information storage. As a point of reference, an alphanumeric character—one keyboard press, such as the letter A—is one byte. A KB (kilobyte) is about one thousand bytes; a MB (megabyte) is one million bytes. And a GB (gigabyte) is a thousand-million bytes (that's nine zeroes after the number. Uffdah!).

Basic types of memory

Before getting into the details of RAM, let's review the basic types of memory used in your PC and their functions. Three basic types of memory are utilized:

➢ Disk drives

➢ ROM

➢ RAM

Disk drives, a magnetic-based memory medium with a very large capacity, are used for long-term storage. Functionally, disk drives are analogous in operation to a blackboard in that they can be written on and maintain their memory indefinitely until they are intentionally (or unintentionally) erased. Much like a blackboard, disk drives can be repeatedly written on and erased. As far as speed is concerned, compared to RAM, disk drives are a relatively slow memory medium to access (many milliseconds). Disk drives comes in two flavors:

➢ Hard

➢ Floppy

Hard disks (a.k.a. fixed disks) are usually permanently mounted in your PC (portable hard drives are also available, see chapter 5). Hard disk storage capacities range from as low as 20MB to hundreds of megabytes to as high as several gigabytes. Hard disks serve a vital function as the basic long-term storage device for the PC, storing the massive amounts of data and software that need to be accessed during the execution of a program. A hard disk retains its

information, whether the power to the PC is on or off. Although hard disks are generally very reliable, they can fail on occasion and need to be backed up onto floppy disks or other backup media.

Floppy disks (although some are no longer "floppy") are a removable magnetic storage medium used primarily to input data from software programs or external sources and to create backup copies of the data stored on the hard disk for security purposes. Storage capacities range from as low as 360K to as high as several MB.

ROM (Read Only Memory) consists of electronic circuitry which stores fixed computer data (such as BIOS) that has been permanently burned into a chip. ROM is analogous to the printed pages of a book. Both ROM and printed pages contain valuable information; however, the stored information is permanent and cannot be changed. The stored information for both ROM and printed pages can only be read. However, you probably won't be concerned with installing ROM unless you have to update your BIOS.

 RAM

Next, let's consider RAM (Random Access Memory), the main topic of this chapter. RAM is the high-speed working memory (access time is in the nano-second range, that's one thousandth of a microsecond) which serves as the storage area required by the software program(s) being used. RAM for PCs ranges in capacity from about 1MB to 32MB and growing. Functionally, RAM is analogous to the picture on your TV set. With power on, the TV functions, your picture glows, or in some TV shows, glowers. However, as soon as you turn power off, the picture is gone forever. Similarly as soon as power is removed, RAM suffers a permanent loss of memory.

RAM is fabricated of millions of tiny capacitors. It is the temporary home for storing your operating environment, the programs being used, and all the data you create. When you add more RAM to your system, it often speeds up the performance of your PC because much of the computer's activities are handled in high-speed, nano-second RAM, instead of having to repeatedly access the slow millisecond disk

memories. In general, added RAM allows you to handle large documents, utilize disk caches, print spoolers, RAMdisks, etc.

With so many memory-hungry programs currently in use, the more RAM you have, the better and faster your PC runs; up to a limit, of course. Windows and DesqView, for example, gobble up enormous chunks of RAM, enabling you to run several programs at the same time. For example, you can be working with your DTP software, then decide you need to add an illustration. You can jump to your graphics program, create the illustration, then import it into your DTP program, and resume your work where you left off. Another feature that more and more software developers are adding is "linking," a process where any changes you make in one program (such as revising a drawing) will automatically be carried over to and update that same drawing in another document, such as a word processing program.

How much RAM do you have?

You don't have to take the cover off your computer to determine how much RAM you have installed. Just input MEM/C/P at the C:\> prompt and you'll receive a tally similar to Fig. 4-1. Rounding it off, this PC has 4MB of RAM.

Figure 4-1

Type of Memory	Total	=	Used +	Free
Conventional	655360 (640K)		24096 (24K)	631264 (616K)
Upper	187456 (183K)		50016 (49K)	137440 (134K)
Adapter RAM/ROM	393216 (384K)		393216 (384K)	0 (0K)
Extended (XMS)	2958272 (2889K)		1270720 (1241K)	1687552 (1648K)
Total memory	4194304 (4096K)		1738048 (1697K)	2456256 (751K)

RAM allocations.

Different CPUs are designed to handle disparate maximums of RAM. The 286 system can usually be expanded to a maximum of 4MB by adding memory modules. The 386SX can address a maximum of 16MB and the 386DX, 486 and Pentium can address up to 4GB of RAM (Let's hope we never get there).

 # How much RAM is needed?

Different types of programs require dissimilar amounts of RAM to function properly. The tables that follow list the RAM you should have installed to run the specified software.

✳ **Level 1: DOS word processors**   For Level 1 upgrades, Table 4-1 lists the minimum RAM your system must have installed to accommodate specific DOS word processors. Where two numbers are listed, such as 450/520, the first number is the minimum recommended by the software developer, the second number provides maximum usability.

RAM requirements—Level 1—DOS word processors   Table 4-1

Program	Minimum RAM
Microsoft Word	384/512K
PC-Write-Advanced Level	384
PFS:Write	512/640
Professional Write	512K
Textra	340K
WordPerfect	450/520K
WordStar	512K/640

✳ **Level 1: Windows word processors**   Table 4-2 lists the minimum RAM your system must have for specific Level 1 Windows word processors. Even though DTP programs claim you can function with the RAM listed in this table, if you want to run multiple applications, you'll need 4MB as a minimum, and up to 8MB if you want to run several applications simultaneously.

RAM requirements—Level 1—Windows word processors   Table 4-2

Program	Minimum RAM
Ami Pro	2MB
DeScribe (OS-2 only)	8MB
Just Write	2MB

Table 4-2   **Continued**

Program	Minimum RAM
Professional Write Plus	1MB
Textor	2MB
Word for Windows	2MB
WordPerfect for Windows	2MB
WordStar for Windows	2MB

✴ **Level 2: DOS desktop publishing software**   For Level 2 upgrades, Table 4-3 lists the minimum RAM your system must have for specific DOS DTPs.

Table 4-3   **RAM requirements—Level 2—DOS DTP**

Program	Minimum RAM
Avagio	1MB
Express Publisher	640K
IMSI Publisher	460/540K
LePrint	384K
PFS:First Publisher	640K
Publish It!	640K
Publish It Lite!	640K

✴ **Level 2: Windows desktop publishing software**   For Level 2 upgrades, Table 4-4 lists the minimum specs your system must have for specific Windows DTP software. To repeat: even though the DTP programs state you can function with the RAM listed in this table, if you need to run several applications, you should have 4MB as a minimum and as much as 8MB if you have several applications to run simultaneously.

Table 4-4   **RAM requirements—Level 2—Windows DTP software**

Program	Minimum RAM
Desktop Publisher	1MB
Express Publisher	2/4MB

Program	Minimum RAM
MicroSoft Publisher	4MB
PFS:Publisher for Windows	2/4MB
Publish It!	640K

✳ **Level 3: DOS desktop publishing software**   For Level 3 upgrades, Table 4-5 lists the minimum RAM your system must have installed for specific DOS DTPs:

RAM requirements—Level 3—DOS DTP   Table 4-5

Program	Minimum RAM
Aldus PageMaker	512K
Envision Publisher	450K
Ventura Publisher	540/640K

✳ **Level 3: Windows desktop publishing software**   To accomplish Level 3 upgrades for specific Windows DTPs, Table 4-6 lists the minimum RAM your system must have installed. To reiterate: even though the DTP programs state you can function with the RAM listed in this table, if you need to run several applications, you should have 4MB as a minimum and as much as 8MB if you have several applications to run simultaneously.

RAM requirements—Level 3—Windows DTP software   Table 4-6

Program	Minimum RAM
Aldus PageMaker	4MB
FrameMaker`	8MB
PagePlus	2/3MB
QuarkXpress	4MB
Ventura Publisher	4/6MB

 # Cache it

One excellent improvement in speed of operation (some claim a fifty percent increase in speed) results if you have some extra RAM and use it to create a disk cache. A disk cache is an area of RAM that is set aside and reserved to buffer data going to and from the hard disk. The cache controller "guesses" which bytes the processor will need next—based on the statistical probability that programs tend to repeatedly work in a relatively small area of memory and data for a fairly long time—and loads these bytes into the disk cache so they are instantly available to perform their designated functions.

With a disk cache in operation, when your program needs to access a disk, it first checks to see if the information stored in the cache is the information it needs. If so, the program snatches the information from high-speed RAM, instead of the slow, hard disks, considerably speeding up operations.

If you have 8MB of RAM, for example, you can allocate 2MB for SmartDrive, the disk cache utility that comes with Windows. To check how much is allocated, input: SMARTDRV/S at the Windows prompt. Figure 4-2 illustrates a typical response.

Figure 4-2

```
C:\WINDOWS>smartdrsv/s
MicroSoft SMARTDrive Disk Cache version 4.0
Copyright 1991, 1992 MicroSoft Corp.

Room for 256 elements of 8,192 bytes each
There have been 129,533 cache hits
      and 30,694 cache misses

Cache size: 2,097,152 bytes
Cache size while running Windows: 2,097,152
```

Typical response to SMARTDRV/S query.

```
      Disk Caching Status
drive read cache  write cache buffering
A:    yes         no          no
B:    yes         no          no
C:    yes         yes         no


For help, Type "Smartdrv /?"
```

As you'll note, there have been lots of cache hits and relatively few misses. (Maybe that's because I have a one-track mind.) Actually this usually happens when you're working in a given program on a specific document for a long period of time.

Another cache used is a RAM cache, not to be confused with the disk cache. The RAM cache is built into the motherboard and located near the CPU. You can't add this cache; it comes with the motherboard. The RAM cache's work assignment is to store the data used most frequently by the CPU to provide instant access to this data and speed up operations. Typical CPU caches are 64K to 256K or more.

Terminate and stay resident (TSR)

Here's another item that significantly affects the RAM you have available for your programs: TSR (Terminate and Stay Resident) programs. A TSR is a program that is squirreled away in RAM when you're working with another program. It uses up some of your RAM, so you should be aware of which TSRs you are using, and how much RAM they devour. A TSR is called up by activating "hot keys," such as CTRL-F1. Once installed, a TSR is on a standby status. The TSR may contain a calculator, a screen capture program, a dictionary, or some other special program that you want to instantly access from other programs.

You can negate or at least minimize the deleterious effects of TSRs by taking advantage of a memory manager to relocate the TSRs above the 640K mark. Memory managers are available in DOS 5 and 6 and in commercial programs such as QEMM and 386MAX.

When a TSR is called into action by hitting the hot key(s), the program you were working with is temporarily suspended. When you're finished using the TSR, you usually hit another hot key combination (or input EXIT) and are taken right back to the other program, right where you left off. One problem with TSRs, however, is that they use up some of that precious 640K RAM, so you'll have less conventional RAM to use with your standard DOS programs.

 # My recommendations

Table 4-7 lists my recommendations for RAM for the various level software programs. The table lists three categories: Minimum, Working, and Future. The minimum amount is the least RAM I feel you can barely function with. The working column is a moderate level of RAM that functions with most programs. The Future number is the RAM you may have to eventually add to be prepared for future software developments. You should install the minimum if that's all your budget allows. But plan to install more RAM as you can afford it and as your requirements change (and when you get tired of seeing that clock on the window and would like to smash it).

Table 4-7   **RAM recommendations**

Level	Minimum RAM	Working RAM	Future RAM
1- DOS	1MB	2MB	4MB
1- Windows	2MB	4MB	8–16MB
2- DOS	1MB	2MB	4MB
2- Windows	2MB	4MB	8–16MB
3- DOS	1MB	2MB	4MB
3- Windows	4MB	8MB	16–32MB

 # RAM physical packages

Most RAM is available in the modern Serial In-line Memory Module (SIMMs) package. Some of the older RAM packages use an SIP (Serial Inline Package) configuration.

SIMMs are plug-ins which use Dynamic Random Access Memory (DRAM) chips. They come in a variety of forms, capacities, speeds, and operating parameters. A SIMM module is a collection of loose chips that are soldered onto a small circuit board (Fig. 4-3). The board is about the size of a couple of postage stamps and provides a single assembly that's easier to handle and install, rather than going

Figure 4-3

SIMM module package.

through the hassle of trying to manipulate and install 9 to 36 individual chips. The capacity of the RAM chip is usually designated by the last three or four numbers inscribed on the chip casing. For example, an HB52B1000AB-7 is a 1MB chip with an access time of 70 nanoseconds. The other letters and numbers are manufacturers' special designations.

The older SIMM versions have 30 pins, the newer ones have 72. The two versions are not interchangeable. The 30 pins are 9-bit devices (8 bits plus a parity bit) and are called X9s (by nines). They come in 256K, 1MB and 4MB capacities. Motherboards usually have sockets for two or four banks of memory. You have to install four matching SIMMs in each bank, or leave them empty. Although 256K RAMs are still available, a better choice is the 1 and 4MB sizes because it takes too many 256Ks to meet current and future RAM needs. Often as few as 4 SIMM sockets are available and only rarely are 16 available. So you should use SIMM modules as large as you can afford.

The 72-pin SIMMs are 36-bit devices (32 data plus 4 for parity) and are referred to as X36s (by thirty sixes). They come in 1MB, 2MB, 4MB, 8MB, and 16MB capacities. You can usually mix and match the X36s, so you have much more flexibility in configuring your system.

Some motherboards may use SIP memory. The SIP module is similar to the SIMM, except that the SIP module has a row of 30 small prongs or pins which are inserted into a corresponding socket strip on the motherboard.

You are not limited to the total amount of memory you can install in the existing memory sockets on the motherboard. Several companies make memory boards which plug into the plug-in slots on the motherboard. Some of these plug-in boards have SIMM connectors that accept up to 32MB of RAM.

RAM access time

Your next consideration is RAM access time, which is rated in nanoseconds (ns or billionths of a second). Access time is the time it takes RAM to fetch random data from one of its memory cells and deliver it to the CPU. SIMMs come in a variety of access times, from 200 (slow) nanoseconds to 60 nanoseconds (fast). Slow chips can't be used in fast computers or they'll slow operations down and errors can occur. Once you have installed RAM that matches the speed required by your CPU, adding faster RAM does not speed up operations. Table 4-8 lists the RAM speeds required for specific CPUs.

Table 4-8   **RAM speeds required for specific CPUs**

Motherboard type/speed	RAM speed (ns)
8088 4.77 MHz	200
8088 8 MHz	150
8088 10 MHz	120
80286 to 20 MHz	100
80386 16 or 20 MHz	100
80386 to 33 MHz	85
80386 to 40 MHz	70
80386SX	70
80486DX	60
80586 (Pentium)	60

 # RAM installation

Most 32-bit systems (386DX, 486, and above) require the installation of SIMMs in matched groups of four. Sixteen-bit systems (286, 386SX, or 386SL) usually require two matched SIMMs per memory bank. A motherboard typically has two memory banks, each with 4 sockets. Only memory chips of equal capacity can be used within the same memory bank. However, chips of different access times can be used within the same memory bank. The sockets are usually identified as Bank 0, Bank 1, Bank 2, etc. with lettering adjacent to the sockets. You should fill in the lower numbered banks first.

Static discharge can destroy a memory module, so before you handle any memory modules, be aware of the potential harmful effects of static discharge. Keep the memory modules in their protective bag or enclosure until you need them. Before you open the bag, touch a metal surface, such as the case of your PC, to discharge any static electricity your body may have created, or attach the static discharge strap illustrated in chapter 3. You may even see a spark discharge when you touch the metal. This spark could cause a permanent loss of memory (of the chips, not yours).

After touching a metal surface, open the bag or enclosure and handle the modules by touching only the sides; that is, the plastic body (usually green) which comprises the area of the board that has no metal or conductors on it. DO NOT touch the electrical contacts or anything on the board. And, as you work with the modules, continue to pause and touch the metal surface of the computer case occasionally to make sure you haven't picked up static electricity as you position yourself around your PC.

 # Remove the motherboard?

On some PCs you may have to partially remove the motherboard (and possibly some other components) to obtain access to the SIMM sockets. (On one of my PCs, I also had to remove all of my plug-in boards.) On the newer PC cases, the motherboard is typically held in

place by several vertical plastic standoffs and anchored by one or two screws installed in the chassis. (See Fig. 4-4.)

Figure 4-4

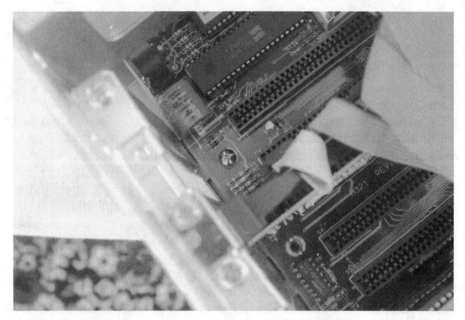

Motherboard anchored by several vertical plastic standoffs and 1-2 screws.

It's relatively simple to partially remove this type of motherboard because the plastic standoffs are mounted in slots. Just remove the one or two screws holding the motherboard in place, then slide the motherboard toward the large hole in the slot (see Fig. 4-5) and the motherboard should be free to move (except for the cables attached to it).

Note also in Fig. 4-5 that the metal chassis that the motherboard is mounted on also has several mounting slots of different sizes and of different spacings so that several different size motherboards can be used with this chassis (nice growth potential). The motherboard depicted in Fig. 4-5 is a Baby AT size.

Be careful of the cables and only move the motherboard far enough to obtain access to the SIMM sockets. If you have to remove a cable, be sure to tag it so you know where to plug it back in. Again, handle

Figure 4-5

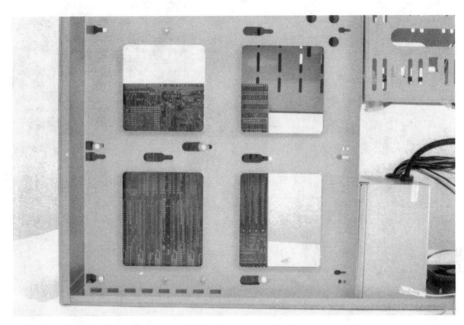

Slots for removing motherboard.

the motherboard gently. If you have to prop it up against something, slip some paper or cloth under it to serve as a cushion and insulator.

⇨ To install SIMMs

Before removing the SIMMs from the package, be sure to discharge your body's static charge by touching your PC's metal chassis and touch it repeatedly during installation. The SIMMs are to be mounted in the slots (8 in this photo) in the lower right quarter of Fig. 4-6.

If you're replacing old SIMMs, note that the installed SIMMs are held in place by a pair of gold (or silver) clamps located at the ends of each socket. (Fig. 4-7). To remove the SIMMs from their socket, gently (very gently) pull these metal clamps outward, away from the installed SIMM board. The board should pop out and tilt away from the socket.

Figure 4-6

Empty SIMM sockets.

Figure 4-7

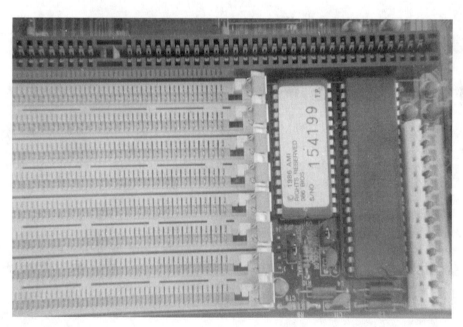

Metal clamps.

Observe also that each SIMM module has a pair of holes, one at each end of the module. These holes match up with the plastic pins that are attached to the sides of the SIMM socket and help hold it in place. After you've pulled the gold pins out away from the module, the SIMM module should be free. Again, touch only the plastic side of the module as you extract it. Place the removed SIMM module aside. Remove the remaining SIMM modules in a similar manner.

To load (or reload) the RAM area, first load up Bank 0. It will probably hold 4 SIMM modules. Pick up the first SIMM module by the plastic body and orient the SIMM module so that the chips on the top of the module face away from the angle of the socket, that is, the chips should be facing upward (Fig. 4-8).

Figure 4-8

The chips on the board face away from the angle of the socket; that is, the chips should be on the top of the board.

Remember that the SIMM module should go in gently and easily. If it doesn't, you may not have it oriented properly. The SIMM module is inserted at a diagonal. Once the SIMM module is positioned properly,

carefully pivot it upright with your thumbs until the locking tabs (at the ends) click in place (Fig. 4-9) and the plastic pins are inserted through the holes at the ends of the SIMM modules.

Repeat for all the other SIMM modules. All of them should be inserted and facing in the same direction.

Figure 4-9

Pivot SIMM upright with thumbs.

⇨ To upgrade RAM

If you have old plug-in chips to remove, it's a good investment to purchase an inexpensive pair of chip extractors from your computer component source (or use the chip extractor from your PC Tool Kit). Be sure to lift the chips up carefully; they should come up with only a modest effort. For SIPs, grasp the modules with both hands on the two upper corners and pull them out slowly.

 # Inform your computer of its new power

After you've installed the memory modules, you need to inform the computer of the additions. Some of the older PCs may require that you change some jumpers, or that you flip some DIP switches on your motherboard. Most modern-day PCs only require that you change your setup on boot-up. To accomplish this, hold the Delete (or Ctrl-Alt-Esc) key down when your computer boots up. Your screen will announce:

```
Keyboard Error
Press <F1> to RESUME
```

Hit F1 and you'll see the AMBIOS SETUP PROGRAM (or something similar) illustrated in Fig. 4-10.

Figure 4-10

```
            STANDARD CMOS SETUP

            ADVANCED CMOS SETUP

          ADVANCED CHIPSET SETUP

   AUTO CONFIGURATION WITH BIOS DEFAULTS

            CHANGE PASSWORD

         AUTO DETECT HARD DISK

           HARD DISK UTILITY

          WRITE TO CMOS AND EXIT

      DO NOT WRITE TO CMOS AND EXIT
```

Hit F1 and you will see the AMBIOS SETUP PROGRAM, or something similar.

Choose STANDARD CMOS SETUP with your cursor arrows and hit Enter. You are then presented with the following warning:

```
Improper Use of Setup may Cause Problems !!
```

plus some more information. Don't be frightened by the warning, just hit Enter and you are presented with the AMBIOS SETUP PROGRAM - STANDARD CMOS SETUP screen of Fig. 4-11.

Figure 4-11

```
                 BIOS SETUP PROGRAM-STANDARD CMOS SETUP
(C)Copyright  1990  American Megatrends Inc., All Rights Reserved

Date(mm/date/year) :Mon, Sep 12 1994    Base memory   :640KB
Time(hour/min/sec) :16 : 42 : 34        Ext. memory   :7168KB
Daylight saving    :Disabled  Cylin Head WPcom LZone Sect Size
Hard disk c type   :47        1025  5    0     0      40   100MB
Hard disk d type   :Not installed
Floppy drive A     :1.2MB 5,"
Floppy drive B     :1.44 MB 3+"
Primary display    :VGA/PGA/EGA
```

Sun	Mon	Tue	Wed	Thu	Fri	Sat
				1	2	3
4	5	6	7	8	9	10
11	12	13	14	15	16	17
18	19	20	21	22	23	24
25	26	27	28	29	30	

```
Month:Jan,Feb,.....Dec
Date:01,02,03,.....31
Year: 1901,1902,...2099
```

```
Esc:  Exit F2/F3:Color  PU/PD:Modify
```

BIOS SETUP PROGRAM.

Check the columns at the upper right of the display which should now automatically acknowledge the base memory (640K), plus the amount of the extended memory you have added. Now all you have to do is hit Esc to leave the presentation. Your computer has acknowledged and can now fully take advantage of this new memory.

If it doesn't recognize the new memory, you may have to manually change the entries in the AMBIOS SETUP PROGRAM table to inform the computer about its new power. You can also determine how much RAM you have installed with the CHKDSK command (the last two lines of the display indicate the total memory and the number of bytes free). Or you can input MEM/C/P at the DOS prompt to obtain a very detailed listing of your memory allocations.

Added hard drive capacity

ONE area which disappears faster than pepperoni pizza at a pajama party is hard disk storage capacity. Not too long ago, a half meg was considered to be adequate storage for a software program. But now 5-to 10MB seems to be about average. Install Windows and 10–12MB are consumed; add Word for Windows and 15MB more are used up; add a few more programs and some utilities and you're pushing 100 megs. One high-end operating system, OS/2, eats up to 50MB of disk space if you install every option. So, hard disks (a.k.a. fixed disks) just keep getting bigger and bigger.

However, with a little care, you can minimize the hard disk capacity consumed by these byte-ravenous behemoths. For example, if you load a tutorial when you install the program, erase it when you're finished with it. If you don't need to access your clip art often, download it onto floppies. Many of the utilities you load onto your disk are seldom used. They may also be downloaded and kept nearby on floppies.

But these are only stop-gap solutions. You're still probably going to be needing more hard disk storage, so here are the basic methods of adding more hard disk capacity:

➤ Use a disk-compression program.

➤ Add a second internal hard disk.

➤ Replace your hard disk with one of increased capacity.

➤ Add a hard disk on a plug-in card.

➤ Add an external fixed hard disk.

All of these upgrade routes are covered in this chapter, along with their advantages, disadvantages, relative cost, and difficulty of upgrading. In addition, this chapter provides step-by-step instructions, along with illustrations and photographs, describing how to install, format, and test the drives for the above upgrades.

⇨ Disk choice is important

As you read computer magazines, you see faster and faster CPUs being touted as the solution to all of your problems. But CPU speed

is only one ingredient in how quickly and efficiently your computer can accomplish the tasks you assign to it. Equally important is the performance of your disk drives. For this reason, careful selection of a hard disk drive and the use of disk caching and file defragmentation are essential to provide optimum performance of your entire computer system.

➡ Some definitions

Before considering the basic upgrades, let's define some terms and unscramble some of the inevitable alphabet soup which must out of necessity be tolerated throughout the discussions.

❋ **Access time**   This specifies the average amount of time it takes the heads to reach the area of the disk which contains the data it needs. Typical hard disk access times are 10 to 30 milliseconds.

❋ **Cache**   A hardware or software cache temporarily stores the most recently used data which has been accessed from the disk in RAM on the assumption that the same data will be used repeatedly. Because of the RAM's high speed, this data is then instantly available to the program being used.

❋ **Capacity**   Rated in megabytes (or gigabytes), this is the total capacity of the storage media. When selecting a new drive, be sure to ask whether the quoted size is the formatted capacity of the disk, because it may lose as much as 10MB or more after formatting.

❋ **Controller**   An electronic circuit that controls the operation of the hard drive. For IDE drives, the controller is located inside the sealed hard drive.

❋ **FAT (File Allocation Table)**   A section of the disk that is set aside to serve as a sort of index that lists which disk clusters are in use, which are available, and which files the scattered clusters belong to.

❋ **FDISK**   A DOS command used to partition your hard disk and prepare it for DOS operations. If you want the disk to hold all of your programs, just hit the Enter key when the FDISK questions are asked and accept the default parameters presented.

✳ **High-level format** This formatting procedure is accomplished by the DOS FORMAT command. It creates the FAT (File Allocation Table) and the root directory. FORMAT makes the disk a system disk which is bootable. You have to effect this format with a new hard disk.

✳ **Low-level format** This basic formatting procedure divides the disk's tracks into sectors. It is not needed for the IDE drives because they contain an integral controller and are low-level formatted at the factory.

If you purchase your SCSI hard drive and controller from the same manufacturer, the low-level format should have been accomplished by the disk manufacturer. If you purchased them separately, you'll have to accomplish this. The controller card should have instructions and a software disk for accomplishing this. This procedure should have to be performed only once for a hard disk.

✳ **MTBF (Mean Time Between Failures)** This calculated figure is the theoretical (mythical) length of time the disk will run before it fails. MTBFs of 100,000 to 300,000 hours are quoted. That translates from 4,000 to over 12,000 days of continuous use. If you believe this figure, I can get you a terrific deal on this low-mileage, pre-owned Cadillac that my old maid aunt kept stored in her garage . . .

This inflated figure is quoted, in spite of the fact that you're lucky if the manufacturer gives you a 1–2 year warranty on the disk. One company claims a 300,000 hour MTBF (34 years) but they only warranty their drives for one of those years. (You figure it out, maybe it's for the 33rd year.)

✳ **Physical size** Hard disks are available for both the 3½-inch and the 5¼-inch hard disk drives in both half-height (1.65 H × 5¼ W inches high) and full-height (3½ × 5¼ inches) configurations. The 3½-inch floppy disk is also available in a low profile (1H × 4W inches) configuration. The half-height is rapidly becoming the more popular size.

✳ **Transfer rate** The maximum rate at which information can be transferred (usually expressed in MB/sec) between the hard drive and the computer.

⇨ Drive system alphabet soup

Several types of recording techniques have been developed and used over the relatively brief lifetime of the PC. I've also included some of the outmoded schemes because you may encounter their names. Here are some of the old, some of the new, some of the borrowed, and some of the true.

❊ **ESDI (Enhanced Small Drive Interface)**   This technique is a modification of the MFM system. ESDI was a competitor to IDE and SCSI, but the ESDI interface can't match the performance of the SCSI drives, nor the low cost of the IDE drives, so ESDIs are practically extinct.

❊ **IDE (Integrated Drive Electronics)**   As its name implies, the electronics required to control this type of drive are integral to and mounted inside the sealed hard drive case and are therefore not accessible. This results in a lower-cost drive. Over 90 percent of all PC disk drives are IDE. Many vendors' motherboards have a built-in interface and connector for the IDE. The IDE is easy to upgrade because all you have to do is remove the old drive and install the new one in its place; all of the electronics are in the drive.

IDE drives continue to be enhanced. The latest models can pack up to 16 times more data than the current 528MB permitted by traditional IDE drives; that's almost 9 gigabytes. So IDE drives will continue to compete with SCSI drives for most applications.

❊ **MFM (Modified Frequency Modulation)**   This technique was an early scheme, but did not lend itself to high capacity drives, so it became obsolete.

❊ **RLL (Run Length Limited, a.k.a. Real Lethargic Loader)**   A modification of the MFM technique which allowed 50 percent more data to be stored than for MFM. Also outmoded.

❊ **SCSI (Small Computer System Interface)**   That's pronounced "scuzzy." This is a high-speed, parallel hard disk scheme that allows multiple drives (including CD-ROM drives, scanners, etc.) to be connected together in parallel. They're about 20 percent faster than the IDE. SCSI is used mostly in server applications where multi-tasking the drive system pays off.

 # How much memory is needed?

Before we can begin to select the type of hard disk memory upgrade to incorporate, it's necessary to estimate how much hard disk capacity is required to accommodate specific levels of DTP. The tables which follow list the hard disk storage requirements for specific software programs for the various levels.

Where two numbers are listed in the tables, such as 1/4, the first number is the minimum recommended by the software developer, and the second number provides maximum usability. You'll often note a wide discrepancy between the two numbers. The first number specifies the disk capacity required to run the basic program. The larger number is the disk capacity required to accommodate all of the possible files, many which are nonessential, such as the tutorial, help, extra printers, and clip-art files. These nonessential files are usually optional when you load the program. They can be added later and deleted when no longer needed.

Table 5-1

**Hard disk capacity requirements—
Level 1—word processors**

	Program	**Minimum hard disk capacity**
DOS	Microsoft Word	1.5/5.5MB
DOS	PC-Write—Advanced Level	2.4MB
DOS	PFS:Write	1.5MB
DOS	Professional Write	2.5MB
DOS	Textra	2MB
DOS	WordPerfect	7/15MB
DOS	WordStar	2.5/14MB
Windows	Ami Pro	15MB
OS/2	DeScribe	4–11MB
Windows	Just Write	5MB
Windows	Professional Write Plus	4MB

	Program	Minimum hard disk capacity
Windows	Textor	4MB
Windows	Word for Windows	5/15MB
Windows	WordPerfect for Windows	8/12MB
Windows	WordStar for Windows	11MB

Note that there are wide variations in the disk capacity required from one program to another, as well as a wide spread within a specific program. In addition, these numbers seem to change with each new version of software, invariably increasing.

Hard disk capacity requirements—Level 2—DTP   Table 5-2

	Program	Minimum hard disk capacity
DOS	Avagio	2–4.2MB
DOS	Express Publisher	12MB
DOS	IMSI Publisher	7.5/9MB
DOS	LePrint	0.85/6.3MB
DOS	PFS:First Publisher	1.5/2.5MB
DOS	Publish It!	2/2.5MB
Windows	Desktop Publisher	3.5MB
Windows	Express Publisher	5/10MB
Windows	MicroSoft Publisher	6/13MB
Windows	PFS:Publisher for Windows	3.5/6.5MB
Windows	Publish It!	1.5/3MB

Hard disk capacity requirements—Level 3—DTP   Table 5-3

	Program	Minimum hard disk capacity
DOS	Envision Publisher	2.5MB
DOS	Ventura Publisher	2/4MB

Table 5-3   **Continued**

	Program	Minimum hard disk capacity
Windows	Aldus PageMaker	8/20MB
Windows	FrameMaker	10–20MB
Windows	PagePlus	4MB
Windows	QuarkXpress	6/8MB
Windows	Ventura Publisher	14MB

From the above tables you can see the amount of hard disk memory each individual program requires. However, you need considerably more disk space to accommodate multiple program use and to store other software programs such as DOS, utilities, and a graphics program, plus other types of software. So, think big.

Types of drives available

At the present time, your realistic drive choices have dwindled down to a precious two: IDE and SCSI. Avoid the MFM, RLL, and ESDI because they are based on outmoded and inefficient technology. The most popular type at the present time for single-user PCs is the IDE, also known as an AT drive. Because their electronics are mounted inside the drive, they're less expensive and simpler to install.

IDEs are available in capacities of up to 1GB; however they're best adapted to systems requiring less than 300MB. (Note that new developments will vault their capacities into the several gigabyte range.) They offer a transfer rate of about 1.7MB, that's about 300 pages per second. The IDE uses a host adapter instead of a controller. The host adapter can usually accommodate two IDE drives.

For large storage and multiple drive requirements, a SCSI drive is needed. SCSIs can daisychain (connect in parallel) up to seven SCSI devices (hard drives and CD-ROMs). An individual hard drive can have a capacity of up to 3GB. However, SCSIs are more expensive than the IDEs, although the price gap closes for the larger capacity sizes.

SCSI offers a burst mode of 5MB per second, but this mode only functions with large, continuous streams of data. A more typical speed is about 1.7MB per second, approximately the same as IDE.

⇨ Disk capacity expansion alternatives

There are a number of avenues that can be taken to increase the disk capacity of your computer. They include:

- ➤ Disk compression
- ➤ Adding a second fixed disk
- ➤ Replacing your current disk
- ➤ Adding a hard disk card
- ➤ Adding an external fixed disk

Of course, each alternative has its tradeoffs in capacity, complexity, and expense.

⇨ Disk compression

The first and easiest alternative for increasing your current hard disk storage is to install a disk compression program. Disk-compression software operates on what is called "on-the-fly," which means they squeeze out the slack and compress and uncompress files so quickly when you access and store them that you won't notice any slowing down of your programs.

Compression programs available include SuperStor, Stacker, and software included with several operating systems. Microsoft DOS' DoubleSpace, DRDOS, and PC-DOS all provide compression programs with their operating systems. Because all of these are constantly being improved, check the latest software reviews to see which performs best for your specific system. Keep in mind that specialty programs such as SuperStor and Stacker are most likely to stay ahead of the pack because their very survival depends on being and remaining the best.

Another consideration is that SuperStor and Stacker add extra value in the form of features such as an automated uninstall. Uninstalling DoubleSpace can be a time-consuming and cumbersome manual procedure.

The resultant degree of compression achieved by this software depends on the type of data. This compression is accomplished by removing inefficiencies in the manner in which files are stored. Here are typical compression ratios for various types of files:

Executable program files	1.4:1 to 2:1
Word processing files	2:1 to 4:1
Database files	2:1 to 8:1
Spreadsheet files	2:1 to 4:1
Video image files	2:1 to 8:1
CAD/CAM	3:1 to 8:1

For a typical hard disk, an overall compression ratio of about 2:1 is attainable. Disk compression programs are available in both software/hardware and software-only versions. The software/hardware version adds a plug-in board to your system and may cost as much as double the software solution. Reputedly the software/hardware solution is a little faster, but I've never noticed any speed problem with the software-only solution.

Disk compression should not be considered a long-term solution because it only doubles your current disk capacity. When you examine your long term goals, you may conclude that you may eventually need 4 to 8 times the storage capacity you have now. However, as a temporary solution, it's an inexpensive and simple one to incorporate.

If you need more capacity than is available from disk compression, you're going to have to install an internal or external hard disk. Read on.

 # Buying guide

Hard disks cost about $1 to $2 per megabyte, depending on the size, type, and quality of the drives. For most current DTP systems, or for lightly accessed LANs, the IDE drive should be adequate. For expansion capability (i.e., the ability to add more hard disks, CD-ROMs, etc.) and huge systems, SCSI technology can run up to 28 disks from four controllers.

You can ignore the MTBFs that the manufacturers quote. Instead, look for a two- or three-year warranty (some give 5 years) and a 30-day money-back guarantee. A hard disk is a significant investment and you want to be assured that it works with all of your system hardware and software. Also, procure a hard disk that has a disk cache or buffer. Typical values are 64K to 256K. Look for an access time of 15 milliseconds or less and a transfer rate of 4MB per second.

Disk drives are usually available in either half-height or full-height versions. The half-height is preferred because it saves space. Make sure the drive has self-parking heads so that the bumps of life don't damage your data. If you have a problem finding out the information you need about a specific drive, here are technical support numbers for obtaining drive settings:

Fijitsu	800-826-6112	Touch tone menu
Maxtor	800-262-9867	Touch tone menu
Micropolis	818-709-3325	Operator assisted
Seagate	408-438-8222	Touch tone menu

 # Add second internal hard disk

If you have a spare bay, you may want to consider adding a second internal hard disk to your PC. Most disk controllers can drive two hard disks, so the electronics are probably already there, waiting to be used.

Adding a second hard disk internally is also advantageous from a reliability standpoint. The likelihood of both drives failing at the same time is small. For very critical operations, you could use the second disk to mirror the first one by writing critical data on both disks at the same time. Your second hard disk can also be used to back up some of your critical files. A hard drive can back up to another hard drive in a very short period of time. And you won't have to discard your old disk; you'll save the investment you made in it originally.

One interesting concept is to use a low-capacity IDE drive to boot and use a high-capacity SCSI drive for working with and storing your data. This gives you the best of both worlds by taking advantage of IDE compatibility and SCSI flexibility and performance. SCSI drives are also faster if you don't boot from them because SCSI controllers are required to imitate the standard PC drive interface for compatibility when the SCSI drive is configured as a boot drive. This slows down the SCSI's performance.

Replace existing disk with a larger capacity disk

With this upgrade, you can make a quantum leap into the largest and most expensive hard disk capacity you can afford. Because of the continuing advances in the state-of-the-art, hard disk drives are becoming smaller, have increased capacity, and the cost per megabyte keeps decreasing. And, because you're replacing an existing hard disk, much of the work has already been accomplished for you. The cables are ready; your software will welcome it.

Add hard disk card

If you don't have enough room in the drive bays of your PC case to add another fixed hard disk, another alternative is to add a hard disk card. A hard disk card (a.k.a. hard card) is a combination hard disk drive and controller mounted on a standard plug-in card. The hard card occupies one or two of your plug-in slots, depending on how

thick it is. The hard card is a little bulky and may block out one of your plug-in slots from being used, or it may have to be mounted in an end slot if the disk drive is too thick. Many hard cards require a full length slot. The hard disk card costs about twice what a fixed hard disk costs. Hard cards range in storage capacity from 20-to about 250MB.

One advantage of the hard card is that it's easy to install and is internally mounted, so you won't lose any precious desk or shelf space. Secondly, you don't need to disturb or reconfigure your existing hard disk and controller at all. You can even set up the hard card as a boot disk.

Software setup is easy, too. You may have to add a driver to your CONFIG.SYS file. And, although it's not too convenient, the hard card can be removed fairly easily and transferred to another computer for shared use. For security purposes, the hard card can be removed and stored in a safe place.

External hard disks— general considerations

The external hard disk is mounted in a separate case and plugs into your computer's parallel port, your SCSI card, or a special interface card. Because most computers have only a single parallel port, and because that port is used for the printer, you need to purchase and install a special interface to be able to share the parallel port. However, some fixed hard drives are equipped with a separate parallel port that you can use for your printer. Alternatively, if a special interface card is needed, you have to pop open the case and install the special interface in a plug-in slot. Both methods use up a plug-in slot.

With a SCSI daisychain system, an external disk drive can plug into your SCSI card via a connector.

 External fixed hard disk tradeoffs

If you need more storage and have run out of room inside your PC's drive bays, consider adding an external hard disk. The external hard disk is basically an internal hard disk that has been mounted in a case, with a connector attached. It costs about twenty percent more than an internal hard disk and is available in similar storage capacities to an internal.

In addition to the added cost, another disadvantage of this approach is that it is another separate unit you have to make space for on your desk or shelf. However, it has the advantage that it can add considerable hard disk storage capacity to your system and doesn't drain power from your PC. Also an external disk can easily be disconnected, physically moved and used on a different computer, or on a portable computer. And it can be stored in a secure location if the information on the disk is confidential.

 My recommendations

You'll find as many recommendations for how large a disk to procure as you will find people quoting them. One formula recommends a base capacity of 40MB, then says to add 15MB for each application you are going to run, then double that. For example, if you are going to run 4 Windows applications, that would require $40 + 4 \times 15 = 100MB$. Double that and you'll end up with 200MB. Another one calls for quadrupling your current disk capacity.

My own recommendations are included in Table 5-4.

Table 5-4   **Hard disk capacity recommendations**

Level	Hard disk capacity
1- DOS	100–150MB
1- Windows	250MB
2- DOS	150–250MB

Level	Hard disk capacity
2- Windows	300–350MB
3- DOS	250MB
3- Windows	350MB–1GB

Now that you have an idea of how much disk capacity you require, you can decide what type of update to accomplish, based not only on the disk storage capacity required, but also on the cost, the ease of installation, the application, and the compatibility with your PC.

Upgrade procedures

This section covers the procedures required to install the upgrades, including listing any extra hardware required and special precautions to observe.

Disk compression

To utilize a disk compression program, you should first back up your hard disk before you begin the compression and also prepare a recovery disk as described in chapter 3.

If your hard disk storage requirements are modest and you feel that doubling your disk capacity will serve your needs, at least for the near future, then by all means install a disk compression program. It's the easiest to accomplish, the least costly, and it almost doubles your storage capacity without having to take the cover off your computer.

Disk upgrade—general guidelines

When you purchase a disk drive, you have the option of obtaining a "bare drive" or a "kit." The bare drive includes the disk drive, mounting hardware and software. Order a bare drive if you're replacing an old disk of the same type that is already installed. And be sure to purchase a disk using the same type of controller, because IDE and SCSI disk types can't use the same controller card.

A kit consists of the disk drive, the controller or host adapter, rails, cables, mounting hardware, a front panel bezel, and any required software. Purchase a kit if you are installing a new type of drive, or if you are adding a second hard drive. Be sure to purchase the disk drive controller (if one is needed), the cables, and the drive from the same manufacturer to ensure compatibility.

When you're installing a new hard drive, be sure to double-check the dimensions to make sure it'll fit in your case and that you have the proper cables and mounting hardware. Hard disks use very little power, so you probably needn't be concerned about upgrading to a new power supply.

If you're installing a half-height drive, locate it at the bottom of the drive bay. Floppy drives, because they can stand the heat better, should be mounted above fixed disks. The lower positions in the drive bay are cooler.

For larger capacity drives (400MB and greater), you may get a full height drive. Often you'll need mounting screws and an adapter kit to mount a 3½-inch drive to fit in a 5¼-inch drive bay. Or you may have, as many of the newer PCs do, a mounting slot ready-made for the smaller drive.

For a second hard drive you may need to buy and install a Y power splitter to divide the power output from the existing power supply connector into two cables.

Upgrade procedures— replace existing disk

Because the most complex hard disk drive procedure is the removal of an old drive and replacing it with a new drive, this procedure will be covered first. The detailed procedure is depicted in Fig. 5-1. Before you start the removal, have your recovery disk handy. Set this disk aside. You'll need it to boot up after you've installed the new disk.

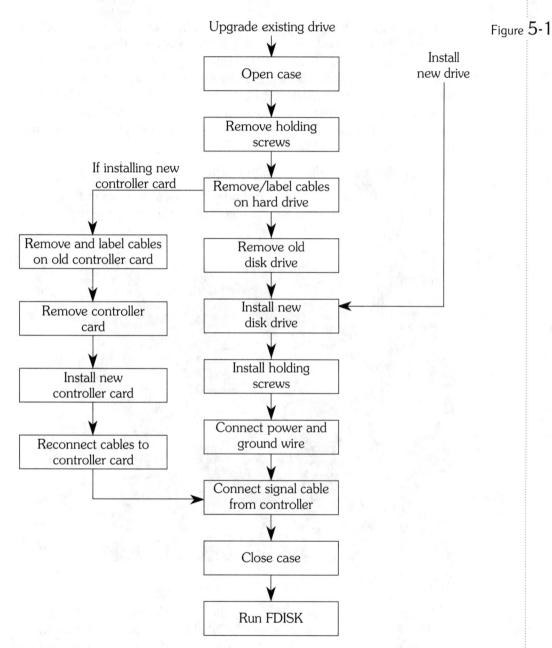

Figure 5-1

Replace disk upgrade procedure.

To begin, follow the procedures described in chapter 3 to remove the case. Set the case aside and check out the position, size, and mounting provisions of the existing disk. If you're lucky, replacement is almost as easy as disconnecting the cables and sliding the old one out and sliding the new one in. But, according to Murphy's Law, it doesn't always turn out that way. You may need to use different mounting hardware if the new disk size differs radically from the one being replaced.

1. Open the case as described in chapter 3.

2. Unscrew the 2 to 4 screws holding the old disk drive in its place (Fig. 5-2). Save the screws in your container, you're going to need them for the new drive.

Figure 5-2

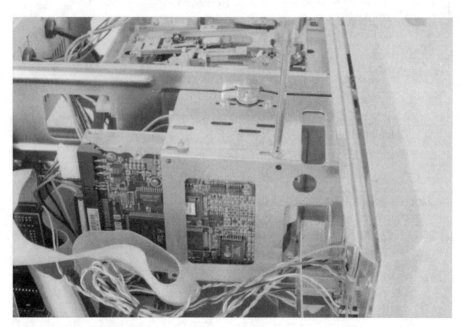

Unscrew holding screws.

3. Disconnect the power cable and the gray, flat control data cable (Fig. 5-3) from the disk drive and label them. If you're going to replace the controller (or adapter for an IDE) card, also disconnect and label all of the cables from the controller card, including those running to the existing hard drive you're going to replace.

Figure 5-3

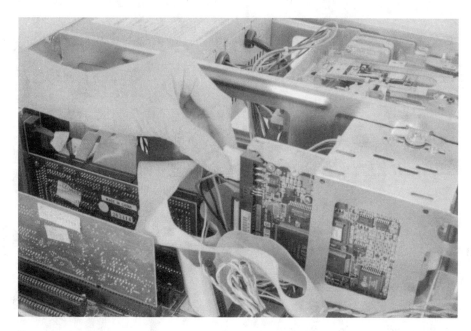

Disconnect cables.

4. Next, if you're replacing the controller (or adapter) card, remove the screw holding the card in its place (chapter 3). Set the screw aside in your container. Lift the controller card out of its slot.

5. Remove the old drive from its bay (Fig. 5-4). It should be free and slip out easily toward the rear of the chassis. Set the old drive aside in case something goes awry with your installation and you have to re-install the old drive to troubleshoot and find out what happened.

6. If the new drive is the same size and configuration as the old one, install it in the same bay. If it's a different size or configuration, use the adapter hardware (Fig. 5-5) that came with the disk and mount it in the same, or different, location.

   If your power cable has been set up for a 5¼-inch drive and you're installing a 3½-inch drive, you'll have to use a 5¼-inch to 3½-inch power adapter cable (Fig. 5-6). If you're installing a slim model (1 inch high), you have many more choices of where to mount the new drive.

Figure 5-4

Remove old drive from its bay.

Figure 5-5

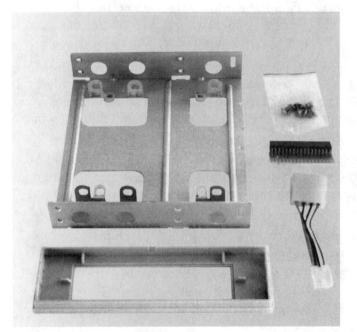

Adapter for 3½-inch to 5¼-inch disk drive.

Figure 5-6

5¼-inch to 3½-inch power adapter.

7. Connect the data and power cables and the ground wire to the rear of the new drive.

8. If you're replacing the controller card, plug the new card in the vacated slot and install the screw that secures it in place.

9. If you've replaced the controller card, reconnect the hard and floppy disk cables to the card.

10. Double-check all that you have done to make sure you have connected everything up correctly and that the cables and the drive (and the controller card if you replaced it) are all firmly seated in their new homes.

11. Reinstall the case, hook up all the external cables, but don't turn the power on yet.

12. Put your bootable disk in Drive A and turn the power on.

When this is accomplished, it's time to introduce your computer to its new resident memory expert. The procedure to be followed depends on what the manufacturer has already accomplished and what you have left to do. From the floppy drive, invoke the FDISK command and follow the procedure covered under the heading Formatting a Hard Disk in the next section.

⇨ Formatting a hard disk

A hard disk requires two levels of formatting: low-level and high-level. Low-level formatting requires sophisticated tools and technical expertise, so disk manufacturers perform this task before the disk is sold.

To begin high-level formatting, boot up with your Recovery Disk (chapter 3) in Drive A (make sure it has the DOS command FDISK on it). Type FDISK at the A prompt. If the disk has been low-level formatted, it will accept the FDISK command. When the command is executed, you'll be presented with a series of questions.

Figure 5-7

```
FDISK Options


Current fixed disk drive:    1


Choose one of the following:

1.   Create DOS partition or logical DOS drive
2.   Set active partition                        FDISK screen.
3.   Delete partition or logical DOS drive
4.   Display partition information



Enter choice:    {1}


Press Esc to exit FDISK
```

Note in this figure that the default choice, {1} in this case, can be chosen by hitting the Enter key. Hit the Enter key to accept this choice and continue to hit the Enter key on the subsequent screens to accept the defaults. When this is accomplished, you next have to format the hard disk as the system disk if you want this hard disk to be the boot disk. At the A prompt, type:

FORMAT C:/S

and the disk will be formatted as a boot disk. Now your disk is prepared to accept your software. Load your software at this time, load DOS first, then Windows if you are using it.

⇨ Upgrade procedures— add second internal hard disk

1. Remove the cover as illustrated in chapter 3.

2. Follow the procedures depicted in Fig. 5-1 and in the text from Step 6 and on, with one exception. If you don't have a second power connector for the added drive, use a Y-splitter power cable (Fig. 5-8) to split one of your existing power connectors into two separate cables.

Figure 5-8

Y-splitter power cable.

3. If you have to install a new controller card for the second drive, follow the procedures depicted in Fig. 5-1 and described in the accompanying text.

 # Upgrade procedures— add hard disk card

A hard disk card is relatively easy to install. First, take the cover off using the procedure described in chapter 3. Next check your documentation to see if any jumpers or DIP switches have to be set on the card and in your computer. Then plug the card into an empty slot and secure the card with a screw. If possible, locate the card near the end slot where it won't block any plug-in slots.

Like a fixed hard drive, a disk card is assigned its own drive letter by your computer. You may have to format the disk once it's installed, some come already formatted by the manufacturer. Follow the directions that came with the hard card to complete the installation.

Upgrade procedures— add external fixed disk

External hard disk drives usually connect to your printer parallel port. The hard disk drive should include an additional parallel port for your printer (the hard drive provides the capability of simultaneous printing) so you won't be deprived of your printer port.

With power off, find a safe place to mount your drive (a place where it can't accidentally be knocked down), then hook the supplied cable between the hard drive and your PC's parallel port. Hook up the power cable from the hard drive to primary power.

From that point on, follow the instructions that came with the hard drive. They'll probably be very similar to the procedures required for an internal hard drive.

External hard drives are also used as supplemental storage for existing systems, including portable computers. For this reason, they are often designed so they can be driven from a standard ac power line, or from internal batteries in case they're used with a portable PC. SCSI versions are available which permit daisychaining up to seven SCSI external drives.

⇨ Wrapup

An ongoing debate continues over the wisdom of leaving your computer run continuously versus turning it off every night. The leave-it-on advocates claim that your PC is susceptible to transients when it is turned on repeatedly, transients which may damage or wear out certain components. They claim that the hard disk (see MTBF earlier in this chapter) and the computer chips never (or seldom ever) wear out, so the PC should be left on continuously. Other advocates ignore these precautions and advise to turn it on in the morning, and turn it off at night.

My personal preference after experimenting with both procedures is to leave my computer on constantly. I never turn it off, unless I'm going on an extended vacation (more than a few days, which doesn't happen often enough to suit me). I tried the other method of turning my computer on and off each day and found that once in a while my computer refused to boot. Panic set in, of course, so I went back to the full-time running computer.

For the display, the situation is different. Most displays have a vacuum CRT with a filament boiling off electrons from a finite supply.

And the filament has a limited life. So I turn my display off each night and turn it on in the morning.

One other thing about displays, you should also have a burn-protect program on your PC, one which is activated when you haven't input any data for a specified period of time (5 to 10 minutes should work). This prevents a phosphor burn-in of a pattern that is constantly being displayed. A burn-protect program should have a small display (a picture or a short sentence) which is displayed and constantly shifted about the screen. One comes with Windows (select Control Panel on the Main Menu, then Desktop on the Control Panel Menu) and provides several different backgrounds to choose from.

⇨ Sell your old hard drive?

When you replace an old hard drive, what can you do with it? You could, of course, put it in your closet along with the software that never lived up to its expectations. But there are some other alternatives.

Perhaps your local high school would like the donation. Most high schools have a few enterprising youths who would love to learn how to install the disk in one of their computers (with their teacher's permission, of course). Or perhaps your local church or charity would like to add another disk to their existing PC system.

Alternatively, you might be able to sell or trade it for something at a local computer swap meet. There are always people there looking for bargains, so you're liable to find someone who can put it to good use.

⇨ Software utility programs for hard disks

When data is continually stored on and read from a disk, the data often grows and shrinks and may not fit in the old sectors it occupied

previously. So related data from the same file cannot be laid down in contiguous (adjacent) sectors. Data has to be split up and stored wherever room is available. The FAT tells what sectors and how much room are available and records where the data have been split up so it can be reconstructed when needed.

After many reads and writes, your disk data may be so fragmented that your software is considerably slowed down because it has to search over many nonadjacent sectors on the disk to locate and reconstruct the fragmented files. When this happens, it's time to defragment the disk.

A defragmenting program searches your hard disk and finds new areas large enough to store your files contiguously so that the next time the data is needed, it is all located in the same area and can be accessed quickly.

Several defragmenting programs are available. DOS and DR DOS both have defrag programs. Norton and Central Point Utilities also have excellent defrag programs. And the shareware market (see appendix C) also has several defragmentation programs available. For busy hard disks, these programs should be run at least once a week to optimize the performance of your hard disk.

Adding or replacing a removable-media drive

MANY modern computers are currently being produced with a single floppy disk drive, usually a 3½-incher. That's a little like chugging along on one cylinder. Just imagine what would happen if your single disk drive wasn't working and you had to download or back up some data on a floppy: you'd have a feeling of utter helplessness. And some PCs are still hobbled with 360K and 720K drives; that's woeful underachieving.

The solution is to add a removable media drive, such as another floppy, a floptical, magneto-optical, or Bernoulli drive that can serve a dual purpose as a secondary backup medium and as a transportable medium for storing and delivering data to your co-workers or customers.

This chapter is dedicated to encouraging you to consider adding an alternative type of removable drive. You could add a second floppy drive if you have a singleton now and modernize those doddering, decrepit, dinosauric drives that just can't disk it anymore. Or you could step up in capacity and capability and add a high-capacity removable-media drive.

This chapter presents the tradeoffs needed in deciding which upgrade approach to take. In addition, the physical installation required for each type of drive is provided, along with detailed step-by-step instructions, photographs, and illustrations. Finally the testing procedures to verify the validity of the upgrades are described.

⇨ Why add a second floppy drive?

Because several million 5¼-inch drives are still in use, some software is still being delivered on the larger disks. Even though a software vendor gives you the option of sending in for the 3½-incher, that's a nuisance. You've purchased the software and are anxious to use it and don't want to wait a few weeks for a replacement. Fortunately several vendors deliver both sizes, or offer you the size option at purchase. But not all do.

Having a second floppy drive is also advantageous if you want to exchange data or software with your co-workers or customers. Some LAN users find that their networks are so busy that they can't tie up their lines to send a large program, voluminous data, or complex drawings and so on, back and forth on the network. They may find it simpler to fill a disk of the proper size and deliver the disk. And if you have to deliver or mail a data-laden disk to a customer, or deliver to a print shop for a high-quality print, you need to remember that some shops accommodate only limited disk sizes and types.

⇨ Why modernize old floppies?

If you have an older model disk drive (e.g., 360K or 720K), you're operating at only partial efficiency. If you back up on low density disks, you need 2 to 4 times the number of disks that would be required if you modernized your drives.

Some new software is also being delivered only on the higher-density disks and this trend will probably increase in the future; so you're again going to be confronted with the nuisance of having to request and wait for the lower-density disks if you don't upgrade. And if you deliver data or software to customers or co-workers, or if you take disks with you on travel or to your home, you have less disks to be concerned with if you use the high-density version.

One important thing to remember is that the high-density drives are downward-compatible with low-density drives. So you can use all of your software, your data disks, whatever you have stored on the lower-density disks in higher-density drives. High-density drives can also format both low and high-density disks; however the low-density drives cannot format the high-density disks. Commands for formatting the various types of disks are included later in this chapter.

Besides, you have to keep up with the Jones's clones in this highly competitive world.

 # Your floppy drive choices

To add a floppy, or to update your floppies, you have these basic choices:

> ➤ Internal drive(s)
> ➤ Combination drive
> ➤ External drive(s)

If you have space in your bays to add a second drive, the internal drive is preferable. It doesn't require shelf or desk space or external cables and your computer is probably already equipped to handle it.

If you're short on space in your drive bays, another possibility is to install a combination 3½/5¼-inch floppy drive in a single drive slot. The combination drive has the advantage that it takes up only one drive bay slot and that the drives share a drive card because only one drive can be used at the same time. The combination drive sells for a little more than the cost of two disk drives, but it's a great space saver.

And if you've run out of space, consider adding an external drive. Available in both sizes, an external drive costs about twice as much as an internal drive; but if you don't have the space, it's your only option.

 # Definitions and acronyms

First a review of some of the disk definitions and specs to clear up any misunderstandings.

✳ **Disk density**   Indicates how closely magnetic information can be stored on a disk. The most common disk types are double-density and high-density disks.

✳ **Sector**   An organization of data storage on a magnetic disk, arranged like slices in a pie.

✳ **Track**   A physical arrangement in the form of concentric rings for storing data on a magnetic disk, much like a phonograph record. Each track is divided into sectors.

The following floppy-disk acronyms have always confused me, I hope this unconfuses them for you. For disks labeled MFD-2DD, the MFD stands for Micro Floppy Disk, the 2 indicates a double-sided disk, the DD stands for double density: 360K for the 5¼ and 720K for the 3½-inch disks. For disks labeled MFD-2HD, HD stands for high density: 1.2MB for the 5¼ and 1.44MB for the 3½-inch disks.

➯ Formatting disks

For reference, here are the basic commands for formatting disks. Uppercase, lowercase, or a mix of the two is accepted.

✳ **FORMAT A:/1**   Formats only one side of a 360K diskette in a standard 360K drive.

✳ **FORMAT A:**   Formats a high-capacity diskette in a high-capacity drive.

✳ **FORMAT A:/4**   Formats a 360K diskette in a high-capacity, 5¼-inch drive.

✳ **FORMAT A:/F:[size](Don't type the brackets)**   Formats a diskette for the capacity specified by [size] and can be used for 160K to 1.44MB diskettes.

✳ **FORMAT A:/S**   Makes your diskette a system diskette. This formats the diskette and copies the files that must be on a System diskette. These files include COMMAND.COM and a few hidden files that are needed for DOS to operate, and which must be stored at specific locations on the diskette.

The /S added to the last command is called a "switch." Switches are used to modify and bolster the basic commands. If you need to reformat a disk to erase the files and subdirectories on it, you can accomplish it quickly with this command:

```
Format A: /Q
```

When you're in a real hurry and want to avoid the "Insert disk," "Label disk," and "Insert another disk" prompts, use this command:

```
Format A: /AUTOTEST
```

To format a series of floppies with this same command, just hit the Function key, F3, to bring the above command back to the prompt, hit Enter and repeat it for each disk to be formatted.

But there is another way to avoid all of this hassle. It takes about 2 minutes to format a 3½-inch disk. If you format a half dozen, it takes about 12 minutes of your precious time to accomplish this. However, you can now purchase preformatted disks for little more than the cost of the unformatted disks and save all of this hassle and wasted time. Check with your local or mail-order supplier the next time you purchase disks to see how reasonable the preformatted disks are.

 # Basic DOS copy programs

The basic DOS copy programs are:

➢ COPY

➢ DISKCOPY

➢ XCOPY

 # COPY

Use COPY to copy a single file from one location (source) C: to another (target) A:. The format is:

```
COPY C:FILENAME.EXT A:
```

However, COPY is a slow command to use for multiple files because it reads and copies only one file at a time, even if you specify a group of files by using wildcards. COPY reads a single file into RAM, copies it to its destination, then moves on to the next file and repeats the procedure. Slow, slower, slowest.

You can also use the COPY command to print an ASCII text file stored on any drive. Use:

```
COPY A:MANUAL.TXT PRN
```

where PRN is the designation for the printer.

 DISKCOPY

To copy the precise contents of one diskette in drive A (or B) to another diskette of the same size and same capacity in drive B (or A), use the DISKCOPY command and this format:

```
DISKCOPY A: B:
```

This DOS command copies the entire contents of diskette A onto diskette B. The target diskette need not be previously formatted before you use this command; DISKCOPY automatically formats the diskette if needed. But remember that this command only works when copying from one diskette to another diskette of the same size and capacity.

You can use the DISKCOPY command even if you have only a single disk drive, Drive A. DISKCOPY is unique among DOS commands in that it accepts the same drive letter for both the source and the destination. Just input:

```
DISKCOPY A: A:
```

The computer prompts you when to remove the source diskette from Drive A and when to insert the target diskette (it may take a few exchanges) as needed to complete the copy process.

XCOPY

To copy all the files from one diskette type (e.g., 5¼-inch disk) in drive A to a different diskette type (e.g., 3½-inch disk) in drive B, use the XCOPY command and this format:

```
XCOPY A: B:
```

127

The advantage of this command is that it's much faster. It copies as many of the files as your RAM can hold, then transfers all of these files stored in RAM to the target disk. Often XCOPY can complete a copy on a single pass if you have enough RAM.

However, to make sure you are copying all the files from A to B, including the subdirectories, use this format:

XCOPY A: B: /S /E

The /S switch makes sure that all of the files in the source directory are copied to the target directory, along with all of the subdirectories. The /E switch does the same thing, but it also creates any needed subdirectories at the destination, even if the subdirectories are empty. The /E switch works only if the /S switch is also specified. The only files XCOPY won't find are hidden and system files.

If the disk in drive A contains hidden and system files that you want to copy, you have to first strip off the hidden and system attributes. To accomplish this, input:

ATTRIB , /S

This strips all attributes from the current directory and its subdirectories. These files can then be copied via XCOPY.

However, this command also strips the archive bit, so use it with care between backups. Every time DOS creates or alters a file, it sets a bit (called the archive bit) in the attribute byte that's stored with the file's name. XCOPY has a switch, /M, that directs it to copy a file only if its archive bit is set and it clears that bit after the file has been copied. So if you are using XCOPY for backup purposes, use this command:

XCOPY C:\DIRNAME A:\BKUP\DIRNAME/S/M

It copies only the files in DIRNAME that are new or modified, then it clears the files' archive bits so the files won't be copied the next time, unless their contents have been changed.

High-capacity removable storage media

If you have an enormous amount of data to store and back up, such as you would from a program with significant graphics, consider adding an external high-capacity hard disk with a removable media. Because the disks are removable, your storage capability is limited only by the number of disks you have. Among the types available are:

> ➤ Magneto-Optical
> ➤ Floptical
> ➤ Bernoulli

The advantages of a removable storage medium are:

> ➤ High storage capacity
> ➤ Security
> ➤ Transportability
> ➤ Data sharing
> ➤ Long-term economy

The advantage of having a high storage capacity of from 21MB to several gigabytes gives you a choice of several different removable media. Security means you can remove the media and store it in a safe place. Because you can transport hundreds of megabytes as easily as swapping floppies, transportability and data sharing are also huge advantages. If you need considerable disk storage, you can sort your data and programs, store them on separate disks, and you'll probably never run out of storage space. You can also move these disks from one computer to another for shared use. Although the initial cost may be high, when you amortize the cost of the removable media as compared to other solutions (floppies), the use of high-density removable media soon results in significant savings.

One of the disadvantages of removable disk media is its initial cost. The initial cost can range from two to four times or more than that of

a similar capacity internal fixed disk. And each individual removable disk can cost as much as (or more than) a single internal fixed disk.

 # Magneto-Optical drives

Magneto-Optical (a.k.a. optical or MO) drives use a laser beam to write data to, and read it from, a plastic disk. The MO offers access time of about 35–50 milliseconds, but has the highest capacity (up to 1.3GB per cartridge), storing almost ten times as much as the other magnetic media listed above. There are also MO "jukeboxes" available that hold several optical disks, giving you access to dozens of gigabytes of data. There is no chance of a head crash with an MO drive and the disk can't be accidentally erased or corrupted by a magnetic field. It's available in 3½-and 5¼-inch sizes. The 3½-inch size is available as an internal or external mount.

 # Floptical drives

The floptical uses a hybrid of magnetic floppy disk and optical disk techniques. It utilizes magnetic technology to store data and optical technology to locate it. The floptical is a low-range storage device (up to 21MB per cartridge), low in cost, and simple to use. It's ideal for transporting low-capacity data to co-workers or customers. But the floptical is slow and its cartridges are vulnerable to magnetic fields. It also has a limited range of cartridge capacities.

 # Bernoulli drives

The Bernoulli (magnetic cartridge) drive uses a cartridge that contains two flexible plastic disks coated with a magnetically sensitive alloy. As the disks spin, air moves outward over them and passes between the disk surfaces and the read/write head. The reduced air pressure causes the disks to position themselves very close, almost in contact with the heads. It uses the same principle that causes lift on airplane wings. The spacing is closer than for a hard disk.

The Bernoulli disk drive is very fast and costs about one eighth as much as an optical drive. With a storage capacity of up to 150MB per cartridge (2 flexible disks in a cartridge), this middle range storage device is ideal for DTP applications where you have considerable graphics you want to keep together in the same package. The Bernoulli is a rugged and reliable disk that can be physically manhandled (personhandled?) and mailed to distant locations by UPS or the U.S. Postal Service. You can conveniently use it to carry your work between home and work. A disadvantage is that the cartridges are vulnerable to dust and magnetic fields.

The choice of which to use is a complex one based on price of the drive, the magnitude of the storage capacity you require of a removable media, and the cost of the individual disks or cartridges. While optical cartridges are less costly, optical drives are much more expensive than the other two. Also, you may not need 650MB of storage; maybe a 20MB or 100MB disk can satisfy most of your needs.

⇨ My recommendations

If you have the space, add the drive(s) internally. You won't use up shelf or desk space, it's neater with no cables dangling around, it's less costly, and your computer was designed to accommodate these changes.

If you're updating two low-density drives, I recommend the use of 2 half-height drives, or the dual 3½/5¼ combination. The two half-height drives use up only two inches of front panel space. The dual-drive combination costs only slightly more than two drives and takes up only one slot in the drive bay. And with more and more exciting peripherals being made available (CD-ROM, Tape Backup, etc.), you need to use the space inside your PC case as efficiently as possible. However, the dual-drive has a disadvantage in that if one fails, you have to replace the entire drive, or limp along on the one good drive for a while.

A 2.88MB drive (called Extended Density, ED) is also available. It costs about twice that of a 1.2-or 1.44MB drive. The disks for the ED drive also cost almost two to three times that of the high-density disks. The ED drive is also downward compatible with the lower-density drives. If you have the money to spend, go for it. Personally, I'm content with my two high-density drives.

If you want to invest in a much bigger and better floppy, consider a floptical drive. This combination floppy and optical drive can handle a 21MB optical disk, as well as a 720K/1.44MB floppy disk in the same drive. Because the floptical can handle all three sizes, you can replace an internal floppy with this unit. It's ideal for backup, large file storage, data interchange, and archiving.

It seems as if you never have enough hard disk storage, and often you'd like to be able to download some of the material you don't use too often onto a floppy. With each 21MB floppy, you can download a great deal of information and store it in folders where they are immediately available without cluttering up your hard disk. The floptical is also available as an external unit which connects to your parallel port, giving it a portability.

Finally, adding an external drive isn't really a choice, it's a necessity if you have no internal room.

Upgrade procedures—general

When you connect the gray, flat-wire cable from the plug-in cards to a floppy disk drive, note that one of the outside wires in the cable has a black (or maybe red) stripe and lettering running down one side (Fig. 6-1). (On some units, one end of the floppy drive cable may be plugged into the motherboard.) This stripe and the accompanying lettering stamped on the cable indicate that that specific outside wire is Number 1 and must be plugged into Pin 1 (surprise) on the I/O card (or motherboard) and on the floppy drive.

The fixed connectors on both the I/O card and the floppy drive have the legend Pin 1 engraved next to the body of the connector. It may

Figure 6-1

Flat cable with stripe down one side.

take a magnifying glass and a penlight to find it (maybe even a young pair of eyes), but it's there. If you can only find a Pin 2, Pin 1 is on the opposite side of the connector. So, whenever you're plugging cables in, be sure to align the stripe on the flat cable with Pin 1 on the connector. There are a lot of pins (34) to line up, so be careful when you mate the plug. Once properly aligned, the cable plug should slide in fairly easily, but push firmly (you may have to use a little rock and roll, back and forth rocking motion) to make sure the plug is completely engaged. The procedures that follow require that you remove the PC case, so refer to chapter 3 for this procedure.

⇨ Add second floppy drive internally

Your PC needs a vacant space in a drive bay to accommodate your second internal drive. The front panel probably has a bezel that can be removed (popped out with a thin screwdriver) (Fig. 6-2) so your drive can be mounted and accessed from the front.

Where you can mount your drive depends on your specific case design. On one of my PCs, my 5¼ inch is mounted horizontally in a large drive bay designed for 5¼-inchers and my 3½ inch drive is mounted on its side in a separate cage designed for 3½-inchers. On one of my other PCs, both drives are mounted horizontally in a bay designed for 5¼-inchers.

If you're going to mount a 3½-incher in a 5¼ inch drive bay, you need an adapter kit (Fig. 6-3) that has to be attached to the side of the small drive and which effectively expands the small drive's width to fit in the cage designed for the larger size.

Figure 6-2

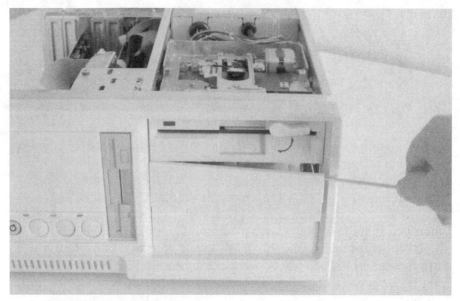

Pop out front bezel.

Figure 6-3

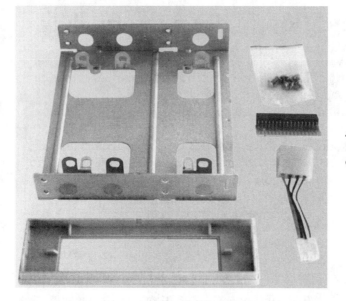

Adapter for 3½-inch to 5¼-inch disk drive.

As far as power is concerned, your power supply should have two power cables (some have three) for disk drives. Check your existing disk drive to see what one looks like and look inside your case for its twin. If you don't have a twin, you'll have to buy a Y-splitter power

Figure 6-4

Flat cable for drive.

cable (chapter 5) which connects in series with one of the existing
power supply cables and expands it to provide two outputs. Note that
the power supply connectors are keyed so they can't be inserted
incorrectly. They should just snap in place and lock.

You also should have a wide, flat cable running from your I/O card to
the existing drive (Fig. 6-4). This cable will have 2 (or 3) connectors
attached along its length and one connector at the end. The
connector on the end nearest the twist in the cable is to be attached
to the A drive. The other connector nearest to the end connector is
to be used if you mount your second drive adjacent to your other
drive in the 5¼-inch drive bay.

⇨ Mounting procedure

The 5¼-inch drive (Fig. 6-5) slips right into one of your bay slots.

To mount the 3½-inch drives, you have to add the adapter depicted in
Fig. 6-3 so it will also fit into the 5¼-inch slot, or you may have a
special slot especially set aside for the 3½-inch drive.

Figure 6-5

5¼-inch floppy drive.

Figure 6-6

Slide drive into drive bay.

Figure 6-7

Connectors at rear of drive.

To mount the drive, slide it into the drive bay you're going to use (Fig. 6-6).

Attach the power cable, the control cable, and the ground cable (Fig. 6-7) to the drive.

Most mounts use a couple of captive screws and offsize washers to secure the drive in its assigned place (Fig. 6-8).

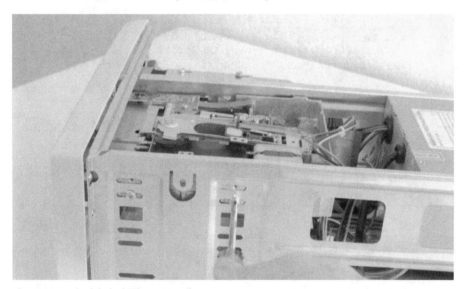

Figure 6-8

Screws to hold disk drive in place.

⇨ Informing your computer

After you've added a second floppy drive where no floppy has tread before, you must inform your computer not only of its existence, but also of its size. To accomplish this, you need to invade your CMOS setup domain. To enter this hallowed hall, hold down the Delete key when you boot up. You will then be presented with a screen similar to that of Fig. 6-9.

Toggle to the first selection, STANDARD CMOS SETUP, and hit the Enter key. The next screen warns you:

```
Improper Use of Setup may Cause Problems !!
```

Figure 6-9

```
                    STANDARD CMOS SETUP

          AUTO CONFIGURATION WITH BIOS DEFAULTS

        AUTO CONFIGURATION WITH POWER-ON DEFAULTS

                    CHANGE PASSWORD

               AUTO DETECT HARD DISK          CMOS setup screen.

                  HARD DISK UTILITY

               WRITE TO CMOS AND EXIT

            DO NOT WRITE TO CMOS AND EXIT
```

You're given an opportunity to escape the setup at this point. Of course, you know what you're going to do, so ignore it. To continue just hit the Enter key again and you'll be presented with another screen of data as shown in Fig. 6-10.

Figure 6-10

```
                   BIOS SETUP PROGRAM-STANDARD CMOS SETUP
    (C)Copyright  1990  American Megatrends Inc., All Rights Reserved

    Date(mm/date/year) :Mon, Sep 12 1994   Base memory   :640KB
    Time(hour/min/sec) :16 : 42 : 34        Ext.  memory  :7168KB
    Daylight saving    :Disabled Cylin Head WPcom LZone Sect Size
    Hard disk c type   :47       1025  5    0     0    40   100MB
    Hard disk d type   :Not installed
    Floppy drive A     :1.2MB 5,"
    Floppy drive B     :Not installed
    Primary display    :VGA/PGA/EGA         Sun Mon Tue Wed Thu Fri Sat
                                                            1   2   3
       Month:Jan,Feb,.....Dec                4   5   6   7   8   9  10
       Date:01,02,03,.....31                11  12  13  14  15  16  17
       Year:1901,1902,...2099               18  19  20  21  22  23  24
                                            25  26  27  28  29  30

    Esc:  Exit F2/F3:Color  PU/PD:Modify
```

BIOS SETUP PROGRAM.

On this screen, keep hitting the right arrow key until the blinking cursor is positioned in the Floppy Drive B : Not Installed menu selection. A listing of the possible floppy drives is then displayed on the bottom of the screen. Keep hitting the Page Down key until the proper disk capacity (probably 1.2 or 1.44, or maybe 2.88) is indicated under the cursor. Then hit the Esc key to accept this selection and leave the menu.

You are then back at the screen depicted in Fig. 6-9. With the down arrow key, toggle down to the WRITE TO CMOS AND EXIT menu entry, then hit the F10 key, which will then Save & Exit. Your computer has now recorded this selection and will boot up. Your new drive is now installed and ready to spin magic moments for you.

 # Upgrade existing floppy drive(s)

The procedure for upgrading existing floppy drives is relatively easy. All you have to do is pop open the PC case and disconnect the cables. Note that there are three cables: the wide flat one is the control cable, the narrow flat one provides power to the drive, and a single wire cable with a lug on the end slips onto the ground lug of your drive. Remove the cables from the old disk drive and label them.

To remove the old drive, there will be at least a couple of screws that secure the drive in place. They may be on the sides, or on the front with a couple of oversized washers that hold it in. Once these restraints are removed, you can easily slide your old drive out.

Install the new drive following the procedure above and you're back in business. You should also follow the procedure for updating the CMOS setup described above.

Add 2-in-1 floppy disk

The procedure for installing the 2-in-1 floppy disk is essentially the same as installing a single disk drive. You can't connect a combination drive as the second drive to a conventional combination that's designed to manage two disk drives. If you have a conventional controller, you have to operate the combination drive as the only drive.

The combination drive mounts in a 5¼-inch drive slot. The combination drive is preset with the 5¼-inch drive as Drive A and the 3½-inch drive as Drive B. However, you can change this by changing the "Drive Select" jumper on the drive. The instruction manual that came with the drive will show you which jumpers to move.

The combination drive requires only one cable, so use the flat cable that already exists and connect the end connector (the connector beyond the twist) to the card connector on the floppy. Only a single power cable and ground wire are also required.

To set up the drives, use the same procedure described above for adding a single drive.

Add external removable-media drive

External removable-media drives usually connect to your printer parallel port. The removable-media drive should provide an additional parallel port for your printer (the external drive provides the capability of simultaneous printing and using the drive), so you won't be deprived of your printer port.

With power off, find a safe place to mount your drive (a place where it can't accidentally be knocked down), then hook the supplied cable between the external drive and your PC's parallel port. Hook up the power cable from the external drive to primary power.

From that point on, follow the instructions that came with the external drive. They'll probably be very similar to the procedures required for an internal drive.

External removable-media drives can be used as supplemental storage for existing systems, including portable computers. For this reason, they are often designed so they can be driven from a standard ac power line (or from internal batteries in case they're used with a portable PC). SCSI versions are available which permit daisy chaining up to seven SCSI external drives.

Care and feeding of disk drives and floppy disks

Floppy disk drives are open to the atmosphere and will accumulate dust, dirt, etc. It's advisable to clean them (cleaning kits are available in many places, including Sears) after 100 hours of computer use.

Concerning diskettes, the 3½-inch disks are not only more rugged, they have a shutter that opens to reveal the recording surface when it's inserted in a drive. The 5¼-inch disk has a slot in the cover that exposes the recording surface to dust and dirt, so the larger disks are more susceptible to contaminants.

Quality diskettes are rated at 30 million passes; with typical use, that's fifty years, give or take a few days. But if a little dirt gets on them, your warranty doesn't cover that. Fingerprints, dust, and other contaminants are anathema and must be avoided. Don't write on your disks with a pen that requires pressure, use a felt-tip pen. Store the disks upright, on their edges, and in the original envelopes. Don't sun them or put them in your car trunk or glove compartment. And don't expose them to the other extreme, freezing temperatures. Keep them away from magnetic fields, stereos, speakers, TVs, and electrical outlets. Airport X-Ray machines are usually safe, however.

If disaster strikes

If someone (not you, of course) spills hot coffee, peanut butter, an adult beverage, or a milk shake on your disk, all may not be lost. Dab it dry with a towel (don't rub) and let it dry for a day or so. Then try to copy it to another disk (here's another reason for having a second drive). You may not recover all of it, but you should be able to recover enough to make the effort worthwhile.

Some experts claim they open the disks, wash them in warm, soapy water, rinse them good, then let them air dry. I make no claims to the

efficacy of any of these methods; I only offer them as suggestions to try.

There are also some special utilities available to recover data from damaged disks. One shareware program, Read My Disk (appendix C), is available from shareware vendors. A commercial program, RESOLVE, is available from AllMicro. RESOLVE can be used to recover data from both a hard disk and a floppy.

So, take care of your drives and your floppies and keep using them until your 50-year warranty expires (hopefully before you do).

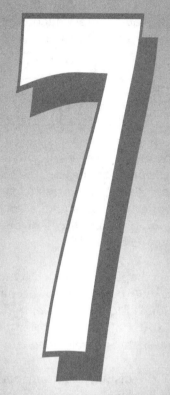

High-resolution display
and display driver

CHAPTER 7

THIS chapter covers the selection and upgrading of the display driver (a.k.a. display adapter, video card or graphics card) and the display (a.k.a. monitor), the combination depicted in Fig. 7-1.

Figure 7-1

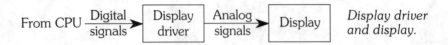

From CPU $\xrightarrow{\text{Digital signals}}$ Display driver $\xrightarrow{\text{Analog signals}}$ Display

Display driver and display.

In Fig. 7-1, the display driver receives digital data from the CPU and converts it into analog signals for driving the display. The display driver can range in complexity from a relatively simple, plain-vanilla, digital-to-analog converter with minimum associated circuitry, to a complex driver with a graphics coprocessor or an accelerator and containing up to a few MB of RAM.

The baseline system of chapter 3 assumed a modest resolution (640 × 480 pixels) 14-inch VGA color display. To function at DTP levels 2 and 3, higher resolution is required. For entry level DTP (Level 2), a 14-inch Super VGA (800 × 600 pixels) color display with a 0.31 dot size (about 82 dots per inch) is barely adequate.

Level 3, full-featured DTP display requirements are more stringent. Noninterlaced, higher-resolution, higher-cost color displays with smaller dot sizes and more complex display drivers (also higher cost) are required. The display size should also be increased. Because these are large expenditures, detailed tradeoffs are provided to help make these purchasing decisions.

Another alternative for high resolution DTP is the use of "paper-white" displays. These displays have resolutions as high as 1,664 × 1,200 with screens as large as 20 inches. They can display two pages of a DTP document side-by-side. This is also a considerable investment, so detailed tradeoff considerations are supplied for considering this alternative.

Each display requires a compatible display driver. The display driver must not only be able to accommodate the display's resolution, it must also have on-board memory so that it can store the image being

displayed, and continually refresh the display without having to rely on the motherboard RAM.

In addition, when DTPs utilize considerable graphics, an accelerator or a graphic coprocessor may be required on the display driver to perform the complex graphic processing required to drive and repaint the display when it is edited or repositioned, without the process being slowed down by having to rely on the already busy CPU on the motherboard. The types of display drivers available, their characteristics, and relative costs are also covered.

Finally this chapter provides the detailed instructions and illustrations needed to install the display driver and to set up the software required to accommodate these additions.

Definitions and acronyms

Here are some definitions and acronyms you'll encounter in the display and display driver discussions.

❋ **Convergence**   This is the ability of a color display to focus the three colors of a pixel on a single point. If the convergence is poor, the display looks fuzzy. As a check for convergence, check a white line on your screen. If it's not near-white, you'll see a tinted haze of whatever color is not converging properly. You can't adjust convergence, however; it's an inherent quality that comes with your CRT. Displays with a smaller pixel size usually have better convergence.

❋ **Dot size**   A measure of the diameter of a dot on the display. The smaller the dot size, the higher the resolution and the sharper the image. Dot size is expressed in millimeters; a .25 mm (millimeter) dot size is 0.25 millimeters, or about 0.01 inches. Why this is expressed in millimeters while screen sizes are expressed in inches is beyond me. Isn't 100 dots per inch (or 10 mils) easier to comprehend than 0.25 mm? To convert from dot size in millimeters to dot size in inches, just divide the millimeter figure by 25.4. The dots per inch are then the reciprocal of this result.

✳ **DRAM** Dynamic RAM. The common type of RAM that is used for most of the PC's functions.

✳ **Horizontal scan frequency** The rate at which each horizontal line is painted on the display screen, expressed in kilohertz.

✳ **Interlace** The process by which the composite image on the display is drawn in two successive passes (Fig. 7-2).

Figure 7-2

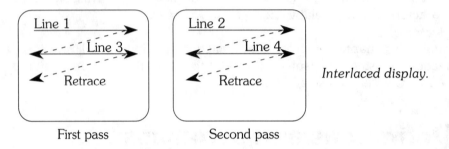

First pass   Second pass

Interlaced display.

The first pass paints the odd numbered horizontal lines {Line 1, retrace (the dotted line), Line 3, retrace, etc.} The second pass shifts down to the spaces between the previously painted lines and paints the even numbered horizontal lines. During the high-speed retrace, the electron beam is turned off.

✳ **Monochrome display** Displays information in only one color. Monochrome displays generally have black backgrounds, with the information being displayed in white, amber, or green.

✳ **Multiscan or multisync** The ability of a display to lock on to and synchronize its refresh or painting rate with a wide range of input scanning frequencies.

✳ **Noninterlace** As opposed to interlace, a noninterlace scan paints all of the odd and even numbered lines in sequence, painting an entire display in one pass (Fig. 7-3).

✳ **Pixel (picture element)** The basic element in a display. A pixel is the diameter of the dot on a display. Although the pixel is shown as a square for illustration purposes, in practice its profile is approximately bell-shaped. The pixels overlap so there is no sharp cutoff at the edges of each dot.

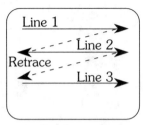

Figure 7-3

Noninterlaced display.

Single pass

In color displays, a pixel is made up of three dots (red, green, and blue) usually arranged in a triangle with overlapping areas; this is true for most screens, except for the Trinitron display which uses parallel slots on the screen.

✳ **Raster scan**   The process by which a picture is painted on the screen by a series of horizontal lines advancing from the top to the bottom of the display as illustrated in Figs. 7-2 and 7-3.

✳ **Refresh rate**   The rate at which a complete picture is painted on the screen. Two passes are required for an interlaced presentation, a single pass for a noninterlaced presentation. For example, a refresh rate of 70 specifies that the screen is completely repainted 70 times a second. Typical refresh rates range from 50 to 90 Hz.

✳ **Resolution**   The number of dots (or pixels) on the screen in each dimension (horizontal and vertical) (Fig. 7-4). Horizontal resolution ranges from as low as 320 to as high as 2,048 dots per screen width. The higher the resolution, the better WYSIWYG presentation you receive of how the printed page will look.

✳ **Screen size**   Expressed in inches, it is the diagonal dimension of your display measured from corner to corner (Fig. 7-5). Screens usually have a 4 (horizontal) to 3 (vertical) aspect ratio.

✳ **VRAM (Video RAM)**   A faster and more expensive memory with a specific architecture for handling video.

Figure 7-4

Horizontal resolution in pixels

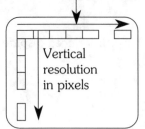

Vertical resolution in pixels

Resolution in pixels.

Figure 7-5

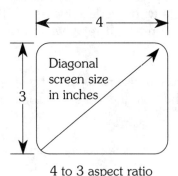

Diagonal screen size in inches

Screen size-diagonal.

4 to 3 aspect ratio

Why use a landscape display?

Most displays are designed with a 4 to 3 aspect ratio. The reason why the horizontal plane is larger than the vertical has its roots in the cinema. When movies were first made, most of the motion and the action occurred in the horizontal plane (horses, trains, people), so this larger dimension was standardized to accommodate the dominant horizontal motion in a landscape format.

Television, because many of its early presentations were movies, simply continued this standard. Although early CRTs were round because this form was easier to fabricate, TV screens were masked off with a bezel to provide a 4 by 3 viewing area.

When rectangular CRTs were later produced for TV, they also had no choice but to continue using the 4 to 3 aspect ratio. Computer displays also adopted this format because they initially used television CRTs.

However, most printed material (books, periodicals, etc.) uses a 3 to 4 format where the horizontal dimension is about 75 percent of the vertical dimension (standard A size is 8½ × 11 inches), also known as the portrait format.

So, why don't computer display manufacturers rotate their CRT ninety degrees and scan the picture vertically, providing the highest resolution on the vertical axis? Are they stuck with a dinosaur? Wouldn't a portrait format be ideal for DTP applications where you can see an entire page displayed in portrait format, occupying the entire screen, wasting none of the display space?

Well, at least one company has. Portrait Display Labs has a 15-inch display with a portrait format. Dot size is 0.28 mm (0.011-inch, 91 dots per inch), resolution is 1,024 × 768. This display can also be physically rotated ninety degrees to provide a landscape presentation. Hopefully other innovative companies will also experiment with and provide the option of a portrait format with their computers.

Video standards

For reference, here's a list of the standard video resolutions that have been adopted by industry. The date in parentheses is when the specific standard originated. Resolutions are specified according to the number of colors they can display. The first number is the horizontal resolution, the second number the vertical resolution.

One important fact to note is that most of the higher-resolution systems are downwards compatible; that is, a high-resolution display driver (e.g., VGA) is compatible with (and functions at) a lower resolution when the software is using a lower resolution (e.g., CGA).

✳ **CGA (Color Graphics Adapter)**   CGA was introduced in 1981. Its color capabilities vary with its resolution setting; e.g., 320 × 200 pixels, 4 colors; 640 × 200, 2 colors; 160 × 100, 16 colors. It was the first graphics-capable display driver, a low to medium resolution color graphics system for PCs. Marginally adequate for lower level DTP.

✳ **EGA (Enhanced Graphics Adapter)**   EGA dates from 1984. A medium resolution color system for PCs, it too has varying resolution and color capabilities: 320 × 200 pixels, 16 colors; 640 × 350, 16 colors; 640 × 200, 16 colors. EGA has its own BIOS.

✳ **HGC (Hercules Graphic Card)**   With 720 × 350 resolution but only one color, the HGC display was introduced in 1982 as a graphics-capable monochrome PC enhancement. Displays well-formed text characters and high-resolution graphics.

✳ **MDA (Monochrome Display Adapter)**   The original display driver, MDA could only display text; it did so at 80 characters by 25 lines, 720 × 350 pixels and one color.

✳ **MGA (Multicolor Graphics Array)**   320 × 200 × 256 colors, or 640 × 480 × 2 colors.

✳ **SVGA (Super VGA)**   800 × 600 resolution with 256 colors, or 1,024 × 768 and 16 colors. SVGA is a very high-resolution color display system. Super VGA requires a multisync display.

✳ **VGA (Video Graphics Adapter)**   Introduced in 1987, SVGA is a high-resolution color system. It displays 640 × 480 pixels in 16 colors, or 320 × 200 in 256 colors. VGA also comes in gray-scale or paper-white versions that are used principally for DTP and display varying shades of gray instead of color.

✳ **XGA (Extended (or Ultra) Graphics Adapter)**   The current resolution king, with 1,024 × 768 pixels. An extremely high-resolution system.

⇨ Basic choices

The display is the most important visual communication device on your PC. It is the primary presentation and working surface which you use to create, compose, review, and revise your publications before committing them to print, or for delivery to the next stage in its process. So the choice of which display to use is one of the most important you will make. And there are many factors to consider in making this choice:

➤ Color or monochrome

➤ Number of colors to display if a color display is selected

➤ Size

➤ Cost

➤ Resolution

➤ Interlace versus noninterlace

➤ Refresh rate

➤ Horizontal scan rate

➤ Ergonomics

➤ Growth potential

All of these factors are interrelated, so the decision is a complex one and will be covered in detail. In the text that follows, I'll try to take some of the mystery out of them.

Monochrome or color?

This is perhaps one of the easiest decisions to make. If you are going to create documents that use color, you need to use a color monitor. However, if all of your work is with monochrome documentation, such as books, drawings, proposals, reports, newsletters, etc., a monochrome display is a less expensive solution.

A monochrome display can present up to 64 gray scales; that's actually 64 levels of white (or whatever color your CRT provides). Monochrome displays are available for a reasonable cost in large sizes (19–21 inches) and can display two readable 8.5-inch pages side-by-side. But they can't display color, so you'll always be working in a monochrome world. That is, unless you configure a dual-display system. With a dual-display system, you can take advantage of the monochrome's high resolution for layout and creation of the basic document and use a color display to add and tweak the color portions of your documents.

 # How many colors?

For color displays, here is the standard terminology used to identify the various color modes. Just hope you never have to count them.

Bits/Pixel	Mode Name	No. of Colors
4	Minimum color	16
8	Pseudo color	256
16	High color	65,536
24	True color	16.7 million

The number of colors you choose to display directly affects the hardware. The more colors you choose, the more computing that is required, so it slows down your system. Some of this can be accommodated by an accelerator or a graphics coprocessor, both of which will be covered later in this chapter. All color displays will support as many colors as your display drivers can generate.

True color offers as many colors as the human eye can detect, it displays images with photographic-like color quality. The human perceptual system interprets true-color images as having higher resolutions than images with fewer colors at the same resolution. For DTP or presentation graphics you should have at least a 256-color capability at all resolutions, even if you don't use color at the present time.

As far as the number of colors needed, here are some recommended guidelines. Most display drivers can accommodate 4-bit (16 colors) and 8-bit (256 colors) systems, which are adequate for applications that don't require a lot of color, such as word processing, spreadsheets, pie charts, etc. And 4-bit (16 gray scales) should be adequate for most black-and-white DTP documents. If you only view, crop, and place images on your documents, 16-bit color (65,536 colors) should be sufficient. If you work with photo-retouching or other high-resolution special effects, you need 24-bit color (16.7 million colors).

 # Display size

Once you've decided on monochrome vs. color and the number of color levels, the next crucial decision you have to make is choosing the size of your display. Displays are manufactured in three basic sizes: 14–15 inches, 17 inches, and 20–21 inches.

In choosing a size, consider the actual useful diagonal of the display; that's the area you can use for previewing images. Diagonals quoted by manufacturers are often exaggerated and include the physical diagonal of the CRT glass. Some manufacturers in quoting their dimensions even include the unused area of the CRT that is hidden behind the bezel. The useful diagonal of the CRT is usually an inch or more less than the manufacturer specifies. For example, a 17-inch CRT has a useful diagonal ranging from 15.5 to 16 inches. Table 7-1 lists average CRT, horizontal and vertical viewing dimensions (based on a 4 to 3 aspect ratio), the viewing areas for various size CRTs, the increase in viewing areas as you use a larger CRT, and a cost comparison figure.

Display size versus cost   Table 7-1

CRT size in.	View diag. in.	Horiz. size in.	Vert. size in.	Area sq. in.	% Viewing area increase	Relative cost
14	13	10.4	7.8	81	Std	1
15	14	11.2	8.4	94	16	1.5–3
17	16	12.8	9.6	123	51	2–4
19	18	14.4	10.8	156	193	3–8
20	19	15.2	11.4	173	214	6–9
21	19.5	15.6	11.7	183	225	8–10

The first column is the CRT size under which the display size is marketed. The second column lists the typical useful diagonal for each size CRT. The useful horizontal and vertical dimensions are listed in the next two columns. The 16-and 17-inch displays are either the same size

or close to it (some manufacturers actually use the same CRT for both advertised sizes), so I only listed the 17-inch display.

The viewing area in square inches is next, the percentage increase in viewing area follows. The increase in viewing area from a 14-inch to a 15-inch is very small. However, a 17-inch provides a fifty percent increase in viewing area over a 14-inch. Moving up to the 20-and 21-inchers doubles, or more than doubles the viewing area of a 14-inch.

Closely allied with the viewing area is the cost. The last column compares the relative cost of the listed display compared to a typical 14-inch display. With displays, cost goes up almost exponentially with the increase in size as illustrated in Table 7-1. In this chart a 14-inch CRT is used for comparison, with a cost of around $300 for a 14-inch at the time of this writing. Note that these figures are averages and can vary widely for different manufacturers' products. When you're purchasing a display, obtain the manufacturer's actual size and cost figures for comparison.

Another important factor to consider is the weight of the display. A computer display can range in weight from as low as 20 pounds for a 14-incher to as high as 80 pounds for the 21-inchers. So if you are going to use one of the larger CRTs (17 inches or larger) arrange your work setup so the display is on a sturdy table or desk in front of you and behind your keyboard. Place your computer chassis nearby where you can readily access the controls and the disk drives.

How much resolution is needed?

The higher the resolution, the easier it is to display and read the information. The higher the resolution, the easier it also is to proof layouts on the screen, rather than having to continuously zoom in and out and print drafts. But the higher the resolution, the higher the cost too, so the choice becomes a compromise of what you need and how much you decide to invest.

The maximum resolution attainable by a specific display is determined by its dot size and the physical dimensions of the viewing area. Dot

sizes range from about .31 mm (.012 inches or 83 dots per inch) to about .25 mm (.010 inches or 100 dots per inch). To give you a better feel for size, a dot size of 0.31 mm (0.012 inches) is about the thickness of a typical business card; so dot size is extremely small.

Trinitrons have the smallest dot size, .25 mm at 14 and 17 inches, and .26 mm at 20 inches. Although going from a .31 dot size to a .25 dot size is a reduction of spot size of only 24 percent, the cost to move from the larger spot size to the smaller spot size is significant because of the more critical manufacturing tolerances required.

Next, let's take a look at the relationships between active screen size and the most common dot sizes as illustrated in Table 7-2. We'll use only the horizontal dimension because the vertical resolution is constant, usually about 0.75 of the horizontal.

Horizontal resolution versus dot size Table 7-2

Display size in.	Horiz. resol. in.	Dot size .31 mm (83 dpi)	Dot size .28 mm (91 dpi)	Dot size .25 mm (100 dpi)
14	10.4	866	945	1040
15	11.2	933	1018	1120
17	12.8	1066	1164	1280
19	14.4	1200	1309	1440
20	15.2	1266	1382	1520
21	15.6	1300	1418	1560

This table gives you the theoretical maximum resolution that can be attained for given dot sizes for specific display sizes and doesn't even account for the fact that the dot size grows at the edges of the screen. In practice the dots are not square but are rounded and the actual extent of the dots exceeds the quoted dot size, but that's acceptable because you need an overlap of dots to provide a continuous (and not a polka-dot) display.

So, if you see vendors quoting a 1,280 horizontal resolution for a .25 dot size on a 14-inch display, be a little skeptical. You have to get

down to about a .20 dot size to accommodate that resolution on a small display.

The resolution given above is only the theoretical maximum possible for perfect displays. The actual resolution of the system is also determined by the display drivers which are covered later in this chapter. As was mentioned earlier, a 17-inch display provides a better than 8½-x-11-inch display. With a .31 or smaller dot size and 1,024 × 768 resolution, you can display a 2-page spread and read 10-point text.

Interlace vs. noninterlace

The mechanics of interlaced versus noninterlaced displays were illustrated earlier in this chapter. Although both are used in current displays, the trend is toward noninterlaced displays. The reason for this is that each half of an interlaced display is rewritten (refreshed) only about 30 times a second. This is slow enough to be perceived as flicker by the human eye and can lead to all manner of maladies. The solution is to use a noninterlaced display and a refresh rate (discussed below) of over 70 Hz.

Refresh rate

Screen flicker results from a slow screen refresh rate, and/or the use of interlacing. When both the screen and the overhead fluorescent lights are being refreshed at the same 60-Hz rate, the resultant display flickers like a bunch of moths fluttering around a light bulb. Flicker is also more readily perceived when the screen image is static, as it is with computer displays. Flicker is less noticeable with white (or bright) text on a black background. Windows and DTP are especially prone to flicker because of the many white pages and backgrounds they create. Even if you don't notice flicker, it can affect your eyes. Severe flicker can cause headaches, eyestrain, blurred vision, and fatigue when working with a display for extended periods of time (many hours a day).

Current refresh rates range from about 50 to 120 Hz. A refresh rate of 70 Hz and higher will pretty much guarantee a flicker-free scan, even under the hard fluorescent lights found in many office and home environments. VESA (Video Electronics Standards Association) has established 72 Hz as the minimum acceptable refresh rate for screen resolutions below $1,024 \times 768$ and 70 Hz for higher resolutions. So make sure your display should not only be able to provide these rates, but, for backward compatibility, it should also be able to synchronize at any refresh rate of from 50 to 100–120 Hz.

Horizontal scan rate

The horizontal scan rate is interrelated with, and determined by, the refresh rate and the number of lines the display has to paint for each screen refresh. For a specific example, consider a $1,024 \times 768$ resolution display that is refreshed at 72 Hz. Because the CRT must draw 768 horizontal lines at a 72-Hz rate, the required horizontal scan rate is the product of the two or $768 \times 72 = 55.3$ kHz. (In practice the horizontal scan rate has to be slightly higher to allow for horizontal and vertical retrace times, say about 60 kHz.) To accommodate a wide range of resolutions and refresh rates, the display should be able to synchronize at all horizontal scan rates between 30 and 75 kHz.

Ergonomics

Applying an anti-glare treatment to the face of a CRT reduces the reflections on a display screen caused by a working environment. This light and other reflections can wash out the image and make it unreadable, or interfere enough to increase eyestrain and cause headaches. You can obtain CRTs with anti-glare coatings on their faces, or several third-party anti-glare products are available that you can affix to the face of your CRT.

Flat screens are now becoming common, particularly among larger displays. (Actually, they're only flat in the vertical plane.) A flat screen produces less glare, which makes images rendered up to its

edges much easier to view. Flat screens tend to minimize pin-cushioning and barrelling also. Unfortunately flat-square screens are more likely to have flaws, unless they are manufactured to high standards. Such standards cost more.

Another ergonomic factor affecting usability is if the display is mounted in a swivel that can be tilted. The display should be capable of being rotated in both the vertical and horizontal planes so it can be adjusted for an optimum position suited to the tastes of each individual tall, short, farsighted, or nearsighted viewer.

ELF (extremely low frequency) and VLF (very low frequency) electromagnetic radiation emitted by the display are also of increasing concern as to their effect on the user's health. If you're concerned about this aspect, select a display that has been tested to the Swedish government's National Board of Measurement and Testing, usually a subset of the so-called MPRII standards.

Growth potential

A display doesn't have inherent growth potential. You can't change the dot size, nor the screen dimensions, nor any other item. However, a display driver does have growth potential, so if your funds are limited, splurge and procure the largest and highest resolution, smallest spot size CRT you can afford and temporarily settle for a moderately priced display driver that's upgradable. You can add more DRAM or VRAM later to achieve more color.

Alternatively you could purchase a modest priced display with the knowledge that some day in the future you're going to replace it with a better one. You may be able to sell your old display at a computer swap-meet or a computer store may sell it for you on consignment. You may not receive much for the old display, but it's better than putting it in a closet. Or you could donate it to your local school, church, or charity.

Display driver

Because a display has a very short memory (a fraction of a second), it needs some device to keep reminding it of what it has to do, and where, how, and how much to shine. Once a display is painted, the CRT phosphor quickly fades away, having no visible memory of what was once there. The device that is needed must keep track of every pixel, where each is located, and at what color and intensity each pixel is supposed to glitter. That's the function of either the CPU and its RAM, or the display driver.

For all but the simplest applications, the CPU and its RAM are much too busy with other tasks to continue to take time out to continually refresh and rewrite the display. It is a waste of computing power, particularly when the display is static and presenting unchanging information sixty to seventy times a second. So, help is needed. Hence the need for a display driver.

Display drivers range in complexity from a relatively simple VGA driver that displays 640 × 480 pixels (the resolution used by most DOS applications which most display drivers also support) to high-speed and high-resolution Windows accelerators and coprocessors that accommodate resolutions of 1,024 × 768 pixels and even higher.

As higher and higher display resolutions have been developed, demands on the display driver have increased to the point where two basic types of display drivers were developed to meet these increased requirements:

> ➢ Accelerators

> ➢ Graphics coprocessors

An accelerator is dedicated to perform a limited number of fixed and defined functions. A graphics coprocessor is a small graphics computer that works with the main CPU on the motherboard, relieving the CPU of many of its display tasks. The graphics coprocessor has its own graphics programming language.

159

The villain in the piece, the program with an insatiable appetite for RAM, is the GUI; that is, the graphical user interface, such as is used in Windows. GUIs are composed of bit maps. These bit maps require that each of their elements be stored and delivered to the display on command, 60 to 70 times a second. This is an enormous amount of information that has to be continually processed.

What causes this complexity, and how much resolution and memory you need to incorporate for functioning at various DTP levels, are covered in the text that follows.

Bit map vs. vector displays

A bit map is an image composed entirely of pixels or CRT dots. For example, a bit map drawing of a rectangle is not composed of a set of simple, straight lines on a CRT, but of thousands of tiny pixels next to each other, all arranged to form the four lines that depict the rectangle. To create this rectangle, the CPU or the display driver must keep track of each pixel's location and color. When the rectangle is resized, reshaped, or moved, all of these pixels must then be erased from memory and the rectangle must be recreated at a new position. Further, its color must be reloaded into new memory locations corresponding to the rectangle's new position and size.

A vector or drawing program functions much differently. Most basic geometric figures can be described by a few values; a circle, for example, can be completely specified by a radius, a horizontal and vertical position, its color, etc. So a large circle can be described using only a few bytes.

To get back to GUIs, when an entire screen must be drawn via the bit map method, the quantity of pixels involved may be anywhere from a few hundred thousand (a 640 × 480 display requires over 300,000 pixels) to a few million (a 1,280 × 1,024 display requires over 1.3 million pixels). In addition to this, the color of each pixel must be stored, so it's easy to appreciate the magnitude of the problem.

⇨ Memory required

Two factors determine the amount of memory required to paint the display:

➤ Resolution

➤ Number of colors

To determine the number of colors to be displayed, the display driver's DAC (Digital-to-Analog Converter) converts the digital signal received from the CPU into an analog signal to drive the display and provide the various color combinations. The display driver compares the digital signals with the information stored in a look-up table that contains matching voltage levels for the three primary colors needed to create the color of a single pixel.

Consider, for example, a system where each DAC on the display driver uses a 6-bit data input and can therefore display 2^6 different colors; that is, each color can be displayed in 64 different combinations. Combining the three colors results in $2^6 \times 2^6 \times 2^6 = 2^{18}$ (remember from your algebra classes, you add exponents), which equals a color palette of 2^{18} = 262,144 different colors being theoretically available. So a 6-bit system must choose 256 colors to display out of the 262,144 different colors available. But hold on, this isn't the end, yet. Some systems utilize 8 bits, so they can display ($2^8 \times 2^8 \times 2^8 = 2^{24}$) or 16.7 million colors (whew!), although this would be rather difficult to count with a naked (or even an electronic microscopic) eye.

Here is a formula for calculating display RAM requirements:

Memory	$= (R_h + R_v + N_c) \div 8$
Memory	= The amount of RAM required
R_h	= Horizontal resolution in pixels
R_v	= Vertical resolution in pixels
N_c	= Number of color bits
8	= Number of bits in a byte

To calculate the memory required on a display driver, here is a typical example. Consider a 1,024 × 768 display requiring 256 colors. Substituting in the formula:

Memory = {1024 × 768 × 6} ÷ 8 = 590,000

So nearly 600,000 bytes of RAM are required for this resolution. Table 7-3 lists several combinations of resolutions, number of colors, and their impact on the memory required.

Table 7-3

Colors and resolution versus memory required

No. of colors	Color bits	Resolution	Memory required
16	4	640 × 480	154K
		800 × 600	240K
		1024 × 768	393K
		1280 × 1024	655K
256	8	640 × 480	616K
		800 × 600	960K
		1024 × 768	1.57M
		1280 × 1024	2.62M
32,768	16	640 × 480	1.23M
		800 × 600	1.92M
		1024 × 768	3.14M
		1280 × 1024	5.24M
16.7 M	24	640 × 480	1.85M
		800 × 600	2.88M
		1024 × 768	4.7M
		1280 × 1024	7.86M

Human perceptual system

The visual capabilities of the human perceptual system also enter into these considerations. As far as color is concerned, our senses interpret true-color (24 bit or 16.7 million colors) as having a higher resolution than images with fewer colors, even though we can only distinguish about 256 different colors.

As far as resolution is concerned, about 70 ppi (0.36 mm dot size) to 80 ppi (0.32 mm dot size) gives you about the same resolution that you'll see when you print on paper. Any additional resolution does not benefit the human eye, but it does benefit the printed output.

Table 7-4 lists the various dot sizes resulting from specific resolutions in dots per inch.

Dot size vs. resolution in dots/inch   Table 7-4

Dots/inch	Dot size-in.	Dot size-mm
70	0.0143	0.36
80	0.0125	0.32
90	0.111	0.28
100	0.01	0.25

⇨ DRAM vs. VRAM

Another choice to be made is the type of RAM to be used. Two basic types are used:

> ➤ DRAM
> ➤ VRAM

DRAM (Dynamic RAM) is used in your main memory. It's called dynamic not because it's so energetic, but because it has a short memory and must be dynamically (continuously) refreshed so it doesn't

forget its contents. VRAM (Video RAM) is a different type of RAM with a specific architecture that is better suited for video applications.

For video applications both DRAM and VRAM must accept new display information from the processor. At the same time, they must output the current image to the display. DRAMs have only one port that a processor can use to read and write data. This is acceptable for most system applications, but is not efficient for video applications. VRAMs, however, have two ports that can be written to or read from at the same time, so VRAMs effectively double the bandwidth of the video memory system. VRAM boards run faster because the commands from the CPU do not have to pause while screen refresh is taking place.

The major objection to VRAM is that it costs about twice as much as RAM, so you pay a price for the improved performance. Some board manufacturers use a combination of VRAM and RAM; some use all VRAM.

Accelerators

An accelerator (a.k.a. a graphics or Windows accelerator) is a dedicated display driver that is specially designed to perform Windows graphical tasks. It is not programmable; Windows calls have been programmed into the chips to perform fixed and repetitive functions, such as redrawing the Windows screen, the pulldown menus, etc.

Accelerator cards replace standard display drivers (a.k.a. video cards) and can boost performance by 10 to 20 times by performing much of the needed video processing, rather than relying on the motherboard CPU. Without an accelerator, Windows can take 30 seconds to go from one application to another and generate a new screen. An accelerator can reduce that time to about 2 seconds.

Graphics coprocessors

On the premise that two heads are better than one, some display drivers contain graphic coprocessors to perform the functions needed

to display text and graphics, without help from the CPU. The graphics coprocessor is actually a small graphics computer working with the CPU, but which has its own graphics programming language.

The graphics coprocessor is a programmable processor that handles both DOS and Windows. Rather than using the CPU on the motherboard to calculate the position and color of each pixel, the CPU sends the graphics coprocessor a set of commands for graphics primitives (the fundamental elements that make up an image, lines, circles, rectangles, etc.). The graphics coprocessor then processes this data and turns it into an image, relieving the CPU of this cumbersome burden.

Coprocessors' principal applications are for CAD programs that run best in DOS. They are well-suited to drawing lines and curves and to fill in areas of the screen, but are not too helpful for bit-mapped graphics. Graphics coprocessors perform all graphic functions: line drawing, area filling, memory-to-memory transfer, and raster generation. They are also helpful for special purpose display functions, such as rendering 3-D models. However, they are not much help with bit-mapped graphic programs such as Windows, because of the huge volume of information that has to be moved from the system over to the display driver.

A graphics coprocessor is not required for DOS unless the graphics requirements are strenuous, or unless CAD software is used. A graphics coprocessor costs from 4 to 5 times that of an accelerator display driver.

⇨ My recommendations

For DOS and Windows Level 1, a 15-to 17-inch display should be adequate. And you should have about one half to one megabyte of RAM on your display driver card, plus resolution compatible with the spot size on your display if you are going to use a modest amount of graphics.

For DOS and Windows Level 2, a 15-to 17-inch display should also be adequate, unless you are going to use a large amount of intricate graphics. For considerably complex graphics, a 19-to 21-inch display is needed. One to two megabytes of RAM on your display driver and a resolution compatible with your display should suffice for this level.

For Level 3 DOS and Windows, a 19-to 21-inch display is needed along with two to four megabytes of RAM on your display driver, plus a resolution that matches your display and your controller card resolution.

Even though the paper-white displays have excellent resolution, I wouldn't recommend them unless you are going to be content with creating only black-and-white desktop publishing documents or want to use them in a dual-display configuration. Color sure adds a lot to your documents. Just as color TV leapfrogged black-and-white TV and made it obsolete, so monochrome displays have only a limited use.

If your displays are graphics-intensive, and particularly if you use a lot of bit-map illustrations, you should consider purchasing a fixed-function graphics accelerator. And be sure to obtain one that is RAM or VRAM expandable. If you doubt the need for considerable memory on an accelerator board, review Table 7-3.

If you plan to work with 256 or more colors, at a resolution of 800 × 600 or higher, and want a flicker-free refresh rate of 72 Hz or above, consider buying a graphics coprocessor instead of an accelerator type of display driver.

⇨ Upgrade procedures

Once you have decided which display system components are right for you, you still have to install them, then get them up and running. Here's how.

Installing high-resolution display

The installation of the high-resolution display consists of simply finding a suitable position for the display and a sturdy enough table or desk to hold it if it is one of the larger displays.

The display should be eye-height, about 18–24 inches from your eyes, depending on your eyesight. A swivel base is desirable if it can swivel in all three dimensions to adjust it for different individuals.

With your PC power off, plug the connector into the proper jack at the back of your PC. If you have a power station or a surge suppressor with separate power switches for several peripherals, plug your display into that. You want to be able to control the power to your monitor from an external switch rather than the one on the monitor, because the monitor switch is too difficult to change if it malfunctions.

Installing display driver

Physical installation of a new display driver card is identical to replacing any standard card, a procedure covered in chapter 3. Figure 7-6 is a typical display driver card. Note that it comes with a disk that contains display driver software for driving specified software programs at various resolutions. A manual is also provided.

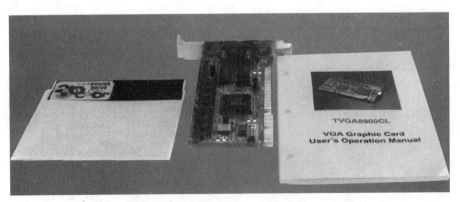

Figure 7-6

Display driver card—1MB RAM, software disk and manual.

Check your documentation to see if you have to flip any DIP switches or move any jumpers before you install the card. Once you have set or moved any needed jumpers or switches, install the new display drive card and button up the case. Plug the new monitor into primary power and connect it to the plug on the rear of your PC. Boot up your computer and you should see some kind of presentation on your new display and display drive combination.

You may have to install new display driver software to match your new display's resolution. If so, refer to the software disk that came with your display driver and input the driver software it provides. You may also have to accomplish this driver upgrade for some of the individual programs you utilize.

CPU/motherboard
transplant

CHAPTER 8

IF your PC wakes up in the morning sluggish, its disk drives creaking in geriatric grief as it agonizingly unveils your opening screen . . . if it is as reluctant to accomplish its assignments as a recalcitrant teenager . . . if your integrated circuits seem to disintegrate and they change screens slower than a bachelor changes his socks . . . if your screen is fading like a teenager's jeans . . . then it's time for an update to the heart of your computer.

To take full advantage of the modern and versatile software you're using, it may be time for a CPU or motherboard transplant. The CPU transplant is the easier of the two; just select the right replacement, pop out the old one, and plug in a shiny new one. The motherboard transplant, however, is a little more involved as you will soon see.

If you don't have a PC, you may decide to purchase and assemble your own. Alternatively you may opt to define and purchase a completely assembled PC with built-in upgrade capability.

Whatever your situation is, read on and you'll learn how to cure your PC's heart failure.

Replacing the CPU and/or motherboard

This chapter covers the selection and replacement of the CPU or the motherboard, key components in all PCs. It also covers the assembly, upgrade, or purchase of a PC to meet your specifications.

Selection and replacement of the CPU and the motherboard are akin to a total ticker transplant, so read through the entire chapter before you select and purchase any components. The PC and the motherboard are truly the heart of your PC; the cables are its life-giving veins. If your PC's heart does not race as fast as a fifth grader galloping out to recess, you have to perform a transplant. This chapter guides you through this vital surgery.

The basic reason for replacing the CPU or motherboard is to upgrade to a more modern and higher-speed system (after listening to high-

speed hype for so long, you've finally surrendered to its temptation). More and more modern computer systems are going at a faster and faster pace, making our work easier (and more complicated). Whether it's fast food or fast computers, the object is to make the most of our precious time.

Fortunately a wide and diverse variety of replacement CPUs have been designed to physically and electrically function in an expansion slot, or with an in-place motherboard; and motherboard replacement is becoming more practical because the cost of motherboards keeps plummeting, just like the stock you just invested in. As far as a CPU and motherboard are concerned, for whatever version you're installing, the replacement procedures are essentially the same.

⇨ If you don't have a PC

For those of you who don't own a PC and want to create your own desktop publishing capability, this chapter shows you how to make the proper choices in purchasing a used PC and upgrading it, or purchasing the components and assembling your own. This chapter also informs you about specifying and purchasing an already assembled PC.

If you're considering assembling your own computer, this chapter only covers the step-by-step instructions to assemble the case (including the power supply) and the motherboard. To add the other components (RAM, hard drive, floppy drive, etc.) refer to the applicable chapters in this book for the detailed procedures.

⇨ Definitions, acronyms, and numbers

Personal computers are blessed (or cursed) with more acronyms than a fifty-gallon vat of alphabet soup. Even this exceptional electronic equipment does not speak its name, but goes by the designation "PC." So it was inevitable that many acronyms and numbers would

be associated with its progeny. Table 8-1 lists some of the models past and present, their dates of birth and other pertinent data. It should help bring a modicum of understanding to this PC Tower of Babel.

In addition to the enormous advances in speed and in the quantity of transistors used, note that each advance in a PC model has a gestation period of about four years (are you listening IRS?). So you can count on continuing to upgrade your PC several times for the rest of its hopefully ten-year or so lifetime.

Table 8-1   PC evolution

Style	Model	Date of birth	No. of transistors	Speed in MHz
XT	8086/8088	1978/79	29,000	4.77–10
AT	80286	1982	134,000	12–20
AT	80386SX	1985	275,000	16–33
AT	80386DX	1985	275,000	16–33
AT	80486SX	1989	900,000	16–33
AT	80486DX	1989	1.2 million	25–50
AT	486DLC	1990	600,000	20–40
AT	80586 a.k.a Pentium	1993	2.1 million	60–66 and 100

For reference, here are some more details of recent bygone CPUs and some of the latest hot shots:

✳ **XT**   The original PC used an 8086 and 8088. The 8088 has an 8-bit bus, the 8086 16-bit internal and 8-bit external buses. Addressable memory is 1MB.

✳ **80286**   This first of the AT class has 16-bit internal and external buses and addresses 16MB of memory.

✳ **80386SX**   32-bit internal data path and a 16-bit external bus. Addressable memory - 16MB.

* **80386DX** 32-bit internal and external bus that transfers data at twice the speed of a 386SX running at the same clock speed. Addressable memory - 4GB. According to Intel, the 386DX can scan the entire Encyclopedia Britannica in just 12.5 seconds. (Now that's what I call speed reading.)

* **80486SX** Slightly more refined design than the 386/386SX design, with 8K internal cache 32-bit internal and external data paths. Addressable memory - 4GB.

* **80486DX** Everything an 80486SX has, plus a built-in math co-processor. Performs more than 50 times faster than the venerable 8088. There is also an 80486DX2 model, a clock doubler chip that's internally operated at twice as fast as normal (is a triple-speed far away?). Operations outside the CPU take place at the regular chip speed.

* **486DLC** Cyrix's true 486-compatible, 32-bit internal and external buses, a 1K cache and a built in math coprocessor. A low-cost CPU I have in one of my computers. It's faster than a kite in a tornado.

* **CX4860DRu.sup.2** Cyrix's overdrive chip. DRu stands for Direct Replacement upgrade. This chip doubles the speed of the 16-, 20-, and 25-MHz machines; it has a 32-bit internal and external bus.

* **80586 a.k.a. Pentium** 32-bit instruction set, built in coprocessor, 64-bit processing capabilities, and it processes two instructions per clock cycle; so it's more than five times faster than the 33-MHz Intel 486DX. Truly hurricane speed!

The listings above cover mostly the Intel product line, with a couple of Cyrix's thrown in. Several other highly competitive versions (Advanced MicroDevices, IBM, Cyrix, NEC) are also available for most of the above chips.

⇨ How much speed is needed?

The speed you need is directly related to your patience, i.e., the degree of your tolerance in waiting for screens to be written, moved, edited, and redrawn. The faster the CPU, the faster many of its

operations are carried out. For basic word processing, even the slowest CPU keeps ahead of a fast flying fingers' furious typing speed. It is when you utilize considerable graphics or fiddle in Windows or other GUIs that you need the faster CPUs. Still, a faster CPU is not the only answer to increasing speed of operation. There are other solutions to expedite graphic presentations, such as accelerators and graphics coprocessors discussed in chapter 7.

The answer to how much speed is needed for any particular type of program is a complex one. What it boils down to is that speed comes at a price. The decision becomes a compromise between what you can afford to invest and the amount of time you can wait for your PC to write new screens.

One important consideration about speed: you can purchase a slower and less expensive motherboard, and if you make the right decisions, it won't be a dead-end purchase. For example, several 486 CPU upgradable motherboards are available that have 238-pin Zero Insertion Force (ZIF) sockets. When the cost of a higher speed CPU, such as the Pentium, comes down from the stratosphere, all you have to do is buy one, then "raise the lever, slide out the 486 CPU, and slide in a new one."

So, whatever you purchase, plan ahead. (Remember, growth, growth, growth!) Look for easy upgrade potential, it's the best investment you can make to accommodate this technology that advances so rapidly that by the time you've upgraded, it's obsolete.

You may have heard of "Turbo Speed" in your travels (or travails). Motherboards normally operate at what is called a turbo speed. This mode is usually indicated on the front panel of your computer with an indicator and is selected and de-selected by an accompanying push-button. The motherboard can also operate at a slower mode than may be needed for certain programs, such as games which are sensitive to clock speed. You usually access this lower speed by pushing the "TURBO" button on your front panel. When you do, the turbo indicator should go out to let you know that you're functioning in the slower mode.

⇨ Your options

Now it's time to consider the basic choices you have to make. These choices are the most basic and important of all the decisions you will have to make, so consider them carefully. Your basic options covered in this book are:

※ **Option 1**   Assemble a new computer by purchasing all of the components, or specify and purchase a new computer that is already assembled and tested for you.

※ **Option 2**   Purchase a used computer and upgrade it.

※ **Option 3**   Upgrade your present computer by replacing only your CPU with a higher speed CPU.

※ **Option 4**   Replace your existing motherboard with a motherboard having a faster CPU with an upgradable or overdrive socket.

※ **Option 5**   Replace your existing motherboard with the fastest new CPU motherboard available.

The first option assumes you don't have a computer and that you elect to specify and purchase a PC or assemble your own from scratch. Option 2 is a low-budget option: you purchase a used AT class (or maybe XT class if you can find one real cheap) and upgrade it with a new motherboard, plus any other needed accoutrements. If you already have an AT computer, you may opt to take advantage of the third option and replace your present CPU with a faster plug-in CPU.

Option 4 is a wise one if your budget is limited and you want to immediately achieve a modest increase in speed, but are planning for the future. If you install a motherboard with an overdrive upgradable socket, it is only a minor effort to upgrade to a faster speed CPU when the prices come down (as they inevitably do).

If your budget is unlimited, Option 5 is ideal. You can replace your motherboard with the fastest CPU available and achieve instant lightning speed.

Tradeoff considerations

The various options for equipping yourself with a DTP machine all have their advantages and drawbacks. Here are some of them:

Option 1: Assemble/purchase new PC

This choice is easy to make. If you don't have a computer, you can either purchase the components and assemble it yourself, or you can specify and purchase an already assembled computer. I admit I'm biased, but I recommend that you purchase all of the individual components and assemble your own computer for the reasons I covered in the first chapter.

If you're a trifle skittish about building your own PC from scratch at first, the next best approach would be to purchase a minimal computer similar to the baseline specs listed in chapter 3. Then, when you open the cover and look inside and see how simple it is, you'll be convinced that in the future you're going to be anxious to perform all the subsequent upgrades. In this way you can purchase a working computer for a minimal cost and use it for elementary DTP functions. Later you can upgrade it as your capital budget and needs hopefully expand at the same pace.

The first decision to be made is the option of a motherboard. My only advice is to invest in the most advanced motherboard you can afford—one that has growth (there's that word again) potential. Prices range from less than $100 to well over $1,000, so it's not too easy a decision to make. However, when you compare prices, make sure you know what's included in the motherboard. As far as physical size is concerned, choose a "baby AT" motherboard. It will fit in virtually any of the available case configurations and take up very little space. A typical motherboard is illustrated in Fig. 8-1.

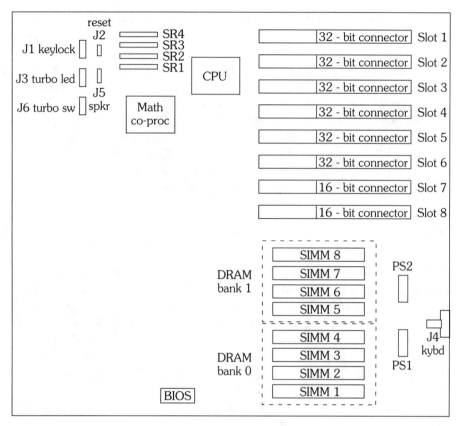

Figure 8-1

Motherboard layout

The motherboard has a CPU, memory sockets for 16MB or more of RAM, several expansion slots (typically six 32-bit and two 16-bit slots) for plug-in boards, a BIOS, a speaker, and a built-in clock and battery. Some of the older versions may have other functions included in the motherboard, such as serial and parallel ports, an IDE interface built in for hard disk drives, etc. Instructions for connecting your motherboard to the case and to the other components are usually supplied with the motherboard. In addition, motherboard suppliers usually provide technical support in case of problems.

The ROM-BIOS (Read-Only-Memory-Basic-Input-Output-System) includes the source loader, subroutines for system clock, various

check routines, and subroutines for the video generator and the graphic generator.

Concerning ports, there are two basic types of ports: serial (a.k.a. RS-232 port) and parallel (a.k.a. Centronics port). DOS can track up to four serial ports, COM 1 through COM 4. DOS can also track up to three parallel ports. The RS-232 port is based on the recommended standard RS-232 of the Electronic Industry Association (EIA). An RS-232 usually has a 9-pin female DB-9 connector. A parallel port usually has a 25-pin DIP female connector. The printer connector is usually a Centronics 36-pin male.

A new case

Once you have selected a motherboard, you should next consider what type of case to mount it in. When choosing a case, it basically boils down to whether or not you want a desktop computer or a tower computer configuration. Typical case sizes are listed in chapter 3.

The desktop configuration fits (not too surprisingly) on your desktop. Although it takes up desk space, it is very handy to have everything (the floppy drives, the indicators, etc.) close by. If the display is small (14–15 inches), you can set the display on top of your computer case for convenience. Desktop cases are usually limited to 3 to 4 slots for mounting disk drives. Put in two floppy drives and a CD-ROM drive and you're filled up.

The tower case can be placed under your desk, on a nearby table, or on a shelf. Two types of tower cases are available: mini-tower and full-size. Their biggest advantages are that they have outstanding growth potential (love those towers!), can accommodate a lot of hardware, and do not occupy precious desk space.

A minitower case can accommodate 4–5 drives and has 6–8 expandable slots. A full-sized tower case has up to 8 slots and can often accommodate up to four hard drives, as many as six floppies (I really don't know who would want that many), plus several more peripherals. But a tower case should be mounted near your work area

so you can easily access the remote CD-ROM drive, the floppy drives, and any other add-ons you've upgraded with. It sure can grow!

An appropriate power supply is usually provided with the case you procure and should be at least 230–250 watts. It will deliver ± 5 volts and ± 12 volts.

No matter which configuration you choose, the desktop or the tower, you still have to (as a minimum) position the keyboard and monitor in front of you, so you will have to use up some valuable desktop real estate.

An arrangement I use and prefer is to mount the display on a shelf in front of where I sit (a computer desk is an excellent investment) and I place the keyboard directly in front of me. I position the PC case off to one side where I can reach the disk drives when I have to. With this setup you have the two components you use most of the time (your keyboard and your display) right in front of you and you can place them in a way that is optimal for you.

The type of case chosen (desktop vs. tower) should be made based on the eventual type of system you wish to obtain and grow into. If your means and requirements are modest and growth potential is not important, select a desktop. If you want the ultimate in an expandable personal computer, select a mini- or full-size tower model.

Desktop PCs are available in standard and miniature footprint versions and are slightly less expensive than tower cases.

⇨ Option 2: Purchase/upgrade used PC

This is a low-budget approach. If you don't already have a computer (or if you have an older model) and you're operating with a very limited budget, consider the early AT (or XT) models that are no longer manufactured, but which are eminently upgradable. You can probably purchase a fully functional used one (from someone who has just upgraded to the latest model available) for a couple of hundred dollars or so and upgrade it in any sequence that your budget and

needs allow. Older ATs use 16-bit slots; the newer ATs use 32-bit slots.

Most of the software and hardware designed for the earlier models function with all the later models, except that the more recent models operate faster. Much of the hardware can continue to be used for upgrades as you progress to faster and faster CPU speeds.

A very economical DTP system can be configured based on a used XT or AT system. As a beginning, you can use the XT or AT with an inexpensive VGA black-and-white monitor. Add a 9-pin dot matrix printer and you have a complete complement of hardware for a modest, low-cost start. The output of a dot-matrix printer can be enhanced by Shareware software (e.g., LQ Print) listed in appendix C. Some of the 9-pin dot matrix printers also have an NLQ (Near Letter Quality) mode which, although agonizingly slow, does produce an excellent quality output. You can use the low resolution mode for drafts and NLQ for your final output. If this output is still not satisfactory, you can save your final output document(s) on disk and have them printed by a service bureau that uses laser printers.

A wide and diverse variety of complementary software is also available at very low cost from the Shareware market (see appendix C). In addition to the print enhancement software mentioned above, an excellent DTP program called Envision Publisher is available for a modest cost and will vault you right into the desktop publishing profession.

⇨ If you purchase a used computer

Here are some guidelines if you purchase a used computer. Computers generally have a long life. Once they're burned in, the integrated circuits seem to be able to go on forever and ever. The most likely failures are in the electro-mechanical components, such as the disk drives.

You can locate used computers at a computer swap meet, in a computer store, or via the want ads in computer magazines, newspaper classifieds, or local flyers. (The Boston Computer

Exchange has been around a long time and is one of the best for mail-order used computers.) Most of the ads have phone numbers so you can conduct much of your preliminary weeding out the prospects on the phone with these questions:

1. How old is it?

2. What is the price? (If it's not in the ad, of course).

3. Are any other peripherals included with the price?

4. Is any software included?

5. Is everything working well?

6. Why are you selling?

7. What is the capacity and size of the disk drives?

8. What is the type and size of the hard drive?

9. How much RAM does it have?

10. Anything else you can think to ask.

To determine if the price is reasonable, check comparable ads in the newspapers and magazines. If the seller is local, go and see it. Make the seller demonstrate to you that it works. You don't want to have anything to do with a computer if something inside is dead or dying. Exercise the computer yourself until you're satisfied. Listen for any strange noises and watch for intermittent or slow operation. If software on the hard drive is included, be sure to get the original disks and manuals.

If you're buying by mail, it calls for extra caution. Get the seller to give you a limited warranty: you get your money back if the computer breaks down within so many days. Try for a week or two, but settle for a couple of days if that's all you can get. Also try to get the shipping costs shared in case you have to return it.

No matter how you pay, cash, credit card, or check, be sure to get a receipt that lists the seller's and your names and addresses and phone numbers and a list of everything that is included, plus the selling price (the IRS may want to see this piece of paper).

Once you get your computer working, you may want to make a clean start. Back up what's in the hard disk onto floppies in case there is something there you may want to use. Then reformat the disk, install your own software, and prepare to upgrade.

Option 3: CPU transplant

This approach is a relatively simple one to undertake. All it involves is removing your old CPU and replacing it with a new CPU. Manufacturers claim a five to tenfold increase in performance over the old CPUs. However, replacing the CPU is almost as costly as purchasing a new and faster motherboard. In addition, you have to be careful to make sure that your new CPU is compatible with all of your existing hardware and software. Also note that the daughterboard approach, if used, is going to use up one of your available expansion slots. Check the prices involved in this approach to help make your decision.

Upgrading a 286 with a 386 CPU won't help much in giving you a faster system because the bus and the rest of the computer's components will slow everything down. If you're upgrading from a 286, your best route is a new 386 or 486 motherboard, because it replaces many of the slower components. However, replacing a 386 CPU with a 486 CPU does make sense; it will considerably speed up your system.

Option 4: Motherboard transplant with upgradable socket

This is an excellent approach because you are installing a new motherboard that has been designed for easy growth and upgrade potential, one that will be compatible with all of your existing hardware and software.

Figure 8-2 is a photo of a 386DX 40-MHz motherboard. Note the empty socket in the lower left corner. Next to the empty socket is the 386DX, the main CPU.

Figure 8-2

*386 motherboard upgradable
to 486.*

The spare socket (Fig. 8-3) is for a 486, so this board is easily
upgradable from the existing 386 to a 486. All you have to do is pop
out the old 386 CPU and install the new 486 CPU in the empty
socket and install some jumpers.

This unique design serves another function, also. If you have a 386
(which doesn't have a math coprocessor) and you want to add a math
coprocessor, the circuitry has been designed so that the math

Figure 8-3

Upgradable socket.

coprocessor can be plugged into the central section of the spare socket of Fig. 8-3. This same design allows you to use a 486SX, 486DX, 386DX, 487SX math coprocessor, or the Cyrix 33/40 or Cyrix 25 in the spare socket. Now, that's what I call excellent growth potential!

Another potential upgrade is to take advantage of a clock doubler CPU. Many motherboards have a separate socket built in for the purpose of installing a clock-doubling 486 chip. It replaces the original CPU by completely disabling it and taking over its functions.

The clock doubler, not surprisingly, doubles the speed of the clock and of the functions within the CPU (e.g., changes a 33-MHz to a 66-MHz clock). So certain tasks that make extensive use of the CPU (calculations, record sorting, word searching, etc.) are accomplished at the higher speed. However, functions that are performed external to the CPU (e.g., disk reads and writes, repainting the screen, etc.) still function at the slower speed. Overall you won't double the speed of the system, but some claim a seventy percent increase in performance. If you have a computer without an extra socket, you simply upgrade by replacing the original CPU chip.

Two basic motherboard sizes are in common use: standard AT, which is used in full-size desktops and towers and the narrower "baby" AT, which is used in small-footprint desktops and mini-towers. Either type of motherboard usually fits in most cases. The baby AT is the most common and the most desirable.

Option 5: Motherboard transplant with fastest of the fast

If your budget is unlimited, you may prefer this approach. But keep in mind that as soon as you install a motherboard with the fastest CPU available, a new and faster CPU is going to become available. According to Bjelland's Upgrade Logistics Law (BULL), "As soon as you plug it in, it's obsolete." So you're eventually going to have to replace the old fastest with the new fastest.

Upgrade procedures

One of the most important precepts of upgrading is simple: plan
ahead. Review in your mind what you are going to do before you pick
up any tools. Have a pad and pen (do people still use pencils?)
available for making notes before you start the disassembly. Make
checklists covering all components; make sure the motherboard has a
CPU (some don't), some plug-in slots (8 are preferred), room for
memory and expanded memory, etc.

If you're going to disassemble, sketch the cables and boards, their
locations, etc. It also helps to take a few Polaroid shots before you
disassemble. Label all the cables with both their origin and
destination. Save all screws, mounting brackets, and miscellaneous
hardware in some container so they won't be misplaced.

If you're replacing a motherboard and your old motherboard has
some I/O circuitry on it, you probably won't find I/O ports on your
new motherboard; there just isn't room on the new and smaller
motherboards for the I/O circuitry. So you may have to add an I/O
card and a cable(s). You can purchase a card that controls two hard
drives, two floppy drives and which also has a parallel port for a
printer, a serial port for a mouse, plus a game port. This card costs
less than twenty dollars.

Assembling or upgrading your PC

Because the procedure for removing a motherboard and installing a
new one is the most complicated, this procedure will be covered first.
The procedure diagrammed in Fig. 8-4 covers both the removal of a
motherboard and the replacement of it with a new motherboard, as
well as the procedure for installing a new motherboard in a unit you
are building.

1. Before removing the old motherboard, record on paper any
   information from the CMOS-RAM (RAM that is powered by a
   battery and retains the settings even when your PC's power is
   turned off). To get this information, hold down the Delete key

Figure 8-4

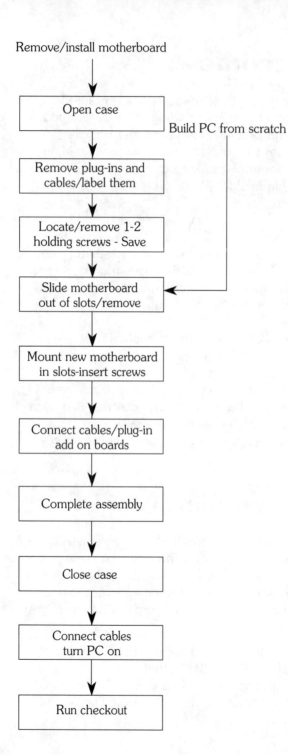

Remove/install motherboard

Open case

Build PC from scratch

Remove plug-ins and
cables/label them

Locate/remove 1-2
holding screws - Save

Slide motherboard
out of slots/remove

Mount new motherboard
in slots-insert screws

Connect cables/plug-in
add on boards

Complete assembly

Close case

Connect cables
turn PC on

Run checkout

*Remove/replace
motherboard procedure.*

186

when booting up (or hold down the Ctrl-Alt-Esc keys simultaneously). Write down (or use Print Screen key to obtain a copy of the screen) the drive type, number of cylinders, number of heads, write precompensation, landing zone, number of sectors, and capacity. After this is accomplished, you can turn everything off and open the case (chapter 3).

2. Remove all plug-in modules and cables that are connected to the existing motherboard. Label them all clearly with both their origin and destination. The cables running from the motherboard to the front of the PC are usually for the:

- Speaker
- Reset button
- Turbo switch (usually also has an LED indicator)
- Keylock/power LED

The turbo switch-LED wire will be one or two wires running from the motherboard to the front panel. This wire is polarized; the positive wire must be connected to the pin designated 1 or +. There are normally three wires from the turbo switch and a two-pin connector on the motherboard. The keylock/power LED usually has a five-pin connector on the motherboard designated as "keylock." The power LED usually connects to pins 1 & 3. The LED wire is polarized, and the positive wire (usually green) must be connected to the positive pin (usually 1). The keylock wire is connected to the remaining two pins. The hard disk indicator lights when the hard disk is running.

The tower cases also have an ON/OFF switch on the front panel. The front panel is a convenient position where I think all PC power switches should be mounted, instead of being hidden near to (or on) the rear of the case.

3. The motherboard is held in place by a number of plastic stand-offs on the motherboard (Fig. 8-5) that fit snugly in slots in the PC case and one or two screws that lock the motherboard in a fixed position. Inspect the top of the motherboard and locate the one or two anchoring screws. Remove the screws and save them.

Figure 8-5

Plastic standoff.

4. The motherboard should now be loose from its moorings, so slide the motherboard out of its slotted mounting holes and remove the old motherboard from the PC case.

5. When you deal with your new motherboard, handle it only by the edges. Don't touch the chips or the copper traces. Your new motherboard should have several plastic standoffs with it. The standoffs elevate your motherboard up off the chassis so the circuitry won't short to the metal case. Before you insert the standoffs in the new motherboard, line up the new board with the old one and insert the standoffs in the new motherboard in the same holes to match those in the old motherboard.

If you're building your own computer from scratch, position the new motherboard where it is supposed to fit inside the PC case and note where the holding screws are going to be inserted as well as the plastic standoffs which should line up with the slotted holes on the case. Mark these holes on the motherboard with a piece of tape, then push the plastic standoffs through the holes in the bottom of the motherboard (Fig. 8-6). They'll protrude a short distance above the motherboard surface.

If you accidentally insert one of the plastic standoffs in the wrong hole, you can remove it by carefully grasping the top of

Figure 8-6

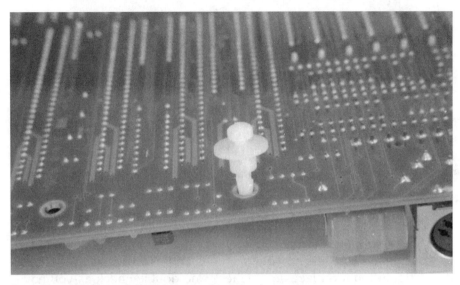

Inserting plastic standoff into motherboard.

the standoffs with a pair of needlenose pliers (or strong tweezers). Pinch the top of the standoff, then push the standoff back through the bottom of the motherboard.

NOTE If you are updating an XT, you'll also have to replace the XT power supply with a new, higher-powered supply. A 230-watt AT supply is reasonably priced.

While the motherboard is out of the case, install the RAM you are going to use. The SIMM sockets may be difficult to reach after the motherboard is mounted. Review the RAM installation procedures in chapter 4.

Review the manual that accompanied your motherboard to determine if you have to set any jumpers for your specific configuration. On the more modern motherboards, most of the settings are controlled by the BIOS setup program as described under software setup.

6. Place the motherboard in the chassis, slide it in the slots until the holding screw holes in the motherboard line up with the threaded holes in the PC chassis. Insert the holding screws and

tighten the screws. Do not over-tighten the screws or you'll deform the motherboard.

7. If any switches or jumpers have to be changed on your add-on boards to accommodate the new motherboard, do so at this time. Install all of the add-on boards.

8. Reinstall all the cables. (If you're building your own PC, follow the directions that came with your motherboard and install all of the necessary cables. To install the other components, e.g., disk drive, RAM, etc. follow the instructions given in the appropriate chapters in this book.)

9. Complete the assembly; make sure power is applied to all of the needed components. Double-check all of your connections, refer to the motherboard documentation and the appropriate chapters in this book. Refer to your sketches and Polaroid shots if you are attempting a replacement. Check and double-check all you have done. The moment of truth is about to come.

10. Close up the case and connect up your keyboard and your display. Make sure all of the power switches on the individual units are off, then plug each unit into ac power.

11. Put your recovery disk in Drive A (or if you are building from scratch, put a DOS disk in Drive A), then turn the unit on.

12. Your A: drive indicator should light up and you should see some information on your display. If this is a new machine, follow the directions on the DOS disk to install DOS on your hard drive. If this is a motherboard replacement, your PC should be working with its newfound muscle and speed.

⇨ Upgrading the CPU

A CPU transplant is much simpler to accomplish than a motherboard replacement. First open the case and locate the CPU. It's probably the biggest chip on the motherboard; it may also have a "Warranty Voided if Removed" or similar warning sticker on it. To remove the old CPU, use the chip puller provided with the new CPU (or use the chip puller from your tool kit). Be sure to ground yourself to the chassis before you start.

Note that the old CPU has one of its corners cut off at an angle; this will be your reference point. Mark this point somehow on the chassis to show how the old CPU chip is oriented. The old CPU may not be easy to remove; after all, it's been in your motherboard for a long time, and has expanded and contracted as it was turned on and off. It may be a trifle reluctant to leave its comfortable home.

The chip puller that came with your new CPU is usually a many-toothed tool, or it may look like a shoehorn. Put the pulling part of the tool under the CPU and pull up gently to try to ease it out of its residence. Pull it up only a fraction of an inch at a time. Move around the various sides of the CPU and continue easing the chip up a little at a time until it's loose.

To install the new chip, locate the corner with the cutoff edge and line it up with the spot you marked (or photographed or remembered) on the motherboard socket. Very, very carefully (there are probably over 150 pins on the CPU chip) line the new CPU up with its socket. Apply a gentle pressure and slowly push the chip down into the socket until it is fully seated. If it isn't fully seated, your motherboard won't work.

Voila! You have a new, hyperspeed CPU that will make monumental miracles happen for you. In case you're lucky enough to have a ZIF (Zero Insertion Force) socket on your motherboard, the process is considerably simplified. The ZIFs have a little lever built-in that lets you pop out the old CPU and install the new one.

When you're finished, button everything up, hook up all of the external cables, and power up your PC. Finally, run the diagnostic program that came with your new CPU.

Software setup

When you turn your PC on, if you receive a picture on your display, everything is probably all right with the world (and your PC, too). If you are greeted with a blank screen, you have to disassemble it and check for loose or improperly connected cables, or the motherboard may be in contact with the metal chassis.

If it's working, boot up again as you hold down the Delete key. You'll be presented with the menu of Fig. 6-9. Again select the STANDARD CMOS SETUP menu selection, hit Enter, and a display similar to Fig. 8-7 should pop up.

Figure 8-7

```
                BIOS SETUP PROGRAM-STANDARD CMOS SETUP
(C)Copyright   1990   American Megatrends Inc., All Rights Reserved

Date(mm/date/year) :Mon, Sep 12 1994   Base memory    :640KB
Time(hour/min/sec) :16 : 42 : 34        Ext. memory   :7168KB
Daylight saving    :Disabled Cylin Head WPcom LZone Sect Size
Hard disk c type   :47        1025 5    0     0      40   100MB
Hard disk d type   :Not installed
Floppy drive A     :1.2MB 5,"
Floppy drive B     :Not installed
Primary display    :VGA/PGA/EGA
```

Sun	Mon	Tue	Wed	Thu	Fri	Sat
				1	2	3
4	5	6	7	8	9	10
11	12	13	14	15	16	17
18	19	20	21	22	23	24
25	26	27	28	29	30	

```
Month:Jan,Feb,.....Dec
Date:01,02,03,.....31
Year:1901,1902,...2099

Esc:   Exit F2/F3:Color PU/PD:Modify
```

BIOS SETUP PROGRAM.

Check the entries. Your PC should have picked up most of the settings. Review your notes and update any entries needing it. Once you have everything functioning, hit your Reset button and watch your PC as it boots. The screen goes blank and the PC will follow a sequence similar to this.

1. VGA/EGA BIOS message
2. BIOS message
3. RAM test is performed
4. Drives A: and B: are accessed briefly
5. Drive C: is accessed briefly
6. The loudspeaker emits a beep to indicate boot is occurring

7. Drive A: is accessed, computer tries to boot from A:

8. Drive C: is accessed, computer tries to boot from C:

9. The operating system (typically DOS) is loaded from the hard drive

10. Your C:\ prompt or menu is presented; you're ready to compute.

Enjoy your upgraded computer.

Printers

PRINTERS are an essential part of a desktop publishing system. They vary in quality and cost according to this order, beginning from lowest to highest:

➢ Dot matrix

➢ Inkjet

➢ Laser (a.k.a. HP-compatible)

➢ PostScript laser

Even though the dot matrix is limited in its ability to provide final copy, it still can be used effectively for drafting documents, drafting illustrations, and for printing multi-page forms. Dot matrix printers are also available for printing color documents.

The inkjet printer is similar in design to the dot matrix. Instead of a pin impacting on a ribbon, the inkjet shoots ink at the paper. The resolution is better than that of a dot matrix, and print quality can approach that of a laser printer. The inkjet is also available in both black-and-white and color versions.

The HP-compatible laser printer produces high-quality output, uses regular single-sheet paper, and is quiet in operation. It can turn out near-lithograph quality text copy. It uses PCL (Printer Command Language), a language which was initially based on bit maps in which text and graphics are converted directly to individual dots to form an overall image. Some versions also are PostScript compatible.

PostScript laser printers use the Page Description Language (PDL) to describe the printed image. PostScript is a mathematical language that the printer interprets and converts to a bit map. PostScript capabilities can also be added later to some laser printers (those that have inherent growth potential) by using add-on boards, emulation software, or emulation cartridges.

Detailed consideration is given in this chapter to the tradeoffs involved in laser printing. There are large costs involved and complicated decisions to be made. The relative advantages and disadvantages, as well as the applications and costs of all the printer types, are covered in this chapter.

⇨ Definitions, acronyms, and numbers

Printers, like every other aspect of the microcomputer world, have more than their share of jargon. Here are some explanations:

✳ **ATM (Adobe Type Manager)**   A font utility used by Windows and OS/2 which produces WYSIWYG screen fonts. For non-PostScript printers, ATM also produces printer fonts. Competitive with True Type.

✳ **bit map**   The contents of a graphics data structure where a bit or byte is used to represent each pixel.

✳ **Cartridge font**   A hard font permanently recorded on ROM memory in a cartridge. The cartridge is inserted into a slot in a laser printer.

✳ **dpi**   Resolution in dots per inch.

✳ **Font**   A set of printable letters and characters with a common typeface, size, weight, style, and orientation. Includes uppercase, lowercase, numerals, punctuation marks, etc.

✳ **Half tone**   A tone or shading between white and black.

✳ **Hard font**   A type of printer font permanently written into ROM.

✳ **Inkjet printer**   An output device that prints by spraying a thin stream of ink onto the paper.

✳ **Kerning**   Adjusting the amount of space between characters to eliminate unsightly gaps; makes a line of text look better.

✳ **Laser printer**   A high speed, nonimpact, high-print-quality printer in which a laser "writes" on a drum, then the drum prints on paper. Easily handles alphanumerics, graphics, and special fonts.

✳ **Leading**   Vertical space between lines of type.

❋ **NLQ (Near Letter Quality)**   Pertains to the output of dot matrix and inkjet printers where the quality of the print approaches the quality of a laser printer.

❋ **PCL (Printer Control Language)**   Software standard used by Hewlett Packard printers. PCL 5 includes support for scalable fonts.

❋ **PDL**   The generic abbreviation for Page Description Language or Page Definition Language.

❋ **Point size**   A standard unit of linear measurement, equal to $\frac{1}{12}$ of a pica, or about $\frac{1}{72}$ of an inch.

❋ **PostScript**   A device-independent language; for example, it can drive a 300-dpi laser printer, as well as a 2,000-dpi typesetter.

❋ **Rasterize**   To convert a mathematical function to a fixed pattern of pixels tailored to the resolution of a particular screen or output device.

❋ **Resident font**   Font permanently written into ROM and stored inside a printer.

❋ **Resolution**   The number of dots that can be printed.

❋ **Sans serif**   Letters without the fine lines at the top and bottom, e.g., Helvetica. See serifs.

❋ **Serif**   A tiny counterstroke that runs approximately perpendicular to the main stroke of a character in some fonts, for example Times Roman. Serifs help move the eye from letter to letter.

❋ **Soft fonts**   A font located on a floppy or hard disk. The font is loaded into a laser's RAM.

❋ **Speed**   The rate at which characters are printed is usually measured in cps (characters per second) or, for laser printers, ppm (pages per minute).

❋ **Style**   Vertical slant of the font, e.g., normal (upright) or italic (oblique).

* **True Type**   A standard utilized by a rapidly expanding library of scalable screen and printer fonts, used by Windows.

* **Typeface**   A collection of fonts with a common appearance, but different point sizes, styles, and weights; e.g., Courier.

* **Weight**   The thickness of the characters.

 # How much resolution is available?

Resolution on 9-pin dot matrix printers ranges from 60 to 180 dpi, compared to the lower laser resolution of 300 dpi. The 24-pin printer features resolutions up to 360 dpi.

Inkjet printers provide a resolution ranging from 180 to 360 dpi. The resolution of laser printers ranges from 300 dpi for the lower cost models to 600 dpi for the more expensive ones. Higher resolutions (1,200 dpi) are also becoming available. As a point of reference, typeset quality needed for books and magazines is greater than 1,200 dpi and often as high as 2,000 dpi.

 # What speeds are available?

Assuming a typical rough draft page contains 80 characters per line and 25 lines of characters; that's 2,000 characters per page. So a 200 cps printer requires about 10 seconds to print a rough draft page.

Typical dot matrix printer speed ranges are:

9-pin   240–300 cps high speed draft
190–285 draft
32 cps NLQ

24-pin   240–330 cps high speed draft
160–225 cps draft
50–70 cps LQ

Inkjet printers range in speed from 110–300 cps draft, 150 cps quality and 20–85 cps in letter quality; this is similar in speed to the dot matrix. Laser printer speeds are considerably faster and range from 4–12 ppm (that's from 12 seconds per page to 5 seconds per page); the more expensive models can output as high as 16 ppm.

For many applications, however, you need not be overly concerned about speed, unless you are impatiently standing by the printer waiting for your fifty-page output. For most routine work, printer buffers can store your document to be printed and allow you to go back to work on another project while the printer prints out your masterpieces. Besides, you should take an occasional break (at least every hour) and get away from your PC; when you're printing, that's a good excuse for getting up and doing something else for a few minutes.

Developments are constantly occurring to increase printer speed. Windows accelerators speed up the process. Combination hardware-software solutions use computer memory to expedite printing. Souped-up printer drivers accelerate printing as much as ten times over that achieved by printers not using such drivers. As with computer speeds, printer speeds continue to increase until we will someday have true "instant printing" that will output pages faster than a government bureaucracy.

Tradeoffs

Like every other equipment choice you will make in outfitting your DTP workstation, printer selection is not a simple issue. Here are some considerations that will weigh against each other when you make your choice:

Gray scale

Although a printer has higher resolution than a display, it can only print one color (usually black), whereas a display can present many shades of gray (or color). Thus the printed version of a document can look mottled when compared to a display presentation.

To simulate gray scale, a printer must create a group of dots, much like the technique used in a newspaper for printing photographs. For example, to obtain 256 shades of gray, a 16×16 dot matrix (16 dots horizontally by 16 dots vertically) is needed. One dot in this square matrix provides the first level of gray; all 256 dots being printed provide the other extreme (black) by filling up the entire matrix of dots. However, if your printer has a resolution of 300 dpi, your effective gray scale resolution is reduced to 300/16 or about 19 dpi of halftone cells.

In practice, however, most 300 dpi printers use a 6×6 matrix, giving 36 levels of gray. The 600 dpi printers use an 8×8 matrix, providing 64 gray levels.

 # Dot matrix

The dot matrix printer is an impact printer that produces characters or graphics by hammering miniature metal rods (pins) against an inked ribbon. The closer the dots, the better the quality of the print and the higher the resulting resolution.

The actual print mechanism (or print head) contains one or more vertical columns of pins. The 9-pin heads usually have all 9 pins lined up in a single vertical column. The 24-pin heads usually arrange the pins in three vertical columns, with each column containing 8 pins.

In operation, the print head travels horizontally, printing in a bi-directional path (no flyback needed here). The print head slams the pins against the ribbon and paper, making noise in the process. Considerable engineering has gone into reducing this noise factor to 45 dBA. If you're extra sensitive to noise, sound absorbent cases and low-noise printers are also available.

Because it's an impact printer, the dot matrix is the only printer that can print multiple forms. Most can handle paper up to 14×11 inches and accommodate either tractor-fed or sheet-fed paper.

Dot matrix printers function in two modes:

> Text

> Graphics

In the text mode, they use bit-mapped fonts resident inside the printer. In the graphics mode, they print scalable or nonscalable fonts as bit-mapped graphics. A typical dot matrix printer has 10 resident and 12 scalable fonts.

Your dot matrix printer choice is between a 9- and 24-pin model. The cost difference between the two is relatively small and the output of the 24-pin is so superior to the 9-pin that you should only consider the 24-pin, unless you're severely budget limited. Surprisingly, however, you can achieve excellent quality on a 9-pin if you have the patience to wait for the printer's NLQ mode to make its snail-paced multiple passes.

As far as applications for using the dot-matrix, it is excellent for drafts. It's reasonably fast, the cost per page is low and it is relatively maintenance free. Considering its printer quality, it is considered acceptable for letters, resumes, and general correspondence, as well as for certain DTP applications like low-circulation newsletters, flyers, and announcements.

Some dot-matrix printers offer optional color kits.

Inkjet

The inkjet printer uses a moving print head, much like the dot matrix. It sprays droplets of ink from minute nozzles; the droplets are forced out by the twitch of a piezoelectric crystal. Inkjet printers use a matrix of precisely placed dots to print characters on the paper. An entire row of characters can be printed in one pass.

The inkjet printer is quiet; about the only sound you hear is the carriage going back and forth. However, most inkjet printers require special paper for best results. On close inspection you can see sloppy character edges created by ink seeping into the paper's fibers as it

dries. Also, it's easy to smear inkjet pages in their first few seconds of life.

The resolution of the inkjet is between that of the dot matrix and the laser printer; however, it is much slower than a laser printer. The inkjet also has color capable versions.

Laser printer

A laser printer utilizes a spinning mirror that deflects the laser beam in a horizontal line on a drum. Switching the laser beam on and off as it is deflected writes tiny points of light on the photo-conducting drum (300–600 points of light per inch). A sheet of paper to be printed is pulled across an electrically charged wire which transfers a static electric charge to the paper. Where each point of laser light hits the drum, it causes the film (usually zinc-oxide) on the surface of the drum to change its charge so that the dots have the same electrical charge as the paper.

The drum then comes in contact with a black powder called the toner. The toner sticks to the charged areas. As the drum continues to turn, it contacts the paper. The sheet of paper then pulls the charges off the drum and onto the paper. As the drum continues to rotate, it passes by a thin wire which returns the entire surface of the drum back to its normal charge, ready to process a new page.

The charged paper is pulled through a fuser which applies pressure and heat to bind the toner to the paper; it melts and presses a wax that is part of the toner, creating a permanent image on the paper. Voila! The page of your unforgettable prose is ejected from the printer into your waiting hands (or the paper tray if you're not by the printer's side).

Laser printers are available for standard size paper as well as for the 11 × 17 size. Most laser printers accommodate single sheets of paper, and a few handle tractor feed. Color laser printers are also available, but costly.

Laser printers use RAM to store text, graphics, and font information which is supplied by your PC. The printer accumulates all of the data required for an entire page, then prints that page. The higher the resolution required, the more RAM is needed. For example, to print a full-page graphic at 300 dpi requires 2MB of RAM. In contrast, 4MB is required for PostScript. (RAM is used to store downloaded fonts and graphics information.) Laser printers usually come with a megabyte of RAM installed. You can add more RAM; 1, 2 or 4MB more by installing a memory expansion board.

Currently, PostScript and PCL5 are battling it out in the laser marketplace. PostScript was first to develop scalable fonts and held a monopoly on the market for some time. To compete, PCL was developed by Hewlett-Packard for their LaserJet series. PCL advanced through a series of improvements, from PCL4, which used bit-mapped fonts, to PCL5, which incorporates the capability of using internal scalable fonts. PCL5 is supported by virtually all PC software applications.

The major advantage a PostScript printer has over a PCL5 laser printer is that the PostScript is machine independent; that is, PostScript is transportable over a wide range of platforms. So if you are going to take your output to a high-resolution (2,000 dpi) Lintronics typesetting machine, you need a laser printer that accommodates PostScript.

Improvements continue to be made with laser printers; the 600 dpi printer is being marketed at a cost lower than the 300 dpi. Some of the new laser printers use microfine toner to increase the sharpness of the image. But the best news of all is that prices still continue to decrease. Costs are less than $500 for some of the more economical models, and some higher quality laser printers can be obtained for under $1,000.

⇨ Fonts

First of all: serif vs. sans serif. Most people find that serif is much easier to read for body text. Either serif or sans serif works for headlines.

The arrival of scalable font technology caused a mini-revolution in printing and display. Before scalable fonts, printers created hard copy from fixed-size, bit-map fonts resident in the printer. Printers could only store a limited number of these fonts. Each had a specific size, style, and weight (for example: 12 pitch, Prestige, bold).

However, displays have a lower resolution (about 100 dots per inch) as compared to printers (300 dpi or more), so a lot of trial and error was necessary in composing certain types of documents.

Scalable fonts implement a unique approach by specifying characters mathematically as outlines of lines and curves. As a result of this technique the fonts can be scaled to virtually any size by changing their mathematical properties. Thus only a single outline font file is needed to obtain almost any size of a specific character set.

Another advantage of scalable fonts is that they are device independent; that is, they're not limited to a specific type or manufacturer of printer or display.

Laser printers can generally use three types of fonts:

> Resident Fonts—built-in at the factory.

> Cartridge Fonts—permanent fonts on plug-in cartridges.

> Soft Fonts—loaded from a disk.

Resident fonts are limited in number, but they are quick, always available and do not take up valuable space in a laser printer's RAM. Cartridge fonts, permanently encoded into cartridges slightly smaller than a videotape, can hold from 4 to over 200 different fonts. Cartridge fonts are also quick; in addition, they are available to a printer at any time and do not occupy a laser's RAM.

A laser printer can hold up to 32 fonts downloaded from a disk. Soft fonts provide a great diversity of fonts, but they must be downloaded from the computer memory to the laser RAM, which can be a slow process (taking as much as 15 minutes).

Bit-mapped fonts are used by resident and cartridge fonts. Bit-mapped fonts are hand-designed for each font. Soft fonts are usually based on outline fonts, where each font is a mathematical description of the characters. A font generator is required to convert the soft fonts to bit maps before they can be used by the laser printer. The font generator can produce bit-mapped fonts from 2 to 144 points.

⇨ Costs of consumables

For printers, it's not only the initial cost of the printer that is of concern; the continuing costs of the consumables are also important considerations. Not only do printers consume paper, they also use up their ribbons, cartridges, and print heads. Also, being at least partially electro-mechanical, they require periodic servicing and maintenance.

The dot matrix is probably the least expensive and most maintenance-free of all the printers. I personally have both a 9- and a 24-pin and they have printed thousands upon thousands of pages without a problem. All they need is paper, a ribbon once in a while, and an occasional TLC cleaning with a vacuum cleaner and a cotton swab. You can purchase a box of 2,500 sheets of tractor-feed paper for around $15; that's 0.6 cents per page. A generic ribbon (read "inexpensive") should be good for about 400 pages (I really get mileage out of my drafts) before the print fades off into the sunset. With a ribbon costing about $3, that's another 0.75 cents per page. Making a little allowance (0.15 cents per page) for wear and tear on the printer, a dot matrix printer can deliver copy for about 1.5 cents a page.

Inkjet printers use cartridges that sell for about $25 for 2,000 draft-quality pages of print or 1.25 cents per page. Paper for the inkjet is about $6 for 500 sheets or 1.2 cents a page (many inkjet cartridges contain a replacement print head, as well as ink). Allowing about 0.55 cents for repair and maintenance, the cost comes to about 3 cents per page.

For a laser printer, a cartridge costs about $75 for 4,000 pages of text or 1.88 cents per page. Paper cost is the same as for the inkjet, at about 1.25 cents a page. Allowing a nominal sum (0.37 cents per page) for maintenance, the cost per page for a laser printer is about 3.5 cents per page.

These figures are only typical (isn't it amazing how they all came out rounded to the half-cent?). You might be able to do better on some and worse on others, but the relative costs shouldn't change radically. And there are several ways of reducing the cost of the consumables. If you're doing drafts, you can print on both sides of the paper for inkjets and lasers. Dot matrix ribbons can be recycled, or you can re-ink them. Inkjet cartridge refills are available. Laser toner cartridges can also be recycled.

Upgrade procedures

Printers usually plug into the single parallel port (with a DB-25 connector) you have mounted on the rear of your computer and a 36-pin Centronics connector that plugs into your printer. Don't buy a six-foot cable because it severely limits the placement of your printer. A 10-foot cable should be adequate for most installations; if necessary, longer cables can be used.

Installation

Printer installation is relatively simple. It's best to locate your printer where you can see it printing, even if you have to get out of your comfortable chair to check on it. That way if you've output something in error, you can stop the printer before it wastes 50 pages of paper and much of your time. For tractor feed, a printer table with a shelf below to hold the paper supply box is very desirable. Most laser printers are sheet-fed; they can be placed on a table. Also make sure when you buy a laser printer that you receive a tray that holds about 500 sheets of paper, so you won't be paperless at a crucial time.

The printer cable connects from your parallel port on the back of your PC to the printer. Plug the power cord into a power strip or surge suppressor, and use the power strip or surge suppressor switch to turn your printer on and off. That way you won't wear out the hard-to-replace switch on your printer.

For software, you have to instruct most of your programs what type of printer you have. Your computer can't tell what types of printers you will be using (especially when it's not turned on), so you have to load or select the right printer drivers for your specific model(s). If you can't find your specific model or type, see what printers yours emulates and select one of the emulated modes.

My recommendations

If you're severely budget-limited and are going to turn out single-sheet flyers or a simple newsletter, a 9- or 24-pin dot matrix will suffice. Use the 9-pin if you're really strapped for cash, but stretch your budget a few dollars and get a 24-pin if you can. The cost difference between the 9- and 24-pin is almost negligible. Remember that dot matrix printers do not have growth potential, but many printing miracles have been wrought by the software designers in making the best possible printers out of the dot matrix genre.

For letters, spreadsheets, routine brochures, etc., a 300 dpi resolution is adequate. This is available from low-cost lasers and inkjets. All three printer types can handle the 11-x-17-inch paper size. Dot matrix and inkjet can also handle letters, as well as smaller sizes. Printing envelopes on the laser is iffy, as is printing mailing labels.

But for newsletters, presentations, sales proposals, and quality desktop publications you need 600 dpi or better. This is especially true if you're going to run xerox copies, because some resolution is lost in the translation. Another factor to consider is the gray scale and graphics resolution. The 300 dpi resolution printers are afflicted with what is called the "jaggies," which result from dots too large to fill in or smooth out. The 600 dpi smooths out graphics.

Similarly, because a printer can print only a single color intensity (usually black), shades of gray must be simulated by various dot patterns. Because the 600 dpi has smaller dots, it can better simulate gray scale. Printers with 300 dpi can simulate about 24 shades of gray; the 600 dpi can simulate more than 100 shades of gray. For many applications, 600 dpi is even adequate for camera-ready art that is to be reproduced. But when a 600 dpi resolution is quoted, make sure it is a true 600 dpi and not a virtual 600 dpi that is obtained by overlapping dots.

As far as printer drivers are concerned, most modern software programs can drive all three types of printers. And most of the printers have emulation modes that allow them to emulate the more popular printers.

Even though you settle on and buy a laser printer, I recommend that you also buy an economical 24-pin dot matrix printer for your drafts and for backup. Laser printers aren't as easy to use as dot matrix and laser printers quit working sometimes for mysterious reasons. Repairs can be costly.

Similar to PCs, you can buy an economy laser printer and upgrade it gradually as your needs increase and your finances allow. Your laser printer should be able to emulate several dot matrix printers (e.g., IBM and Epson). When selecting a printer, inquire about growth potential. You should have the option to upgrade to PostScript, even though it may be costly. An RISC processor in the laser is also highly desirable, especially for PostScript and complex graphics. Also consider halftone enhancement technology if you're involved with photograph images. Several laser models provide upgrade options such as more RAM, additional fonts, etc. Some printers even allow you to upgrade from 300 to 600 dpi.

⇨ In summary

Table 9-1 summarizes the major features of the main types of printers for a quick comparison. Resolution is expressed in dots per inch (dpi); the fastest and slowest speeds are given in characters per second,

except that the laser printer speeds are expressed in pages per minute. To make a comparison easier to understand, I assumed a page of 2,000 characters was to be printed and expressed the printing speed in the number of seconds it takes to print a page of alphanumerics. The cost per page follows. The 24-pin dot matrix (at about $250) is used as a comparison for the comparative cost column.

Comparative printer costs   Table 9-1

Printer type	Resolution in dpi	Speed char/sec	Secs. /page	Cents/ page	Rel. cost
Dot matrix 9-pin	60–180	30 NLQ – 300 draft	67 to 6.7	1.5	0.8
Dot matrix 24-pin	360	30 NLQ – 340 draft	67 to 5.9	1.5	1
Inkjet	180–360	20 LQ – 300 draft	100 to 6.7	3	2
Laser	300	5–12 ppm	12 to 5	3.5	3
Laser	600	5–12 ppm	12 to 5	3.5	4

10
CD-ROM drives

CD-ROM discs are going to be the libraries of the future; they're rapidly becoming the library of the present for many professions. (Note that "disc" is becoming the accepted spelling for CD-ROM discs as opposed to "disks" for magnetic disks.) Possessing enormous capacity (640MB and increasing), they store an immense amount of data, software, information, clip art, dictionaries, thesauri, encyclopedias and so on in a very small space. A single CD-ROM disc (4.72 inches, 12 cm in diameter), for example, stores 14,000 clip-art images for use in DTP.

A single disc can store the text of 200 Webster's dictionaries, the data stored on 1,500 5¼-inch floppies, or a quarter of a million pages of text. Not only do they store a stupendous amount of information, you can easily and effortlessly (on your part) quickly search for and locate the single bit you need with the sophisticated search-engine routines that come with the drive. If you are going to rely heavily on clip art or huge amounts of archival data, and require access to many large reference tomes (e.g., the Oxford English Dictionary, general and technical reference encyclopedias, etc.), then a CD-ROM drive becomes a necessity.

CD-ROM drives continue to be improved, prices continue to decline, and a variety of CD-ROM discs continues to be created for all professions and for all interests. As the storage requirements of software and data continue to explode, new and high-capacity storage media are needed. The CD-ROM fulfills this need, providing a physical media that is transportable, is low in cost per byte, and has a mountainous storage capacity. In addition, CD-ROM adds another feature to a PC: multimedia capability, or the ability to add sound and animation to presentations, tutorials, and communications.

The specs for various types of CD-ROMs, along with detailed tradeoffs on their performance, characteristics, and cost, are covered in this chapter. The remainder of the chapter illustrates the CD-ROM hardware installation procedures, along with the software (e.g., add CD-ROM driver and MSCDEX.EXE) installation and modifications that have to be done.

 # Definitions and acronyms

✳ **Access time**   The average time it takes a drive to locate a random piece of information.

✳ **Green Book**   Defines CD-I (Compact Disc-Interactive) hardware and software standards for drives which may contain a mix of audio, video, and text that can be "streamed" into synchronicity.

✳ **ISO-9660**   The international file-format standard for most of the current CD-ROMs; it is an updated version of the High Sierra format developed in 1985.

✳ **Red Book**   Standards covering CD-DA (Compact Disc-Digital Audio) or standard CD audio, the same format as compact discs.

✳ **Multispeed**   The ability of a drive to spin the disc at two different speeds.

✳ **Transfer rate**   The rate at which data is transferred from the CD-ROM to the CPU.

✳ **WORM (Write Once, Read Many)**   A CD-ROM type of recording medium in which the user can write information once and read it many times.

✳ **Yellow Book**   Describes the manner in which data is physically organized on data CD-ROMs.

✳ **XA (eXtended Architecture)**   A standard which, among other capabilities, lets you interlace audio and data on the disc for more efficient multimedia playback.

 # Typical DTP CD-ROMs

As the volume of software increases (some commercial software programs require 24 discs or more to install), more and more software companies are delivering their software programs on

CD-ROMs. And reference works are increasingly being stored on CD-ROMs. Here are several examples of this growing trend:

✳ **Adobe Photoshop**   For creating artwork, correcting and retouching color and black-and-white scanned images and preparing high-quality color separators and outputs.

✳ **Compton's Interactive and New Grolier's Multimedia Encyclopedias**   These two references incorporate millions of words and thousands of articles and illustrations on a single disc. An entire 20 volumes of printed information are compacted and made available on a single disc.

✳ **CorelDraw**   This disc provides powerful tools for illustrating, charting,bit map editing and drawing and is combined with 12,000 clip-art images and 250 fonts.

✳ **Desktop Publishing Collection**   Contains over 150 fonts, over 1,000 EPS files, over 200 BMP files, and over 200 GIF files.

✳ **Full Page Images**   This disc provides high-quality background images that add a professional touch to any DTP layout.

✳ **McGraw Hill Science and Technical Reference**   Contains 7,700 scientific and technical articles, 117,000 scientific terms with definitions, 1,700 VGA photographs and line drawings, and hundreds of tables, charts, graphs, diagrams and formulae. It also provides hypertext search.

✳ **MicroSoft Publisher**   The disc includes a DTP program which provides layout, text and graphics tools, and it features the Publisher Design Pack, all on a single CD-ROM disc.

✳ **OED (Oxford English Dictionary)**   An etymologist's dream; the paper dictionary's 60 million words in a printed version require 20 phone-book sized volumes, take up four feet of sturdy shelf space and weigh 137 pounds. The entire digital version fits on a single CD-ROM and you can flip through and search all 20 volumes in seconds without leaving the comfort of your computer chair.

❋ **Quick Art Lite**   Over 1,500 images in TIFF, IMG, and PCX formats; ideal for DTP.

❋ **The Talking Dictionary**   Merriam Webster's Ninth New College Dictionary offers 160,000 entries and 200,000 definitions. All words are pronounced by a professional radio announcer. Graphics and illustrations are included along with the text.

Whew! And this is only a tiny sample of what is available and only a tiny taste of what is yet to come.

CD-ROM discs vs. magnetic disks

CD-ROM discs are configured differently from magnetic disks such as those used on fixed hard drives and floppies. Magnetic disks lay their data down in concentric circles, called tracks, which are in turn divided up into sectors. The magnetic disk spins at a constant speed; thus the tracks on the outer parts of the disk are longer. Although this wastes space, it provides a fast data retrieval rate.

CD-ROMs, however, lay their data down in a single 3-mile-long track (divided into "sectors" or "blocks") that spirals from the center of the disc to its outer edge, much like a phonograph record (although the phonograph record spirals the opposite direction, from the outside periphery to the inside). Thus each sector on the CD-ROM disc is the same length and the disc storage area is used as efficiently as possible. However, this arrangement causes a problem, because to obtain a constant data rate, the CD-ROM disc must vary its speed as the laser-reading beam moves from the central part of the disc to the longer outside portion of the disc. To provide this constant data rate, the speed of the CD-ROM disc must be high when reading data from the center, and be reduced as the reading beam approaches the outer periphery of the disc.

How it works

A motor rotates the CD-ROM disc at a speed inversely proportional to the distance of the laser reading beam from the center so that the

data rate is constant. A low-power gallium-arsenide laser projects a beam of laser light at the spinning disc, penetrating a protective layer of tough plastic (the same type that is used for bulletproof glass) and impinging on a reflective layer that looks like aluminum foil. This reflective layer is not flat, but is composed of bumps (pits) and flat surfaces (lands). The pits and lands create the 1s and 0s; the transition from a land to a pit is a 1 and the nontransition is a 0.

Laser light hitting the bumps is scattered, but light hitting the flat surfaces is reflected from a mirror, passed through a one-way reflective mirror. The mirror deflects the reflected laser beam to a light-sensing diode, generating pulses. These pulses are the 1s and 0s which represent stored data. The CD-ROM driver reads the data into your PC in a language your computer can interpret and convert into a usable format.

 Photo CD

Another version of CD-ROM is Kodak's Photo CD, a medium in which several high quality photographs can be compressed and stored digitally on a single disc.

To use the Photo CD, you take any 35 mm roll of film (or slides) and drop it off at a convenient Photo CD outlet, which can be anything from a corner drugstore to a professional photography lab. Within a few days (5 to 7 are quoted) you receive a shiny gold CD. Each Photo CD disc contains five scans of each image at resolutions ranging from 128 lines by 192 pixels to 2,048 lines by 3,072 pixels (photographic resolution). Each pack of 5 is compressed to about 4.5MB. The cost is less than one dollar per image.

A single Photo CD stores 100 to 150 images, depending on whether they're black-and-white or color. You can load this disc in your CD-ROM drive, access the images you want, and save them as TIFF, PICT or EPS files on your hard drive, then edit them as you would with any digitized image. You can import the images in a page layout or other program. Because you have 5 different scan resolutions of each image, you can use the low-resolution image for positioning and a higher resolution scan for output.

The Photo CD is an excellent method to archive photographs on inexpensive CDs. When you work with high-resolution photographs, you should also have a graphics accelerator in your PC (chapter 7). Some of the more advanced DTP software programs can import Photo CD images directly.

Make your own CD-ROMs

The Write Once Read Many (WORM) technology allows you to create your own CD-ROMs. WORM drives read and write using a laser beam with a variable intensity writing on a special disc. At high intensity the laser beam records data. At low intensity (about one-tenth of the high), the laser beam reads the previously recorded data. Once written, data can be read out as many times as you choose. The WORM provides an excellent medium for recording your own graphics and data for archival filing.

Tradeoffs

First, make sure that any CD-ROM drive that you purchase meets or exceeds the MPC (Multimedia PC) performance standards, which means the drive must be able to sustain a data transfer rate of 150K per second, while using no more than 40 percent of your main CPU's resources. Most drives meet this standard, but check to make sure.

There are two types of disc loading methods. One method accepts the disc on a tray, just like an audio CD player. The other type uses a caddy (Fig. 10-1 and Fig. 10-2) that you load the CD into, then insert the caddy into the CD-ROM drive.

The caddy protects the disc and the drive from dust and fingerprints. Preferring the security of the caddy, I invested in a half dozen caddies in which I keep my most often used discs. Whichever type of drive loading method you use, make sure your drive has an extra set of doors or a seal that keeps out dirt and protects the drive. Those bumps and valleys on the disc are woefully small and don't tolerate dirt or fingerprints.

Figure 10-1

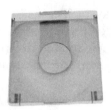

CD-ROM caddy (empty).

Figure 10-2

CD-ROM caddy (loaded).

When ordering a drive, make sure the quoted price includes the drive, the add-in controller card, a cable if needed, and any required software and mounting hardware. Your drive should also have two RCA jacks that allow you to plug stereo speakers into it for multimedia applications.

Access time

Access time is the time required for the CD-ROM drive and circuitry to locate, access, and deliver the requested data to the computer. CD-ROM access time has been reduced from the 800ms of a few years ago to about 280ms for the better drives. Try to obtain a drive with an access time of less than 300ms. For comparison, a hard drive has an access time of about 12–14ms, more than twenty times faster than a CD-ROM drive.

Data transfer rate

The data transfer rate is the speed at which data is read out of the disc and delivered to the PC. Most drives are rated at 150 Kbps (kilobytes per second), the MPC standard. "Double Speed" drives have become

more common and achieve transfer rates as high as 300–330 Kbps. A recently developed "quad speed" drive can reach 600 Kbps. It's desirable that the faster drives also be able to shift down and accommodate the 150 Kbps speed required for the audio discs.

If the disk drives have an on-board capacity of 128K to 256K, that's also a plus because it helps minimize pauses when retrieving large images from the disk.

Internal vs. external

One major tradeoff to consider is whether to purchase an internally or externally mounted CD-ROM drive. The internal drive must be mounted in a half-height, 5¼-inch bay, so it uses up one bay. The internal is a little less expensive than the external. You also have to make sure your power supply has a spare connector.

Some internal PC power cables come with three connectors, two for disc drives and one spare. If you don't have a spare, you'll have to use a Y-splitter power cable (chapter 6) which connects to, and splits the existing single cable into two cables with two separate connectors. One significant advantage of the internal mount is that it is securely and safely mounted and out of the way, with no external cables or placement problems.

The external CD-ROM Disk Drive (Fig. 10-3) is a little larger (about 2 inches high) and has its own power supply. For an external, make sure the cable that connects to your interface board is at least 18 inches long; a shorter cord makes it hard to find a suitable place for the drive.

Whether you use the internal or the external, you still need to install an add-in card in one of your spare plug-in slots. The plug-in card should be supplied with your drive, along with physical mounting and software installation instructions.

Portable CD-ROM drives are also available. These external drives have their own power supply and controller card which plug into your printer port. However, a portable unit is slower when connected to a parallel port.

Figure 10-3

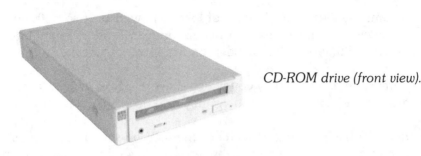

CD-ROM drive (front view).

⇨ Compatibility

So that all CD-ROM discs from different manufacturers are compatible and can be read by all CD-ROM drives produced by still different manufacturers, operating standards are essential. The High Sierra format has been adopted as a standard, and has since been modified by the ISO-9660 standard; make sure your purchase meets the latest standards. Other standards have been adopted for other CD-ROM configurations and have been dubbed "books." The Red Book covers the standards for CD audio and CD graphics, the Yellow Book for CD-ROM, and the Green Book for CD-I.

⇨ Interface

A CD-ROM controller card must be mounted inside your PC case in one of your expansion slots. This card provides the proper signals to access and control your CD-ROM drive. If your drive is external, the card also provides a connector for the interconnecting cable. Be sure you obtain the card and drive from the same manufacturer to ensure compatibility.

⇨ Controls/indicators

Very few controls and indicators are required for the drive. An indicator on the front panel lights up when the disc is spinning. An eject pushbutton is provided for ejecting the discs when power is applied to the drive. A good CD-ROM drive should also have a paper-clip sized (large paper clip) hole on the front of the drive which allows

you to manually eject discs in case of loss of power, or if something goes awry with the mechanism. A headphone jack and a headphone volume control may also be included on the front.

On the rear panel (Fig. 10-4) you should have a power switch, a pair of audio output jacks, a power-in connector, and a bus connector.

You may also have some DIP switches that can be set so you can use the drive in a SCSI daisy chain arrangement. Several CD-ROMs may be connected in parallel using the daisy chain arrangement.

Figure 10-4

CD-ROM drive (rear view).

⇨ CD-ROM changers

If your DTP setup requires frequent access to several CD-ROM discs, the tedious and time-consuming procedure of having to manually change the discs can be eliminated by installing a CD-ROM disc changer. A typical changer can accommodate up to six discs. With a single mechanism you can access only one of the six discs at a time. It takes about 5 or 6 seconds to access a new disc.

If your installation requires that several different users be able to access different discs often, a better arrangement would be to daisy chain several individual CD-ROM drives so each one can be individually accessed. However, if users do not need frequent access, the multi-disc changer (at about half the cost of 6 individual changers) is a better arrangement. A six-disc changer can store about 4 gigabytes of information.

 # How to search CD-ROMs

CD-ROMs aren't just an excellent medium because of their huge storage capacity, but also because you can locate any specific randomly stored bits of data in seconds, while seated in front of your PC. No more huge, dusty, heavy printed volumes to carry around and page through. No more rifling through overstuffed filing cabinets searching for something you can never find. With CD-ROM, you just let your fingers and your PC do the walking and searching for you.

A variety of sophisticated "search engines" have been developed to enable locating and accessing this data quickly and effortlessly. Most search engines allow you to input a word or two and conduct a search on these specific words. Increasingly, search engines allow the use of Boolean algebra for searches. Boolean algebra lets you use the operators AND, OR, and NOT in conducting searches. For example, you can search for Telephones AND Dial to limit your search to clip art or text about dial telephones. Input Telephones NOT Dial results in a search for information about nondial telephones. Telephones AND (Dial OR Push-button) would locate all dial and pushbutton citations.

In addition, the use of wild cards is also permitted in searches. Input TELE* and you receive the citations of all documents containing the words telephone, telegraph, telepathy, and all of the other derivatives. You can also use Boolean algebra to locate combinations of words that are within a specific distance from each other in the text. For example, search for Telephones and Alaska within 5 words of each other to learn about telephones in the state of Alaska.

The subject is much too involved to be fully covered here, so I'll refer you to one of my books (here comes a commercial) listed in the bibliography which discusses the topic in more detail.

 # Installation

Physical installation consists of installing a plug-in controller board inside your PC and, for an internal drive, mounting the drive inside a bay. An external drive requires access to ac power and a shelf or

other place to mount the drive (I mount my external drive on top of my PC). External drives also require a cable connection between the drive and the plug on the rear of your PC. Software installation is accomplished by the software disk included in your drive package.

⇨ Hardware

The controller card plugs into a vacant slot inside your PC. Remove the PC case as described in chapter 3. Before you plug in the controller card, check your documentation to see if any DIP switches or jumpers have to be set on the controller card (or on the drive) for your specific configuration. Once this is accomplished, plug the card in and secure it as described in chapter 3.

For an internal drive, the mounting is basically the same as for a disk drive as covered in chapter 6. You will probably need a Y-splitter power cable (chapter 6) to supply power to the internal drive.

⇨ Software

An Install program should be included on the disc that came with your CD-ROM kit. Run it. The Install program modifies your AUTOEXEC.BAT and CONFIG.SYS files for you to inform your computer that it has another peripheral ready to serve you. The AUTOEXEC.BAT program welcomes your CD-ROM drive as a peripheral on boot-up.

Because DOS does not directly support CD-ROM drives, you need a device driver and Microsoft's extension driver (MSCDEX). This software should be included with your drive.

⇨ Future technology

CD-ROM technology continues to evolve and will continue to develop for many years to come as users learn more about this incredible storage medium. Future desktop publishing of books, manuals,

references, catalogs, etc. will begin a slow conversion to CD-ROM and other competitive technologies, instead of paper. When 60 million words printed on paper require twenty telephone-sized volumes at an enormous cost, take up four feet of strong shelf space, and weigh 137 pounds, there has to be a better way to disseminate information. CD-ROMs are the answer.

Storage capacity of CD-ROM discs will continue to increase. Scientists are working on a blue-laser technique that should triple the storage capacity of conventional CD-ROMs; but there is more that has to be done for this fantastic technology than increasing storage capacity. You not only have to store it; you have to be able to locate and use it. So significant developments are needed to help search and find information needles in data haystacks.

You not only save paper and provide an eminently portable data medium with CD-ROM, you also provide the user with a searchable medium, all in grand and glorious color, plus animation and sound. In addition, a huge volume of information can be located in a few seconds—instant information.

When hyperlink technology is coupled with this, you have an ideal combination for presenting information that need not be read serially, as is required with books and most current printed media, but which can be read in a lucid and more logical manner that is more suited to the mind of the individual reader, rather than to the mind of the writer.

Publications such as manuals, catalogs, books, and other types of documents that must be frequently updated are ideally suited to CD-ROM. It's so much easier to submit an updated CD-ROM disc containing all of the new and revised material than to supply a pile of replacement sheets with hard-to-follow instructions.

CD-ROM is an exciting and rapidly expanding technology, one in which every DTP professional should invest.

Scanners and
screen capture

IT seems as though desktop publishers are always searching for the best technique to add graphics, photos, and drawings to their documents. Two excellent means for inputting graphics and text into DTP are optical scanners and screen-capture programs.

Scanners convert black-and-white, gray scale, and color images into a digital form that can be incorporated into a DTP file, then manipulated, cropped, edited, sized, etc. With a scanner, photographs, line art, drawings, text and illustrations from printed copy can be digitized for processing, then imported into DTP documents. Scanners using optical character recognition software can take much of the tedium out of inputting text by converting optically scanned printed text to digital codes, thus replacing hours of re-keying text, a tedious process often fraught with errors.

Screen-capture programs can capture all or part of a display on your screen and store it for later recall and importation into your documents for editing, cropping, sizing, etc. These programs can capture black-and-white, gray scale, and full-color screen images.

Definitions and acronyms

Here are some of the more common terms and acronyms (I hate to keep throwing alphabet soup at you, but it's so common in the profession that you can't avoid it) you'll encounter when studying this topic.

✳ **bmp**   The Windows bit map format

✳ **bpi**   Resolution, expressed in bits per inch.

✳ **OCR**   Optical Character Recognition. The process by which the graphic images of text characters are recognized and converted to text data.

✳ **PCX**   A common graphics format originally created by PC Paintbrush.

✳ **ppi**   Resolution expressed in pixels per inch.

225

❋ **TIFF (Tagged Image File Format)**   An image format designed specifically for scanned images.

❋ **TWAIN**   The industry standard for communication between TWAIN-compliant imaging devices, such as scanners and digital cameras, and TWAIN-compliant software.

➡ Graphic formats

You'll undoubtedly encounter a wide variety of graphic formats in your daily peregrinations. Table 11-1 lists some of the more popular graphic formats so you can see from whence they came.

Table 11-1   **Graphics file extensions**

File ext.	Usually defines
BMP	Windows device-independent bit map
CDR	Corel Draw graphics file
CGM	Computer Graphics Metafile
DHP	Dr. Halo PIC
DXF	AutoCAD
EPS	Encapsulated PostScript
GEM	GEM Draw
GIF	Graphic Interchange Format file
HPG	Hewlett-Packard Graphics Plotter File
IMG	GEM Image paint format file
MSP	Microsoft Windows Paint
PCX	PC Paintbrush
PIC	Lotus 1-2-3 graphic file, object oriented
PPI	Paint Plus
RLE	Windows bit-mapped run length encoded
TFF	TIFF formatted graphics file
TIF	Tagged Image Format, scanned graphics
WMF	Windows MetaFile, vector format
WPG	WordPerfect Graphics

⇨ Scanners

Two basic types of scanners are in popular use: handheld and flatbed. A handheld scanner covers a limited swipe, about 4.5 inches wide. You hand-scan by manually pulling the scanner down the document to be digitized.

Flatbed scanners, however, can accommodate an entire standard 8½-x-11-inch document (some handle documents up to 14 inches long) and perform the scanning automatically. Flatbeds are, of course, more costly (about four to eight times more costly than a handheld). Some flatbed scanners also have page-feeders to feed multiple-page scans. A unique type of color scanner allows you to scan 3-dimensional objects up to 1.5 inches high.

Another special type used is the drum scanner. Used only for special applications, drum scanners are extra precise, very expensive (100 times the cost of a flatbed), and require special skill and knowledge to operate. The drum type is used mainly for high-quality magazines, art reproduction, and advertising.

Slide scanners are another special type. They provide resolutions of up to 4,000 dpi, a necessary resolution because they scan 35 mm slides. Slide scanners cost from 5 to 30 times the cost of flatbeds. Tradeoffs of the handheld and flatbed types available and their relative advantages and disadvantages are covered in this chapter.

⇨ How scanners work

Both handheld and flatbed scanners use essentially the same technique, except that one's hand moves the handheld scanner and a motor drives the scan head of a flatbed unit.

The scanner illuminates the item to be scanned. Dark areas reflect the least light, white areas the most. The reflected light is directed toward the heart of the scanner, a charge-coupled device which consists of hundreds of photocells arranged along the horizontal dimension of the scanner head. When the reflected light strikes the

photocells, they generate an analog voltage whose magnitude is proportional to the gray scale (or color hue) of the image being scanned (dark areas-low voltage, bright areas-high voltage). This configuration registers a single thin horizontal line of an image at a time, then moves on down, one line at a time, to continue scanning in the vertical dimension.

The analog voltages output by the scanner are then processed by an analog-to-digital converter, which converts them to a digital signal and outputs the information in a digital code that can be processed by your PC. Your PC, in turn, converts these digital signals back into an image, which should be a near duplicate of the original scanned image.

Color scanners function in a similar manner, except that they use three different colored lights and scan the image on three passes. Some scanners utilize three different colored lights simultaneously and can scan the image in a single pass.

Handheld scanner

Handheld scanners are T-shaped (Fig. 11-1) and measure about 5.4 inches wide, 5.5 inches long (with a 6-foot cord attached at the back) and are about 1.4 inches thick. They are inexpensive, but difficult to use.

Controls and indicators on the body of the scanner include an LED indicator, which lights to inform you that you're scanning at an acceptable rate. If you scan too fast, the light goes out (some versions change the color of the light to warn you). A Start button is provided so you can inform your PC that you're beginning your scan. A resolution switch allows you to select the proper resolution (mine has 100, 200, 300, and 400 dpi) and a light/dark control lets you adjust for proper contrast. Another control lets you select a photo (with 3 halftone settings) and a fourth switch position is provided for a text scanning, black-and-white mode. For scanning shades of gray, one of the 3 photo modes should be used.

Figure 11-1

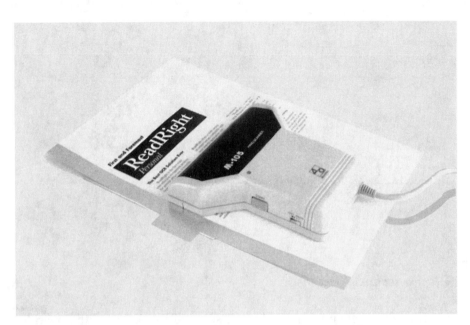

Handheld scanner.

Crucial to obtaining good scans is not only a steady hand, but also some kind of a sturdy mechanical guide to help you pull the scanner down the image in a straight line.

Other mechanisms are available to help provide proper scans. Even with special care, digitized images sometimes appear distorted and fuzzy where your hand twitched or moved too quickly. However, most scanner drivers allow for human frailties and can compensate for a skew of between 10 and 15 percent. Figure 11-1 shows the scanner in operation using a mechanical guide to maintain a straight scan.

A typical active scanning width is 4.13 inches (105 mm). Maximum scanning speeds range from 2.7 inches per second at 100 dpi (4 seconds for a full page) to 0.68 inches per second at 400 dpi (16 seconds for a full page). A yellow-green LED is typically used as a light source.

Many software scanning packages (Fig. 11-2) allow what is called "auto merge," a technique that lets you scan images larger than the 4.13-inch scanning width. First you perform a left-half scan, then

Figure 11-2

Software scanning package.

immediately follow it with a right-half scan, allowing for a little overlap between the scans. The software then permits you to manipulate one of the scans, lining it up with the other, creating a merging point and thus "stitching" the two together to create a full-page scan. This is an awkward process and the graphic may reveal the seams of your stitching on close inspection.

Color handheld scanners are also available, but they cost almost as much as a flatbed, so several manufacturers have discontinued their color handheld scanner line.

Flatbed scanner

For many applications, the ideal scanner is the flatbed; a standard peripheral that can scan multiple pages, one at a time. Flatbeds function much like a photocopier (a.k.a. Xerox copier). You place a document face down on the glass plate and a light source illuminates the material you want to copy which is above the scanning mechanism. (Some scanners include an attachment for scanning transparencies.) Under the page a motor moves the scan head and the scan head picks up the light reflected off the page, digitizing the image line-by-line as it travels down the page.

Another version of the flatbed accommodates sheet fed images. In this version the image to be scanned is fed into the scanner and the image is pulled past the stationary scan reading head.

⇨ How OCR works

OCR is the process by which the scanner and its accompanying software analyze the bit-map image of individual characters and convert the character images into digital codes that can be utilized by your word processor. As you can readily appreciate, it's a gargantuan task, recognizing and converting alphanumerics of many sizes and different fonts, bolded, italicized, underlined, capitalized, and often with inadequate contrast on the image.

Yet the geniuses who developed OCR have designed hardware and software that can recognize 16,000 fonts in sizes between 6 and 28 points. A high-quality system can scan and convert each page of text in a single pass.

A file containing a bit-map image of a printed page can require an enormous amount of memory, as much as 1MB of disk space. For comparison, once this print is converted to ASCII characters by the optical character reader, it requires only 1 byte per character. That works out to only 2K to 3K per page, resulting in a huge reduction in storage requirements.

Optical character recognition software is designed to "read" the loops, bars, and stems of printed words on the page. But, instead of interpreting them as graphics (as scanners do), OCR software actually identifies these components as individual letters, words, and sentences. Whether your text is Prestige, Courier, or any font (fixed or proportional spaced), OCR can read it with uncanny accuracy.

Once the letters are converted, you can process them in any way that your word processor is capable of. You can change their font, erase them, incorporate them in another document, etc. Before using them, however, you should run them through your word processor's

spell-checker to pick up as many of the errors as you can. (Some OCR programs have built-in spell-checkers.)

There are many applications for this capability. You can use OCR to analyze and convert old typewritten or printed archival documents, memos, books, reports, newspaper, and periodical text into a digital format which can then be edited by any word processor.

 # Multi-purpose applications

The combination of a scanner and a fax/modem board (chapter 12) is the rough equivalent of a fax machine. The scanner can first convert an image into the proper digital format, then the fax/modem board can transmit this image to a distant location over the telephone lines.

For text facsimile, a scanner, working in conjunction with an OCR program, can convert a scanned page of fax text into ASCII or some specific word processor format (e.g., WordPerfect). You can import this converted text into your word processor, run a spell check, proof, and edit it, then transmit it via your fax/modem board.

The scanner-PC combination can also serve as an emergency photocopy or duplicating machine if you have only a few copies to make and don't want to take the time to truck on down to the copy store. Scan the page to be duplicated with the scanner, then print it out on your printer.

 # Tradeoffs

Most scanners require at least a 286 CPU. To edit gray scale, you need a VGA or higher to accommodate gray scales. Some scanners can function with 640K of system RAM, while others are more complex and require up to 4MB. Some run in DOS, some of the more advanced require Windows.

Hand scanners are somewhat inept at OCR because the higher the resolution you use, the slower you must move the scanner. The longer

time it takes, the more likely you'll end up with an undecipherable image.

⇨ File format

Most grayscale scanners save images in the TIFF (Tagged Image File Format) (Uffdah! I did it again, more alphabet soup). Some of the simpler scanners (usually the binary type) use the popular PCX format.

Whatever native format your scanner uses, make sure you have the software to convert it to a format you can use, one that's acceptable to your DTP software.

⇨ Gray scale scanners

Gray scale scanners are preferred over black-and-white because if you scan in black-and-white, all you receive is a fixed pattern of dots. When you reduce the image size, the dots are scrunched together, which produces blots and distracting patterns. When the image is expanded, its sharpness is reduced.

However, a gray scale image remains a gray scale image when you process it and until you print it out, at which time it becomes a more uniform dot pattern in your printout.

⇨ Resolution

Scanning resolution is usually expressed in dots per inch and color resolution is further expressed in bits per color. State-of-the-art range is about 300 to 400 dpi, 24-bit color, and 8-bit gray scale. Some manufacturers use an interpolation technique. Interpolation is a pixel averaging process where adjacent pixels are compared, and a new pixel is created which splits the gray scale or color difference between the two. The new pixel is then placed between the scanned pixels, effectively doubling the resolution. If you see a scanner advertised as having 600 dpi vertical resolution and 300 dpi

horizontal or optical resolution, the true resolution is 300 dpi. The 600 dpi is obtained through interpolation.

Recent developments in flatbed scanners have upped the ante to 1,200 dpi. But a 1,200-dpi, 24-bit color image requires over 20MB of disk space per image and scanning it can take hours. Even with a high-speed 24-bit accelerator in a PC, it takes 20 minutes just to draw the image on the screen, which makes editing a rather long and boring process. And if you try to move or expand the image . . .!

Most scanners give you a choice of resolution specified in dpi or ppi (pixels per inch). A compromise must be made between scanning at a low resolution and obtaining poor quality results, versus scanning at a high resolution and creating unmanageably huge files that take forever to redraw and print.

Your hard drive may be loaded with text, graphics, DTP documents, and clip art, but you won't appreciate data overload until you've scanned some high-resolution images. A 4-x-5-inch image scanned at 300 dpi, with 256 levels of gray (about the number of shades that a human can discern) requires about 1.8MB of memory. A single 8-x-10-inch image scanned at 400 dpi with 256 shades of gray requires almost 13MB of memory space on your hard disk.

So you have to experiment to find the right combinations for your applications, one that allows you to store huge images on your hard disk without an overload. You really need a hard disk in the 200 to 350MB magnitude if you work with many high-resolution scanned images. (Talk about information glut!)

If you intend to crop your image, or use only part of it, it's advisable to only scan the part you are going to use so you won't have such a large image to store on your already overcrowded disk.

Twain compliance

Twain (from "never the twain shall meet,") seeks to invalidate the aforementioned claim made by Rudyard Kipling in the "Ballad of East and West" that the two would never meet. Twain (not Mark) is an

application program interface and protocol which allows you to input an image into any DOS or Mac application as long as both the software and hardware support Twain.

 # OCR considerations

There are, of course, some limitations in OCR's capability to read strange fonts, large or nonstandard characters, and text of limited contrast. OCR specs usually quote a certain percentage accuracy of translation; often this is in the ninety-some percent category. You probably have to do some editing of the scanned text, but it does take much of the work out of manually keying in your text.

Manufacturers claim a 98.5 to 99.5 percent accuracy, but this is for ideal copy (the proper fonts, the right contrast, clean copy, etc.). This may sound high, but a 98.5 percent accuracy means you have 1.5 percent errors, that's about one error per line. A 95 to 97 percent accuracy of conversion is considered marginal. If the accuracy is as low as 90 percent (that's one error every other word) it would probably be easier to retype the text, rather than struggling to proofread it.

Another problem with accuracy is that while much of the text can be edited and corrected by reading the words in context, if numbers, unusual words or spellings, or tables, or a spreadsheet are to be converted, much may be lost in the translation and the original copy must be referred to and the output carefully proofread.

OCR software cannot read most handwritten text, although this capability is being developed for hand-written inputs (imagine trying to read a doctor's prescription) using a light pen or other mechanism.

 # Scanner installation

Installation is relatively easy and consists of installing the controller board, connecting up the signal and power cables and loading the software.

For both the handheld and flatbed scanners, the controller board must be installed inside the case in a spare plug-in slot. The board provides a connector at the rear of the chassis which connects to the scanner over a signal cable. The scanner also needs 110-volt ac power; a plug is provided for this.

Some handheld scanners plug directly into a parallel port and do not require a controller card; thus they can be used as a portable. But these types are very slow; you have to move at the pace of a teenager dragging himself to an English class. For the board installation, follow the directions given in chapter 3.

The handheld scanner should be placed near your PC on some flat surface so you can use the surface for holding your scanned material. There should also be some extra free length in the cable because you have to move the scanner down the item to be scanned without its motion being hindered by the signal cable. For storage, you might be able to keep your scanner in a drawer so it's out of harm's way. Don't plug and unplug your scanner with the power on; turn the power off first.

The flatbed scanner must also be mounted near the PC, and is connected to the socket at the back of the PC via a cable.

Software

The software that accompanies your scanner should have an installation program that installs all of the needed software, plus the OCR software if that is also provided. The installation program should automatically modify your AUTOEXEC.BAT and CONFIG.SYS files to inform them of your new peripheral.

Screen capture: how it works

Several methods of screen capture are currently in use. One comes with Windows and is best used for smaller, less complex screen captures that require little or no editing. Here are the procedures for

capturing screens via Windows, first for DOS programs, then for Windows programs.

⇨ DOS capture by Windows

You can capture DOS screens if you are running a DOS program under Windows. Here is how you do it.

1. You should be in Windows. First open the DOS application you want to copy. If you don't have an icon to use, pull down the File Menu in the Windows Program Manager and input in the command line block the executable file of the program you want to run, for example, if I input:

    ```
    C:\PR20\PR
    ```

    and hit OK, it causes my WordPerfect Presentations for DOS program to run. If you don't remember your executable file name, hit the Browse button on the RUN submenu and you can browse through your files to find the precise name of the executable file you want to run.

2. Next, press the Alt and Enter keys simultaneously. This reduces the size of your application and it appears in a window.

NOTE

On some of the more complex screens, your PC will refuse to capture a portion of a screen. If this happens, use the procedure described in the next section Windows Capture. Using that procedure will capture the entire screen and place it on the Clipboard where you can access it, then edit the image with a graphics program.

3. Click the control menu box on the application you have in the window.

4. Pull down the control menu box (that's the little bar in the upper-left-hand corner that pulls down a menu).

5. From this menu, choose Edit.

6. From the Edit menu, choose Mark.

7. Press the Alt-Print Screen keys simultaneously and you'll capture the image inside the window. If you want to capture the entire screen, just press the Print Screen key.

8. You can now access the clipboard and pull this screen-captured image into your word processor or graphics program for further processing or use.

Windows capture program

If you are running a Windows program and want to capture a screen, here is the procedure. First set up your screen with the picture you want to capture. Then hit the Print Screen key. This saves the screen on the Windows clipboard.

Next, switch back to the Windows File Manager screen and open up the Paintbrush program by clicking the icon you will find on the Accessories menu. Pull down the Options menu, select Image Attributes and click on the pels radio button, then hit the Okay button.

Next, pull down the View menu and select Zoom-Out. Then pull down the Edit menu and select Paste. You are now presented with a crosshatched area covering most of the screen and a rectangular gray area to the left of this area. In addition, your cursor has now changed to a crosshair. Position the cursor in the gray area and click the left button of your mouse. The screen you have captured will now appear in miniature. Finally, pull down the View menu again and click on the Zoom-In entry.

Your screen has now been captured, and you need to save it as a file. Pull down the File menu, select Save As and you will be presented with a box. Input the directory and the file name you have chosen in the box. Be sure the file name has a bmp extension so you'll be able to recognize it later, then click on the Okay button.

You can now import this image into a word processing program, or use a graphics program to convert it to some other format and accomplish whatever editing you need to. I pull mine into my WordPerfect Presentations program and convert and export it as a

PCX file. Doing so cuts down a typical storage requirement from about 250,000 bytes to about 40,000 bytes.

Figure 11-3 is a screen I captured of the Envision Publisher program with Windows. I saved it as a bit-map graphic, then converted it to a PCX graphic with WordPerfect Presentations.

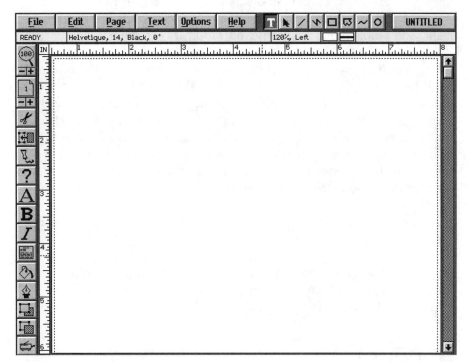

Figure 11-3

Envision Publisher *DTP opening screen.*

If you decide that you only want to capture the active window (this only works for Windows programs), hold down the Alt key and press the Print Screen key. This provides a smaller work area in Paintbrush. Just pull down the Edit menu and select the Paste entry and your active window will appear.

If you find your files are getting too big, go into Setup in Windows and choose the VGA with monochrome as your display driver. Not only will your screenshots be improved, they'll only be one-eighth the memory size.

Commercial screen-capture programs

For bigger, more colorful, and more complex screens, several excellent commercial screen-capture software, such as PizzazPlus (my favorite), HiJaak, or Collage Plus are available. This type of software can select any specific part of a screen and save it in memory. This image can then be incorporated into DTP. Black-and-white, gray scale, and color images can be captured in this manner.

Screen-capture programs provide substantially more versatility than the Windows capture method. Commercial programs let you perform considerable editing and massaging of the images before you capture them. These screen-capture programs allow you to adjust the size in pixels, select only a portion of the screen to be captured, crop the image, select background color fill, reverse black and white, adjust the colors, set the number of gray shades, etc. Dither, Diffuse, and Match are also available as reduction methods.

Images can be rotated or mirrored; smoothing is available to smooth out the jaggies.

Commercial screen-capture programs also perform many different file conversions and can save the images in over 20 different graphic formats, including TIFF, PCX, EPS, and BMP.

Installation

Only software installation is required for screen-capture programs. All of them have their own installation programs. You may have to indicate the type of display and resolution you have, but most of the installation is automatic.

My recommendations

Black-and-white scanners (a.k.a. binary or two-tone) are the lowest in cost and are adequate for scanning line art and scanned text. Note that all scanners can scan black and white.

Grayscale, handheld scanners are best suited to low-end DTP and word processing. They can be used effectively to scan small photos for brochures, newsletters, and other laser-printed documents, or to scan logos, signatures, and other art to create forms or letterheads.

A low-cost hand scanner is adequate if your scanning load is only a few pages a week, or if you're just scanning spot graphics. However, if your OCR demands are heavy, you need a more expensive flatbed scanner, plus a sheet-feed attachment if you need to read multiple page documents. For bound materials (books, magazines, etc.), you need a flatbed scanner. Hand scanners are generally unsatisfactory for the higher resolutions that enlargements, color slides, and commercial laser typesetters require.

If you're printing black-and-white line art on a 300 dpi laser, use a 300 dpi scanning resolution. Lasers do only a so-so job of printing halftones. When printing halftones on the same laser printer, only 75–100 dpi scanning resolution is required because dithering reduces the effective resolution of the printed image to just over 50 dpi, which is a little coarser than newspaper half-tone quality.

As you switch from one type of scanning to another, you'll probably have to use some trial and error to obtain what you want. It's an inexact science, so be sure you erase your old images and discard them so they won't overload your disk memory.

For OCR, when scanning 8–16 point type, use 300 dpi. For 6 point type, you need 400 dpi. With larger point type, lower resolution will suffice. Be sure to set the brightness controls also. For overly dark or smeared copy, use lighter settings; for light type, use darker settings. OCR usually works best for sans serif fonts, such as Helvetica. Serif fonts such as Times or Palantino often confuse the recognition engines of many OCR software programs.

Newspapers usually have dark, often smudged text and need to be scanned at a light setting. For magazines, use a medium setting. For high-resolution text on high-gloss paper, use a darker setting.

If your finances permit and if your needs can justify it, the flatbed scanner is the best choice. First of all, there is a greater variety of

models and features to choose from. They range from 300 dpi, 8-bit grayscale to 1,200 dpi color that can scan originals up to 11.7×17 inches. Some include attachments for scanning transparencies.

Flatbeds provide a better scan quality because the sensing motion is driven by a precision motor that doesn't wobble like one's hand. And the timing of the scan is always right. Flatbeds also provide better resolution than comparable handhelds which use the interpolation technique.

As far as the difference between black-and-white and color, again select the color, even if you're not presently using it. It's best to pay a little extra for color rather than trying to save money by buying a lower cost black-and-white scanner that you'll soon outgrow. Sooner or later you'll have to graduate to color. Color scanners continue to improve in quality and resolution and their cost continues to plunge. Remember that color scanners can also scan in black-and-white.

If you purchase a commercial screen-capture program, be sure it can capture images in both DOS and Windows.

12

Modems, facsimile, and FAX/modems

CHAPTER 12

"That's an amazing invention, but who would ever want to use one?"
President Rutherford Hayes, referring to the telephone.

ONE of the least utilized but extremely valuable applications of the personal computer is telecommunications (telecomm). With a modem or fax, you can telecommunicate with virtually anyone with a modem or facsimile machine, anywhere in the world. You can compose letters and drawings and have them delivered instantly to distant mailboxes and receive a reply in much less time than it takes the post office to cancel the stamp on your envelope. You can request information from distant places and receive it in a few seconds. The age of instant information has arrived.

A modem, for example, lets you transmit and receive information to and from remote locations over telephone lines. The modem sends and receives only digital information, data that is stored in and received by your PC.

Facsimile performs a similar function; however, it utilizes hard copy (such as a printed page of text or graphics) as the original input media. An image of each page is transmitted to a remote location via the telephone lines, where another fax machine provides a hard copy replica of the input page(s).

The fax/modem merges the best of both media; it is both a facsimile and a modem combined on a single plug-in board. The fax/modem sends computer information from your PC over telephone lines to a distant computer or to a fax machine. The fax/modem can only send information that exists in your computer. It can, however, receive and process information received from both a distant computer and a distant fax machine.

The modem provides instant access to enormous computerized databases such as CompuServe, Dialog, BRS, Mead Data Central, EPIC, and Wilson Line. These online databases, Telelibraries, I call them, are essentially huge databases of computer stored and indexed information, electronic reference libraries that can be accessed and electronically searched to locate and obtain copies of most current and

past magazines and periodicals, newspapers, plus encyclopedic and reference data. Telelibraries also have many thousands of free and low-cost software programs and huge clip-art libraries that can be downloaded via a modem and into your PC. Telelibraries also have professional DTP groups with whom you can communicate and have all types of questions answered. You can also receive updates of software changes that have occurred since you installed your software.

Fax provides a means of transmitting and receiving an entire page of information, virtually anywhere in the world where a compatible fax exists. Fax is "instant mail," and, for our fast moving communication needs, is rapidly becoming a substitute for the postal services.

Software programs, called "archivers," can compress information that is to be transmitted so that it requires less time (and expense) to transmit. Text can be compressed by a factor of about 2 to 1 and graphics can be compressed by a factor as large as 4 to 1.

Tradeoffs included in this chapter compare the various specs, the cost and performance of the modem, fax, and fax/modem. Installation and software updating required to install modem and fax/modem boards are also covered.

Definitions and acronyms

Before we get into telecommunications, here are some important definitions and acronyms:

* **Analog**   A continuously varying signal, the amplitude of which represents the information it contains.

* **Baud rate**   The correct technical definition is the number of discrete signal events per second occurring on a communications channel. Even though it's technically incorrect, baud rate in online systems is usually specified as bits per second (bps). Because it takes roughly 10 bits to send a single character (a letter, a space, etc.), the character rate equals the baud rate divided by 10, e.g., 2,400 baud is roughly equivalent to 240 characters per second.

❋ **BB (Bulletin Board)**   A system consisting of a computer and modem with appropriate software which makes messages over public phone lines available at no charge.

❋ **Data bits**   The number of bits in a character which contain data, usually 7 or 8.

❋ **Full duplex**   Communication occurring in both directions simultaneously. Both your PC and the remote PC can "talk" on the telephone line at the same time.

❋ **Half duplex**   Communications occurring in only one direction at a time.

❋ **Hayes compatible**   Modems that are Hayes compatible use the Hayes command set (sometimes referred to as the "AT command set") because it uses the prefix AT to grab your modem's attention. Originated by Hayes Microcomputer Products, the AT command set was so popular that it became the de-facto standard for modems.

❋ **Parity**   A form of error checking. Your software is capable of accommodating both even and odd parity. Your distant online station may specify that you have to use an even or odd parity in your communications; this is set by your software.

❋ **Protocol**   Several different software protocols are used to transmit data via modems to ensure accuracy of the data. These special error-checking protocols are not as important for text, but they are vital for transmitting scientific and engineering information, spreadsheets, statistics, chemical formulas, part numbers, technical data, etc.

❋ **Stop bits**   Used to inform your computer when a character has been sent. They can be either 1 or 2 bits, as specified by your software.

⇨ Modems—how they work

The basic hardware needed to go online and "let your fingers do the talking" is diagrammed in Fig. 12-1.

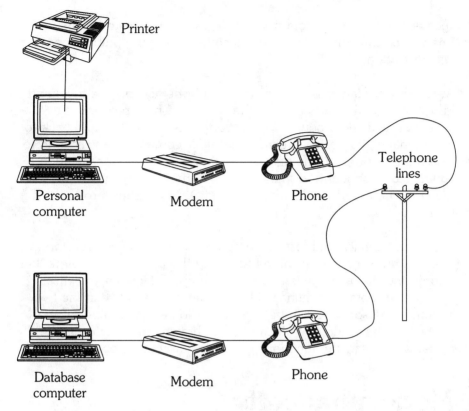

Figure 12-1

Modem communications.

To go online, your PC must be transformed into a "telecomputer," that is, a device capable of "computing at a distance." When you query an online vendor's database computer located a remote distance from your computer, the database computer does most of the work. You compose your query on your keyboard, then your PC dials the host computer, transmits the message over the phone lines, and tells the database computer what to search for. The database computer conducts the search you have requested, then transmits the needed data back to you.

As indicated in Fig. 12-1, your computer creates the information to be transmitted. It is then output to the modem, which converts the PC's digital signal into an analog signal (by a process called "modulation"). Because the PC speaks digital and the telephone

speaks analog, the modem must perform this language translation. The analog information is then transmitted over the phone lines to a distant station.

At the distant database station, the telephone accepts the incoming information and passes it on to the modem, which reconverts it (in a process called "de-modulation," the opposite of modulation) back to its original digital form, a format that your computer can respond to. Communication from the distant location back to the local station is conducted in an identical manner. The term "modem" is derived from the combination of the MOdulation and DEModulation processes it performs.

Considerable back-and-forth communications are necessary, not only before a message is transmitted to set up the proper parameters, but also during the actual message transmission. Telecomm software initiates, accepts, and manages the conversations between the two systems. The software can be considered to be the "brains" of the operation; the modem hardware is the "brawn" that performs the actual work, e.g., the functions the brains direct it to accomplish.

Modem tradeoffs

Tradeoffs in this section cover both the requirements of the modem and the software program that drives the modem.

Speed

Modem speed has continued to increase over the years, taxing the abilities of the hardware that supports it. From the 400 baud of the early years to 14,400 baud and still climbing, each time pseudo-experts claim you can't go any faster, someone ignores them and does.

Currently 2,400 and 9,600 baud modems are available for a very low cost. 14,400 bad modems are increasing in popularity as the prices plummet and as more facilities are able to communicate at this higher

speed. The next step up appears to be 19,200 as the hardware costs continue to decline. Speeds as high as 28,800 are rapidly becoming practical.

 # Standards

Modems should be Hayes compatible and support MNP Level 2–4 error correction and MNP Level 5, the standard for data compression. They should also provide fall-back automatically, shifting down to as low as 300 baud transmission/reception when needed.

 # Software

Modems often have telecomm software bundled with them and a wide variety of competitive commercial and Shareware telecomm programs are also available. For optimum online operation, modem software should have the following capabilities:

➤ Hayes compatibility
➤ 2,400 or 9,600 baud, up to 14,400 baud or higher if you are going to transmit and receive large amounts of data from compatible online services.
➤ Auto speed adjustment
➤ Autodial, redial, manual dial, and busy notification
➤ Handle various protocols
➤ Receive and transmit text and graphic files
➤ Emulate various terminals
➤ Generate script files
➤ Provide a running record of on-time
➤ Auto answer
➤ Text editor
➤ Data compression

Most modem software programs have Hayes compatibility; be sure the one you purchase does.

2,400 or 9,600 baud is usually adequate for most routine communications. However, if you're going to transmit and/or receive large amounts of data, especially graphics, you should be able to operate at 14,400 or 19,200. One thing to keep in mind is that both your modem and the distant modem must operate at the same speed. If you try to operate at a higher speed than the distant station is capable of, your software automatically shifts down and operates your modem at the slower speed. Auto speed adjustment provides this ability.

About autodial, redial, manual dial, and busy notification: your modem software should be able to dial another system without your having to manually dial the number each time. Your program should store all of the telephone numbers you need to dial, so that all you have to do is switch to a dial menu on your screen and tap the proper key(s) to automatically dial into the distant location you selected. The ability to continue to redial a number until it's available is another highly desirable feature.

Some modems also have a "number linking" or "chaining" capability that you can set up to automatically dial a series of numbers, one after the other, skip to the next number if one number is busy, then return and redial the previously busy number(s). Your software program should also permit you to dial numbers manually, when you need to dial a number you use infrequently. And your software should also output a busy signal when your call doesn't go through because the line is not available.

Software protocols

Telephone lines are notoriously noisy. This noise scrambles the data transmitted to and from a distant system. This scrambling may not be too important for normal text, because the loss of a single letter usually does not alter the meaning of the text. However, when technical or scientific information, certain foreign words, formulas, a graphics element, or data are scrambled by noise and interference,

the loss of a single character could be disastrous. To prevent this, error-correcting techniques are used. These techniques use various methods or "protocols" to check the validity of each part of a transmission. If an error is detected, that part of the message is discarded and a request is made for that part of the message to be retransmitted until it is received without error. Various protocols are used by different databases to handle errors in transmission. Your software should be able to handle a variety of these protocols, including XModem, YModem, and ZModem.

The ability to both capture and transmit files is necessary, not only for transmitting information to a remote station, but also so you can capture your two-way "conversation" with the station for later display and printout.

Some distant stations specify that your computer must be able to emulate specific terminals, such as TTY, DEC, IBM 3101, VT 100, ANSI, etc. This is usually specified in the software's setup menu. As a minimum, your software should be able to emulate TTY and ANSI.

The ability to create and use script files is also important. A script file program automates repetitive operations by setting up a mini-program that controls your telecomm software. A typical script program sets up a sequence of events which automatically dials your vendor's phone number, waits 5 seconds, inputs your account number, waits another 2 seconds, then transmits your password, waits another second, transmits another command, etc., all without intervention on your part.

Most quality software programs also have a "learning" feature that records the stream of incoming data and your responses when you go online. This learning feature then generates a script file that copies and automatically repeats your responses at the appropriate times so that the next time you access that station, the stored script accomplishes it automatically for you.

Another script feature that is available, and which uses the computer clock, can be programmed to automatically dial up a distant station at a time you specify, query for a specific topic, or automatically send a message at a specific time that you insert into it.

Your software should also have a running clock that informs you how long you have been online. Also desirable is a log that records the calls you have made, and who they were made to, for later review. It's surprising how quickly you can use up fifteen minutes in a database before you realize how long you've been online.

An auto-answer capability gives your personal computer the ability to automatically answer and accept incoming data when your computer is unattended. If you request information to be delivered to your computer during off-hours, or if you wish to converse with other computer users, your software should also have this ability.

An online text editor serves many functions. First of all, it allows you to compose and edit messages before you go online so you won't waste your online time. You can also use it to compose and edit your messages when you are online and working in the conference mode which requires real-time conversations. The requirements of an online text editor need not be elaborate; it should be able to accomplish the basic editing functions, insert and delete modes, search, search and replace, etc.

Because time is money when connected to an online system, the longer it takes a document to be transmitted, the more the cost. One solution is to compress this information so that it requires less time to transmit it.

And your software should be able to capture and store your entire two-way, on-line conversations in case you want to print them out later for review or analysis.

 Archivers

"Archivers" are software programs that combine and compress several files into a single file. Compressing files has three benefits:

> ➢ They use less disk space than normal files, often less than half of the original storage space required.

➤ Several individual files can be compressed into a single compressed file. This keeps files in a given set or project together and makes file group identification, copying, and transporting faster and easier.

➤ Compressed files can be transmitted and received in much less time via a modem, which reduces telecomm charges.

After one or more files are archived, the original files still remain on the disk, but they are in a compressed form and must be uncompressed before being used. After uncompressing files from an archive file, the compressed file still remains in the archive. What you are doing when you unarchive a file is extracting a copy, or in the case of creating an archive, you are archiving a copy of the original file.

You can recognize archived files by their filename extension. For example, files with an extension of ".ZIP" are archives created by PKZip or a compatible program. Those with extensions of ".LZH" were created by the compression program, LHA.

Archivers were initially popularized by BBSs which use them to save storage space and to reduce the time it takes to transfer files. Archivers are also used to conserve space on hard disks and on backup floppies. Here are some of the best archiving programs.

✳ **ARC**   This is one of the older programs and is seldom used anymore. Some older software may use the ARC archiving program.

✳ **ARJ**   This relatively new archiver has a few extra features, such as allowing extraction to alternate file names, multiple volume creation, merging of archives, file extraction lists and exclusion options, and string searching. The archives are slightly smaller than most of the others.

✳ **LHA**   This archiving program makes the smallest archive files of any general purpose archiver, and the beauty of it is that it's free, unlike ARC and PKZIP which are Shareware and require payment to the author for continued use. LHA is also convenient in that it creates archive files which can self-extract without the end user needing any other extracting programs and you can update the time stamps of all the files in an archive.

✳ **PKWare**   This archiver reduces most files by about half; it also creates self-extracting compressed .EXE files. PKZIP.EXE is the program which quickly compresses files and creates files with a .ZIP extension. PKZIP also handles file maintenance including adding and deleting files, as well as reporting on technical information from within the compressed file.

PKUNZIP is the program's other half; it uncompresses or extracts compressed files. In addition to extracting a complete ZIP file, it can selectively release individual files, show files on the screen for fast viewing, or print them out on a printer. If you don't want to extract all of the files, or if you are limited in storage space, you can selectively extract files from a ZIP file. Instead of extracting everything at once, you can view file size information, then select specific files to be extracted.

⇨ Unarchiving

If you receive archived files from your distant station, before they can be used in your computer they must be unarchived; that is, expanded and returned to their original form. Each of the archive programs also has a unarchiving program that is usually included with the software.

The basic unarchiving procedures are essentially the same; I'll use the popular PKZIP to illustrate how to unarchive. Let's take the file BIRD.ZIP as the file to be unarchived to its original files. The program was initially archived by the program PKZIP.EXE. To "unzip" the archive, use the program, PKUNZIP.EXE.

Assume the archived software is in your C:\TEMP file. (Everyone should have a TEMP or similarly named file to temporarily store programs or information until they are tested, recovered, or erased.) And assume your archive program has BIRD.ZIP and PKUNZIP.EXE stored on it.

First make sure you are at the C:\> prompt. To restore the files to their original state and store the files in C:\TEMP, change to the TEMP directory (CD TEMP), then input at the C:\> prompt:

```
PKUNZIP BIRD C:\TEMP
```

That's all there is to it. Sit back and relax while BIRD is being
unarchived and stored in your C:\TEMP directory. To check your
results, input DIR/P to list the newly unarchived files.

 Fax

A fax machine is a standalone peripheral that scans your document,
makes a bit map of it, and transmits that information over the
telephone lines to a remote fax machine, or to a PC capable of
receiving faxes. A fax machine also prints out the faxes it receives
from other fax machines, or from PCs capable of transmitting faxes.

 Faxes—how they work

Standalone faxes function in two modes: Transmit and Receive. In
the transmit mode, an original sheet (of paper or other suitable
media) containing the image to be sent is loaded into the fax tray.
The paper is pulled into the machine and passes by a reading head
consisting of some 1,600 light sensitive cells arranged in a single line
stretching horizontally across the page. The paper is illuminated by a
green fluorescent light which reflects off the paper and onto the light
sensitive cells, the magnitude of the reflection being proportional to
the level of the gray scale or density of the original. The original
sheet of paper continues traveling past the light sensitive cells and
the information on the paper is read, line-by-line, until the entire
original has been scanned.

In the receive mode, thermal paper is pulled off a roll and passed by
a heat-producing bar synchronized with the information received
from a remote fax transmitter. The bar has about 1,600 points that
can be selectively heated as the thermal paper passes by the bar. The
paper is specially treated so that it turns black when heated,
recreating the image sent by the distant fax machine.

Some fax machines use the same principle as a plain paper copier or
laser printer, using a scanner to copy the page in the transmit mode

and a photosensitive drum and black toner to create the output copy. These are more expensive machines.

Both the thermal fax and some electrostatic fax machines use a roll of continuous paper. Motors and rollers feed the original and the received copy. When each received page is completed, a paper cutter automatically slices the paper to the proper length. Some more expensive plain-paper faxes use regular copier paper, fed from a paper tray.

The electronics section of a fax machine is usually endowed with considerable sophistication and can dial and answer the phone, keep a log of transmissions and receptions, redial if the phone is busy, plus many other options.

Fax tradeoffs

The fax machine requires nothing more than a power line and a telephone jack, so it can be set up anywhere a phone jack and power socket are available. It doesn't tie up your computer when it's transmitting or receiving and often includes a phone (and sometimes an answering machine).

You can transmit virtually any piece of paper (as long as it fits on the scanning bed), including artwork and photographs. When receiving, you see the document immediately, without having to search and display the document as you would if you used a PC fax/modem board. All fax machines can also serve as low-end copiers. Instead of sending an image over the phone, you can send it to yourself and receive a copy.

Fax does have some disadvantages, however. Everything you want to fax must first be printed or drawn on a sheet of paper before you can fax it. Also, a standalone fax machine prints all the messages it receives, whether you want a copy or not, whereas a fax/modem board lets you review a fax on your display to determine if you want to print or discard it. The document feeder sometimes jams or sends two pages through at a time. Received faxes are often of mediocre quality and are blotchy.

 Standards

Group 1 standards for fax transmission, which were adopted in the 1960s, allowed transmission of a page in about 6 minutes. In the 70s, Group 2 reduced this time to about 3 minutes. Group 3, the current standard, transmits pages at speeds of 9,600 and 14,400 bps and incorporates various compression schemes. Now a typical page can be transmitted in 30 to 60 seconds.

The Group 3 standard, an official standard for faxes, calls for a resolution of about 200 × 100 lines per inch; this resolution is better than a dot matrix printer, but not as sharp as the original transmitted. The Group 3 standard also provides for a fine resolution of 200 × 200 lines per inch. Group 3 capability should be available on all models, and the newer models should also be compatible with the older Group 1 and Group 2 fax machines. Some of the more costly machines offer a resolution of 200 × 400 lines per inch. The Group 3 standard mode of transmission takes from 15 to no more than 40 seconds to process a page.

 Fax/modem tradeoffs

A fax/modem card functions as both a fax machine and as a modem. It has most of the capabilities of the internal modem card covered earlier in this chapter, plus some of the capabilities of the standalone fax machine also covered earlier in this chapter.

Functioning as a fax, it allows you to transmit text or graphics over the telephone lines to a remote fax machine, or to a PC equipped to receive faxes. A fax/modem can also receive text and graphics from a remote fax machine or from a PC capable of sending faxes. It accomplishes most of what a standalone fax does, except that it can't transmit a page of information unless that information is first scanned into a PC or created by a PC word processor.

Because the information being faxed to a fax/modem can be displayed and reviewed on the screen, you only need to print the messages you want to retain. In addition, you can print the fax on regular paper on your printer instead of the fragile and curling paper used in most standalone fax machines. You can save the fax in your computer memory in case you decide to relay the information to another station, or incorporate the information in your documents.

Faxes transmitted by a fax/modem are much sharper and cleaner than one from a fax machine because the original image is digitized and not scanned. Another advantage is that you won't have to stand in line or wait for the standalone fax machine to process your ten page report. You can receive your fax on your PC via "instant mail." Most fax/modem programs allow you to schedule your fax transmissions, so if you have a lot of documents to send, you can automatically fax them on a schedule when the phone rates are low.

Your fax/modem should be able to send ASCII (text) as well as PCX (PC Paintbrush) files. For faxing photographs or desktop-published documents, your software should also be able to handle TIFF, the file format commonly supported by grayscale scanners.

There are also disadvantages to using a fax/modem. Your PC must be on to receive a fax. This may not be a problem during normal working hours; however, you have to leave your PC on whenever you expect to receive faxes during off-hours.

If your input and output fax traffic is heavy, consider purchasing a fax/modem board that has an onboard processor which can be used to manage faxing in the background mode while you are using your PC for other tasks. They cost more, of course, but without an onboard processor you'll be unable to use your PC while it is receiving (it could take as long as 10 minutes or more to receive with a graphics-heavy, five-page document) or your fax/board and the program you're using will have to fight to get the CPU's attention.

Another factor to consider is that if you only have one phone line and need to share your fax machine with your voice phone, your setup needs to be able to detect fax calls and direct them to your PC and also let you, or your answering machine, pick up the phone for a

voice call. FAX/Phone switches are available which can automatically detect and switch the incoming signal to the phone or fax machine as appropriate. Some fax/modem boards also have a built-in port for a scanner. This way you won't have to use up an add-on slot in your computer for a scanner board.

Here are some of the things you should look for in a fax/modem board and software combination:

➤ The ability to send the same copy to several different locations.

➤ Automatic generation of cover sheets so you can easily incorporate the pertinent to/from information and a short cover letter.

➤ A scheduler that lets you send faxes during off-hours, at specific times of the day or night, or on specific calendar dates.

➤ Automatic redial in case a busy number is reached.

➤ Auto routing of your faxes to your printer if you have to be gone for a few days and don't want to load up your hard disk with faxes. Faxes gobble up a lot of hard disk space, a page of plain text can take up 80K, a page with a lot of graphics can approach 200K.

➤ Support for both 100 and 200 dpi resolutions. Sending and receiving at 100 dpi is faster, but you need 200 dpi for the documents requiring higher resolution.

➤ Conversion to a graphics format such as PCX or TIFF for minor editing and notation.

➤ A preview feature so you can preview the fax before you send it to make sure everything is all right.

Purchase the fastest speed you can afford. A 2,400 bps modem and a 9,600 bps for fax are considered to be the bare minimum. The fastest modems automatically shift down in speed to accommodate the modem at the distant end, so they will run at the maximum speed of the slowest of the two that are communicating. Some fax/modem boards support only a few printers; make sure yours supports the printers you will be using.

It may seem as though we have forgotten all about the modem half of the fax/modem board, but the modem half should have virtually the same capabilities that were described under the modem section earlier in this chapter.

 # Fax and OCR

A received fax is actually a picture, a bit-map image, even though it consists of nothing but text. This bit-map image cannot be used by your computer as anything but a bit map until some conversion is accomplished. When text is involved, a logical extension of technology is to use OCR (Optical Character Recognition) to process the fax and convert the text to ASCII or a specific word processor format. Fax/OCR accomplishes this.

Although not capable of a one hundred percent conversion accuracy, Fax/OCR can provide better than 97 percent (3 words out of a hundred) accuracy with common 10- and 12-point fonts and a 200 × 200 resolution. Fax/OCR usually offers spell checking also; words not found in their dictionary or words or letters not corrected are indicated by a color different from the color used for the correctly translated text. Once the text is converted and corrected, it can be imported into a word processing program and processed as regular text.

Installation—modem and fax/modem

Both the internal modem and the fax/modem are provided on standard plug-in boards, so follow the procedures described in chapter 3 for installing an add-on board. Before installing, be sure to accomplish any setup (switches or jumpers that have to be set) described in the documentation accompanying the board. A typical fax/modem card is depicted in Fig. 12-2.

Figure 12-2

Fax/modem card.

⇨ Software

A fax/modem card is usually bundled with telecomm and fax software programs and manuals as illustrated in Fig. 12-3. You should also receive a telephone line cord to plug into your telephone jack for both the fax and modem.

Figure 12-3

Fax/modem card, software, and manuals.

After you've installed the modem or fax/modem board, fire your system back up and use the install program to let your computer know about its new companion. You should receive a copy of both a telecomm program for the modem and a copy of a fax program for your fax. Or, if you're adventurous, you can install commercial fax and modem software that will probably provide more capabilities than the software bundled with your hardware.

 # Installation—fax machine

Installation of a fax machine is relatively simple because the unit is a standalone and is not connected to your computer. Just find a shelf or space on a nearby table or desk for mounting it. The fax machine requires only a power connection and access to a telephone jack. If you have the room, place it near enough to your computer so you can hand feed your copies to be transmitted and be alert for any incoming messages.

 # Online databases

Here are several online databases that provide free and low-cost software, access to their periodical archives, and all types of reference material, free advice, and many other services.

 # America Online

This very friendly database vendor service is menu-driven and easy to navigate. America Online (AOL) has no protocols to memorize if you want to send or receive files, no navigation commands to remember, and no dull text-based screens. Their pull-down menus and colorful icons can be accessed with your mouse or your keyboard.

America Online has a graphic interface: for IBMs a Hercules, EGA or VGA monitor is required. It offers a variety of services including software and hardware reviews, product reviews, buyer's guides, E-mail, EAAsy Sabre (make your own airline reservations), clip art, online encyclopedia, bulletin boards for technical support, multi-player games, travel reservations, stock quotes, huge software libraries, sports news, and a "chat" feature. They have tens of thousands of software programs that can be downloaded. One special interest area exclusive with AOL is the Microsoft Small Business Center where you can learn about running a small business. Help is also available from computing experts.

CompuServe

CompuServe is the most comprehensive and diverse selection of the consumer databases. CompuServe's excellent, easy-to-use, front-end program, Communications Information Manager, simplifies navigating in and around the CompuServe databases. They have a Practice Forum (use GO PRACTICE to access it) that you can use to practice using CompuServe commands without incurring connect-time charges.

A diverse variety of software programs can be downloaded from the libraries of CompuServe's forums. To find a forum that features your equipment, type FIND and your computer brand (e.g., FIND IBM).

Libraries are separated by subject to make locating specific software files fast and easy. If you can't locate a specific program, leave a message in the forum addressed to the forum manager (or sysop). PC MagNet, for example, features a utilities database that enables you to download programs to your IBM PC or compatibles.

Dialog

The world's largest and most comprehensive database vendor, Dialog Information Services, Inc., is especially strong on business, science, and technology. It has over 400 databases, with more than 270 million references to over 100,000 publications, including the complete text of over 1,100 periodicals and listings of all the millions of books in the Library of Congress.

Dialog has excellent instructional material. Handbooks, tutorials, videotapes, seminars, user manuals, and extensive documentation for each database are available. Thirty-eight of Dialog's databases have practice versions called ONTAP (ONline Training & Practice) which you can use to learn what information they contain and to practice and learn how these Dialog databases are accessed and searched. The same English commands are used to search all of the full-record and ONTAP databases.

The range of Dialog databases is enormous. Here's a summary listing of their major database categories, with some typical databases listed in parentheses:

- Agriculture, Food, and Nutrition (Agricola)
- Biosciences & Biotechnology (Life Sciences)
- DIALOG Business Connection (Trade and Industry Index)
- Chemistry (Drug Information Fulltext)
- Company Information (D&B Electronic Yellow Pages)
- Computers & Software (Computer Database)
- Energy & Environment (Energyline)
- Engineering (INSPEC)
- Government & Public Affairs (IRS TAXINFO)
- Industry Analysis (Investex)
- Law (Legal Resource Index)
- Medicine & Drug Information (Embase, Medline, Cancerlit, Smoking & Health)
- News & Full Text Publications (Chicago Tribune)
- OAG: Official Airline Guide (Airline Reservations)
- Patents, Trademarks, Copyrights (World Patents Index)
- People, Books, & Consumer News (Consumer Reports)
- Physical Science & Technology (NTIS, Compendex)

⇨ GEnie

GEnie (General Electric Network for Information Exchange) is a bargain. It is also growing and has many forward-looking ideas. GEnie has a number of RoundTables comparable to the Forums of CompuServe. Most RoundTables have libraries attached, with software programs and information files available for access. Thousands of utilities, games, business programs, etc. can be obtained from these libraries. GEnie also has a bi-monthly magazine for all subscribers which provides up-to-date information on the latest services it offers, plus other helpful information.

Removable backup media

CHAPTER 13

GENERAL DISK FAILURE-DRIVE C

THIS dreaded error message is enough to create terror even in the hearts of computer pros. If you haven't seen this horrific pronouncement yet, it will happen to you, sooner or later. Perhaps a virus has infected your system and all of a sudden your hard disk becomes useless. Maybe your 10,000 MTBF disk has died after only a few hundred hours of faithful service. Perhaps some runaway software has scrambled your hard disk's brains.

Fire and theft are also good reasons for backing up. Sudden power losses or fluctuations can cause disk heads to land in the middle of data, or overwrite data, both of which cause unrecoverable losses. If your disk becomes overloaded, you may want to download some of your data on to a backup media to make room for new data. To avoid the devastating feeling accompanying these losses, you must be prepared. To prepare for this disaster, you must back up your data periodically. This chapter shows you how.

When your hard disk is stuffed with considerable vital and irreplaceable data (illustrations, text, documents, etc.) and this data must be preserved to protect against loss, a backup system is essential. In desktop publishing, one publication alone can represent dozens, if not hundreds of hours of work that must not be lost or damaged.

Although current hard disks are quite reliable, they do fail on occasion and sometimes parts of their brains are scrambled. Of course it always happens at the least expected time and without any warning. Without a backup, you could lose all of not only your present work, but also past work you keep stored on your hard disk. So it's essential to periodically back up your data.

Various types of backup media are covered in this chapter and related to the amount and type of work you do, the number of different projects you're working on, and the disk capacity you have. Several types of removable media can also serve a dual purpose as a working memory and for backing up your critical data.

Tradeoffs in this chapter consider the advantages and disadvantages of internal vs. external mounts, comparative characteristics of the various media available, and cost considerations. The remainder of this chapter covers the installation procedures and the required software update.

⇨ An overview

Removable backup media covered in this chapter include:

➤ Floppy disks

➤ Floptical

➤ Bernoulli

➤ SyQuest

➤ Tape

➤ DAT and 8 mm cartridges

➤ Magneto Optical

A floppy disk drive is already installed in your computer and probably has been used for some time for a limited backup. The next type listed above, the floptical, utilizes a special 3½-inch disk. The Bernoulli technique uses a removable cartridge containing a pair of disks. SyQuest is essentially a hard disk encased in a removable plastic package. A tape machine stores backup data on a ¼-inch tape. DAT (Digital Audio Tape) uses 4mm tape. The 8mm cartridge uses the 8mm videotape developed by Sony for camcorders. The Magneto-Optical storage medium is a disk.

⇨ Definitions and acronyms

✳ **DAT (Digital Audio Tape)**   Uses helical scan recording and high density audio tape to stuff considerable data (gigabytes) onto a cartridge that is slightly larger than a credit card.

* **Data transfer rate**   The speed at which data is written to or read from the recording media.

* **Helical scan recording**   Uses two or four heads attached to a rotating drum to read and write tracks diagonally across a tape. The tape curves somewhat around the drum so that each slash of data has a sigmoid shape. The whole pattern of curved, parallel slashes resembles a helix, hence the name helical scan.

* **QIC (Quarter Inch Committee)**   A very small group of people (¼ inch) who establishes standards for tapes and related hardware.

* **QIC 24 standard**   A tape standard which uses one head to write and a second head that immediately checks the material that was written for errors.

* **QIC 40 standard**   Less costly than the QIC 24, this standard uses a single head to write data, then repeats the process to verify the data written. Takes twice as long as the QIC to complete a backup.

* **Serpentine recording**   A technology that uses two stationary recording heads, one for reading, the other for writing.

⇨ Media

To be useful as a backup, the media being used must be low in cost per megabyte and removable so that it can download and duplicate the data on the hard disk, then be stored in some safe location. This removable capability also has another advantage in that you never run out of storage space because you can keep procuring and using as many removable media as you require.

In addition to cost, capacity, etc., another important consideration is the amount of time it takes to accomplish a backup. It's desirable to be able to complete backups without requiring much intervention on the part of the user. Another desirable feature is the ability of the backup technique to be accomplished on an automatically timed

periodic interval, preferably during off-hours when the PC is not being used for productive work.

In practice, no matter what backup medium you use, incremental backups should also be performed throughout the day on low-capacity storage media, such as floppy disks. Major backups should be accomplished during off-hours or nonbusy times.

Floppies

Because you already have a floppy disk drive in your PC, this is the easiest backup system to implement. However, its storage capacity is low: 1.2MB for the 5¼-inch disks and 1.44MB for the 3½-inch disks. Floppies are also available with a 2.88MB storage capacity, if you have this high resolution drive installed. The 2.88MB drive costs about fifty percent more than the 1.44MB floppy drive; the 2.88MB disks cost about two dollars each.

The major problem with using floppies for backup is their small storage capacity. Even if you have only 100MB stored on your hard disk, you have to use 70 or more 1.44MB disks for a backup, which takes a considerable amount of time (an hour or more) and near infinite patience to accomplish. A power glitch or a virus during this lengthy backup could put you out of business. If you have 250MB or more of data (how about one gigabyte?), you must find a better way so you can keep your sanity.

Still, you don't have to give up on floppy disks. If your storage requirements are modest and you're not creating huge amounts of new data, you can invest the time required to accomplish a full backup once, then, via a software backup program, back up only those files you have modified during each day.

A still better technique to use, even if you have an automatic daily backup accomplished by another media (and the method I use for incremental backups) is to label and keep a disk in your floppy drive at all times for each specific project you're working on. Back up your work several times during the day, instead of waiting to accomplish a total backup at the end of each day. If you wait that long to

accomplish a backup and lose an entire day's work . . . ! You'll hate yourself in the morning. If you accomplish incremental backups during the day, you won't lose much of your work in case of a disaster or a software glitch.

Maybe I sound a trifle paranoid about backing up, but as soon as you lose some of your best efforts because of the vagaries of an electro-mechanical drive, or some wayward, incompatible software, you'll be quickly convinced.

Floptical

The floptical has the most intriguing name of all the types of storage. Even though its name is derived from "floppy-optical," the floptical is not floppable, but is encased and as sturdy as the 3½-inch floppies.

The floptical uses a hybrid combination of magnetic floppy disk and optical technologies. Magnetic technology is used to store data and optical technology is used to locate the data. The floptical is a low-range storage device (up to 21MB per disk, 14 times the capacity of floppies) and up to 3 times faster than floppies. A floptical drive can serve a dual purpose role in that it can read and write to 3½-inch 1.44MB and 720KB floppies, as well as to the 21MB disks.

The floptical is low in cost (the same cost per MB as for floppies) and is the least expensive add-on storage device. Simple to use, it's ideal for transporting 21MB of data to coworkers or customers. However, compared to other high-capacity storage media, it's slow and its cartridges are vulnerable to magnetic fields. It also has a limited range of cartridge capacities.

The floptical is available for internal or external mounting and disks may be purchased as singles or in five-packs. The internal version mounts in a 3½-inch half-height slot. The floptical is faster than a floppy, so the typical time required to back up a 100MB disk on to floptical disks is much less than that required for a floppy. However, this backup requires your intervention because you have to remove the full disks and insert new disks. The floptical drive costs about eight to ten times as much as a floppy drive and the floptical disks cost about 20 dollars each.

 Bernoulli

The Bernoulli drive uses a cartridge (a.k.a. multidisk) which contains two flexible plastic disks coated with a magnetically sensitive alloy. As the disks spin, air moves outward over them and passes between the disk surfaces and the read/write heads. The resulting reduced air pressure causes the disks to position themselves almost in contact with the heads. The Bernoulli uses the same principle that causes lift on airplane wings. The spacing is closer than for a hard disk.

The Bernoulli multi-disk drive is fast and has an excellent effective access time: 18 ms. With storage capacities ranging from 35 to 150MB per cartridge (2 flexible disks in a cartridge), the Bernoulli is a mid-range storage device and is ideal for DTP applications where you have considerable graphics you want to keep together in the same package and for backup. The Bernoulli is a very rugged and reliable disk that can be physically handled and mailed to distant locations by UPS or the U.S. Postal Service. You can use it to carry your work between your home and your office. Some of the disadvantages are that the cartridges are vulnerable to dust and magnetic fields. The disks do wear out, but manufacturers provide a five-year warranty. If the disk is kept in cold storage, lifetime is not a problem.

The Bernoulli is available in both internal and external mounts. The internal version mounts in a 5¼-inch, half-height bay slot. Portable versions are also available. Because its capacity exceeds that of most hard disks, backup can be accomplished with a single disk, requiring only a minimum of your intervention.

The Bernoulli drive costs from 10 to 20 times the cost of a floppy drive. Bernoulli disks are very expensive and range from 75 dollars to 150 dollars per disk, depending upon the capacity and quality.

 # SyQuest

The SyQuest drive is, in essence, a hard drive that has a removable disk. It is available in capacities of 44-, 88-, and 105MB. Its access time is about 15 ms.

The hard plastic cartridge contains a highly polished aluminum disk that is plated with a magnetically sensitive metal alloy. When the cartridge is inserted into a drive, the disk's metal hub is held and rotated by a magnetized spindle. Flyweight magnetic heads float above and below the spinning disk platter, resting on a cushion of air.

The SyQuest can be mounted in either a 5¼-inch or a 3½-inch drive bay. The cartridges won't wear out like the Bernoullis, but they are delicate, requiring protected cases for transport and storage. The SyQuest cartridge is widely accepted among service bureaus.

 # Tape

The tape drive system has been the most popular backup media because of its low cost and high capacity. However, it is not of any practical use for storing working data because the data is stored serially and you have to roll the long tape to find your data. Average access time is about 20 seconds, so its application is strictly for backup. Tape systems use tape cassettes much like those used on audio cassette tape recorders, but they're made with greater precision, a faster speed drive, etc.

The designation QIC is derived from "Quarter-Inch-Committee." Most cartridges use ¼-inch tape. The mini-cartridge (DC-2000) and the cartridge (DC-6000) are the principal types used. The mini-cartridge is by far the least expensive media for backup; a 250MB drive and tape are an excellent bargain.

A QIC-1000-standard quarter-inch cartridge is also available and stores a gigabyte in a DC-6000 package. Another type utilized is the Irwin tape. Within these cartridge types, various tape lengths and compression schemes provide a variety of storage capacities.

The DC-2000 is very slow. However, this version is very popular because both the drives and the tape are very inexpensive, widely available, and the drives fit in a 3½-inch disk drive slot. If you're accomplishing a scheduled backup during off-hours, the time required is not too important.

The tapes, referred to as QIC-40 and QIC-80, were originally named because their capacities were 40MB and 80MB. However, extended length tapes increased their capacity by about fifty percent, and compression doubled it, so the 40s became 120MB and the 80s increased to 250MB. The 120 and 250 both use the same blank tape; however, the 250MB is formatted differently to enable it to hold the greater amount of data.

Most of the tape drives can be driven by a floppy controller in your PC. Some require a special controller that must be mounted in a plug-in slot in your PC and are designed specifically for the tape. Some versions use SCSI interfaces. Special controllers and their accompanying software are preferable because they can more than double the speed of the backup, but the proprietary controller cards are expensive.

The time required to back up a 100MB hard disk onto a tape drive (at 2MB per minute) is about 50 minutes. Using a proprietary controller and software (at 7MB per minute) requires about 15 minutes. Also, because the tape storage capacity usually exceeds that of the hard disk, a minimum of human intervention is required.

One factor to note about tape drives is that the capacity quoted for the tapes (120-and 250MB) are based on the fact that the data stored on the tapes is compressed. However, some of your files may already be compressed and some files may not compress to the 2:1 ratio the vendor claims. A compression ratio of about 1.8:1 is more reasonable, so a 250MB tape may only be able to handle about 180- to 250MB of compressed data.

Tape drives are available for internal or external mounting. Also available is a portable model (with its own controller card) that plugs into your printer port. Special cables are available to make this hookup.

273

An internal tape drive costs about five times as much as a floppy drive, an external costs slightly more. An external also requires the installation of a dedicated controller card. However, the portable version may cost as much as double the dedicated internal version. The individual tapes cost about 10 to 25 dollars, depending upon quality and storage capacity.

Backup software is usually included with the tape drive. Purchase a drive that bundles backup software with it (pay extra if you have to) so you can be sure it functions with your drive. Some incompatibility problems exist in tape drives, so be sure you get the proper software for your drive. You have to format the tapes before you can use them; this time-consuming process can take from 1½ to 3 hours or more.

DAT and 8mm

DAT (Digital Audio Tape) is the most popular competitor to QIC tape and is based on technology developed for consumer electronics: 4mm and 8mm tape (as used in some home video recorders). Both use a VCR type helical-scan method of recording in which the read/write heads are mounted on a drum. The drum spins, tracing a helical or spiral path, writing data in diagonal strips on the tape.

DAT, much like tape, cannot be used for storing active data because the data is stored serially and random access is not feasible. Its random access time is of the order of 15 seconds. However, its storage capacity is enormous, from 1 to 4 gigabytes.

A DAT drive costs about six times that of a tape drive; however, DAT drives have a much larger storage capacity. DAT tapes cost from 10 to 20 dollars, depending on size and quality.

The time required to back up a 100MB hard disk (at 6MB per minute) on DAT is a little more than 16 minutes. Also because a single DAT tape exceeds the capacity of most hard disks, only a single tape is required.

An 8mm cartridge comprises one of the highest-capacity backup systems available. Most units store 2.3GB; even larger capacity units

are available. It can also back up at about 6MB per minute. The cost of an 8 mm cartridge drive is about ten times that of a tape drive.

Magneto-Optical

Magneto-Optical (a.k.a. Optical and MO) drives use a laser beam to write data to, and read it from, a plastic disk. The MO offers access time of about 35–50 milliseconds, but has one of the highest capacities (up to 1.3GB per cartridge), storing almost ten times as much as the other magnetic disk media. There are also "jukeboxes" that hold several magneto-optical disks, giving you access to dozens of gigabytes of data. There is no chance of a head crash with an MO drive and the disk can't be accidentally erased or corrupted by a magnetic field. It's available in 3½-inch and 5¼-inch sizes. The 3½-inch size is available as an internal or external mount. The time required to back up a 100MB hard disk (at 0.5MB per second) onto magnetic-optical media is about four minutes.

Magnetic-optical drives are very expensive; they cost about 50 times as much as a floppy drive. Individual magnetic-optical disks cost from about 40 dollars to over a hundred dollars. The disks have a shelf life of 30 years.

My recommendations

If your daily work does not involve a large number of different projects and large amounts of storage requirements, you can get by using floppy disks as a backup medium. The initial backup, of course, will be laborious and time consuming, but once accomplished these disks can be set aside and safely stored. For your daily work, keep separate disks for each project you're working on and update the disks as you work on each project.

The next step up, a nominal increase in capacity, is the floptical with 21MB storage. If you handle several megabytes of data each day, both text and graphics, a floptical drive is a good investment. It serves the dual purpose of serving as a floppy drive for your 3½-inch

disks, but also can be used as supplemental storage on which you can store and access all the data required for large projects. The floptical is an excellent way in which to exchange 21MB of data with co-workers or to deliver to customers. Finally, it can serve as a backup if used in a manner described above for floppy disks.

For another step up the storage ladder, the Bernoulli drive provides from 44MB to 150MB, and several steps in between. With its 18ms access time, it can double as a second hard disk. Because the recording media is removable, the multi-disks can be used to deliver 44–150MB of data to co-workers and customers. It can be used to back up a huge volume of data.

The Bernoulli is one of the most rugged storage media available and can withstand considerable shock and rough handling (in case you want the Post Office to deliver it). Although the Bernoulli drive is not overly expensive for what it accomplishes, the individual disks are very costly.

If you need a drive to serve as an extra hard drive, and if your work requires that you deliver a large volume of data to distant locations, the Bernoulli is a good choice. However, for most straight backup applications, a tape system is ideal. With a capacity as high as 250MB, it can back up most hard disks with a minimum of user intervention required. Tapes are very inexpensive, so it's an excellent, cost-effective medium if you need to archive considerable data and also to keep earlier versions of documents.

For very high storage capacity backups, 2–8 gigabytes, the DAT is the clear choice. Both the drive and the tapes are inexpensive and the time required for backup is minimal.

With a 35 ms seek time, the magneto-optical drive can also serve as another somewhat slower hard disk. With a 1 gigabyte capacity, it can back up most common disks and will be ready for the larger hard disks that will become commonplace in the future. The MO disks have a 30-year shelf life.

⇨ Hardware installation

The procedure for the physical installation of plug-in cards was covered in chapter 3. The physical installation of an internal hard drive or tape drive is essentially the same as installing a disk drive, which was covered in chapter 6. The overall installation procedures for installing a tape drive are diagrammed in Fig. 13-1.

Figure 13-1

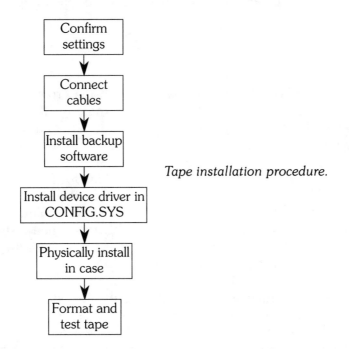

Tape installation procedure.

For internal drives, if you don't have a spare connector on your disk drive signal cable (some forward-looking manufacturers include 3 plugs on a disk drive signal cable) and you want to use your disk drive controller, you need to replace the cable with a Y-splitter signal cable.

A similar situation holds true for the power supply cable. If you don't have a spare disk drive power cable, you'll need to purchase a Y-splitter power cable (chapter 6) which converts one of the power cables into two separate power cables with connectors. Last, but not least, be sure to connect the grounding wire to the case of your installed drive.

Some external units also require a dedicated controller card to be installed. Before installation of any cards, refer to the documentation that came with your drive to see if you have to set any DIP switches or jumpers on the card. Don't assume everything is all set and ready to be used as it came from the factory.

After installing the internal card and buttoning up your case, attach the supplied cable between the controller connector and the external drive. Plug in the power cable and you should be ready to go.

Software

Most of the removable media drives provide install programs that automatically update your CONFIG.SYS file and copy the drivers you need to your boot disk. If you use the floppy driver controller card that is already in your PC, you shouldn't need any new software.

Once everything is working, follow the directions for formatting your storage media. This takes an especially long time for tapes. For tapes, after you've formatted them, create a test file on your hard disk. To test your system, back up this test file on your tape, then restore this test file back on to your hard disk and check to make sure it made the trip out and back without any loss of data.

The software accompanying your drive should also be smart enough to tell you when your backup media is full and that you have to exchange disks or cartridges. Software should be able to split an average hard drive into 2 or more backup disks or cartridges and not lose any of the data in the process.

14

Special upgrades

CHAPTER 14

THE earlier chapters of this book described some of the more prevalent upgrades for creating a desktop publishing system. This chapter covers some of the lesser utilized, but still important special upgrades you can add to enhance an existing DTP system.

For example, a faster CPU can increase the overall speed of most operations. A higher resolution mouse improves the accuracy and speed of operation for DTP. Other input media also considered in this chapter include the use of different keyboards, a trackball, a PC Stylus, and a graphic tablet for inputting and manipulating text and graphics.

Printer switch boxes to enable a number of PC stations to share a high-cost printer is another potential upgrade. Power surge protectors are also an important addition to a DTP station, as is a UPS (Uninterruptible Power System) which provides temporary power in case of the loss of primary ac power. The UPS provides power for an adequate interval to give you time to save whatever you're working on before your data is lost forever. A larger power supply may be needed to power your upgrades.

Here are the add-ons covered in this chapter:

➢ Keyboard

➢ Mouse/PC stylus

➢ Trackball

➢ Math coprocessor

➢ Graphic tablet

➢ Peripheral sharing switches

➢ Add serial ports

➢ Add parallel port

➢ Larger power supply

➢ Surge suppressors

➢ Uninterruptible power supply

➢ Fan/heat sink/fan card

Keyboard

The keyboard is the hardware item you use the most often, so make sure this valuable input device suits you. Its functioning has a direct effect on your productivity and your satisfaction with your system. The one-size-fits-all design doesn't apply to keyboards, any more than it does to people's houses.

Most PCs come equipped with a relatively standard 101-key keyboard. A wide number of variations are available to suit special applications. You can obtain a keyboard with an audible click, one with the function keys on the left side for lefties, one version has a built-in calculator. Some keyboards offer keys with a springy, relatively stiff feel; others offer a light touch to suit different individuals. Some keyboards feature little bumps on the F and J keys so your hands can easily find the Home keys without looking, a nice touch for touch-typists.

One of my keyboards (Model 2001, Focus Electronic Company Ltd.) has another excellent feature: a sturdy, plastic cover that swings down and covers the keys when the keyboard is not being used. The cover swings up on a pair of hinges to expose the keys and also serves to hold any sheets of paper I'm working with. The cover can also be easily removed.

Some keyboards have switches that you can set for an XT, Enhanced XT, PC/AT, or Enhanced AT PS-2. (You need the enhanced for the ATs; it provides the F11 and F12 function keys, plus extra Alt and Ctrl keys.) You'll probably find the switches under the logo pad on the top of the keyboard. And you'll probably find the logo under the template (doesn't everybody use templates?) you've affixed to the top of your keyboard.

Carpal tunnel syndrome is becoming more commonplace. Considerable research is being accomplished to find a suitable keyboard, but some of the proposed solutions are so far-fetched that they will never be adopted. Some manufacturers have devised a keyboard that reposes at an angle (they have legs in the back that can be extended) to better fit the natural position of the user's hands.

Another proposed solution is to use a pad that fits under your keyboard and supports your wrists as you type (I use this and it seems to help a little). Even with these gimmicks, you should rest your hands every hour or more often. Take a break and go outside and smell the roses (I live in rural Minnesota, so I go outside and make snowpeople).

 # Keyboard installation

Keyboard installation is relatively simple. To install your new keyboard, first turn your PC off. Simply unplug the old connector from the rear of your PC and plug in your new connector (it's probably a five pin, AT-standard, round plug—about ⁹⁄₁₆ of an inch in diameter). The keyboard connector has a dimple on top that must be aligned with the dimple on the rear of your PC case where the internal PC connector is mounted. Once connected, turn your computer back on. Your PC should welcome the new addition without any problems.

If you get a message that says:
```
Keyboard is locked...Unlock it
Keyboard error
Press <F1> to resume
```

then you have not plugged the connector in properly. Turn your computer back off and be more careful next time. Look inside the recessed connector at the back of your PC (you may need a flashlight) and note that it has a series of five holes and a small square hole, probably at the top of the connector. Be sure the dimple on the keyboard cable plug is aligned with this square hole. Don't force it in, the connectors were made for each other and should mate easily.

 # Mouse/PC stylus

You probably also received a mouse (Fig. 14-1) with your PC, but you may not be obtaining all the value you can from this essential and versatile peripheral.

 Figure 14-1

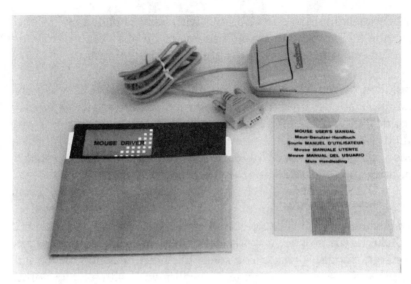

Mouse with software.

Even if a mouse does nothing spectacular, it at least helps reduce the amount of manual keying-in you have to accomplish by using pull-down menus, thus saving your wrists from having to search out and hit key after key, resulting in the dreaded carpal tunnel syndrome that sooner or later affects all of us keyboarders.

A mouse increases your efficiency of operation and it's essential for paint, design, and desktop publishing programs. The mouse is your paintbrush, the screen your canvas.

It's available either as a bus mouse (which connects to a plug-in card you have to install in your computer), or as a serial mouse that connects to a serial port on the back of your PC. The serial mouse is the most common and the easiest to install because you don't even have to open the PC box. If you only have a two-button, you can exchange it for a three-button. Many software programs have special uses for the third button.

Mice also vary in their capabilities. Their precision varies from 200 to 400 dots-per-inch resolution. Some offer resolutions as high as 2,600 dpi. Most mice can be adjusted by software for left-handed operation. Cordless mice are also available. Much experimentation

has been accomplished to come up with what is called an "ergonomic" mouse, but no one seems to be able to agree on the ergonomics, so no design has had universal acceptance.

Resolution of a mechanical or opto-mechanical mouse is adequate for most applications. Precision position readings are available when using an optical mouse, a design that contains no moving parts. For precise CAD drawings or complex paint and draw requirements, an optical mouse is a good choice. However, optical mice are considerably more expensive than mechanical or opto-mechanical mice.

Another interesting version, or rather replacement for a conventional mouse is the PC Stylus depicted in Fig. 14-2. Patterned after a pen, the PC Stylus needs no pad. It works on paper, magazine covers, or any other soft, smooth surface. The stylus has been designed for maximum comfort and ease of use. It's guaranteed to work with all your software and hardware and boasts a resolution of from 100–1,600 dpi, which makes it easy to work with fine details, such as if you were tracing a drawing or sketch to be input into a graphics program.

Figure 14-2

PC Stylus.

The PC stylus has a metal ball which protrudes from the bottom and which rolls with movement to deliver a signal to the tracking software. Three easily reachable buttons are located on the body of the stylus. One serves as an "enter" or "selection" key, analogous to the left key of a 2 or 3 button mouse. A smaller right button is an "exit" key and works like the right key on a mouse. The smaller left button is an alternate key for expanded software applications and functions, such as the middle key of a 3-button mouse.

The PC Stylus may also be used as a trackball which is convenient when your desktop space is limited (of if you're using a portable PC). To function in this mode, turn the PC Stylus upside down so the trackball faces up and the buttons face down. Position your thumb over the ball, with your index or middle finger over the large enter key. Use your thumb to move the ball, following the cursor on the screen. Click on the large button to enter information, just as with the stylus in normal operation.

 Mouse/PC stylus installation

Most mice use a serial port, usually COMM1. Installation consists of turning your PC off and plugging the cable into a serial port. The mouse has a molded connector with a pair of thumbscrews that you turn to securely attach the mouse to the connector on your PC case. The mouse has to be secured because it is the only thing in your setup that is physically moved.

Your mouse should have come with a software installation program on disk. Load both the DOS and Windows software versions if you're using both operating systems. Your software should state that it is "Microsoft-compatible," which means it complies with the widely accepted Microsoft standards. Mouse software also should allow you to change the mouse's sensitivity (how much you have to move it for a given response) and how quickly it responds to the clicks of its buttons. Software for the PC stylus is installed in a similar manner. The stylus may be used for both DOS and Windows.

To maintain your mouse in top working order, clean it occasionally because dust and dregs can collect on the rollers inside the mouse, causing it to stick and move randomly. You can clean these unwanted debris with a little isopropyl-alcohol solution and use cotton swabs to clean its innards. Let it dry before you use it again.

⇨ Trackball

A trackball is a captive ball that remains in a fixed horizontal plane but which is rotated by the user's hand to move a corresponding cursor on the screen. It's almost like flipping a mouse on its back. The trackball takes up less room on a desktop because it doesn't move in the horizontal plane. Trackballs provide finer control than mice. In general, the larger the size of the ball, the better the resolution.

One annoying trackball problem is in click-and-drag. To highlight text with a mouse, you position the cursor at the beginning of the text to be moved, hold down the button and move the cursor to encompass the text. With a trackball, this operation requires two hands, one to hold the button and one to rotate the trackball to the proper position.

Some people claim that a trackball is less likely to cause carpal tunnel syndrome problems than a mouse, but I don't agree with that, unless you are performing long term mouse-intensive operations. My mouse serves my right hand well; it's my left hand that gives me trouble.

⇨ Trackball installation

Trackball installation is essentially the same as for the mouse. Some of the more specialized programs have their own software.

⇨ Math coprocessor

Some of the early PC systems did not provide a math coprocessor, but included provisions for adding one later. A math coprocessor

becomes a necessity if you're running big spreadsheets, large databases, or using CAD.

The specific reason that a math coprocessor is needed is because a typical CPU handles only integer mathematics. For floating-point computations, the CPU represents floating-point values in memory and manipulates them using only integer operations. This requires many, many clock cycles to perform floating-point calculations. A math coprocessor accomplishes floating-point calculations directly.

Most motherboards without a built-in coprocessor have a socket set aside for a math coprocessor chip. The math coprocessor must be matched up with the CPU used on the motherboard. Table 14-1 lists some of the math coprocessors used:

Math coprocessors   Table 14-1

CPU	Math coprocessor
8088	8087
80286	80287
80386	80387
80486SX	80487
80486DX	Built-in
Pentium	Built-in

Note that the coprocessors all have an 87 suffix and note that the later CPU versions include the math coprocessor integral with the CPU.

Math coprocessor installation

Installation is relatively easy. You have to open the PC case and find the coprocessor socket. After cracking the case open, discharge yourself by touching the PC chassis. The coprocessor socket should be empty and located near the CPU.

Handle the coprocessor carefully; align the coprocessor with its socket and gently press it into place. It should fit with just a little pressure; again, they were made for each other.

Put the case back on and run the CMOS setup program by pressing the Delete key when you boot up. Your computer should now acknowledge the presence of the coprocessor by an entry in the "Advanced or Extended CMOS" place on the menu.

Graphic tablet

To provide the precision required for graphic arts and CAD, a graphic tablet is required. Although they cost considerably more than a mouse and consume a lot of desk space (or require their own special work space), they provide a productivity and precision that is not otherwise attainable.

A digitizing tablet functions essentially as a pen drawing on paper, except that the pen (cursor) transmits x and y positions (within a fixed coordinate space) directly to your software. The center of the tablet is the center of the drawing space. A digitizing tablet consists of a flat tablet or work surface and a pen-like stylus or flat "hockey puck" cursor. The pen or stylus is best for sketching and freehand drawing. The hockey puck cursor with crosshairs is best for precision digitizing and geometric creations. Digitizers convert position on the tablet into x and y coordinates within a fixed horizontal plane.

Tablets can be used to digitize already existing drawings by tracing the cursor over the lines. Paper images and blueprints can be digitized in this manner. You can also use it as a sketch pad for creating high resolution drawings. And your drawings become digitized sketches in editable form that can be fine-tuned, or worked up into engineering drawings with relative ease. Tablets offer a much more natural and precise freehand drawing capability than other input devices.

Models are also available with a pressure sensitive stylus that lets you emulate fairly convincingly the range of gray scale strokes and effects you can obtain with pen, pencil, and charcoal.

Small format graphic tablets range from about 12×12 active inches to 12×18 active inches and support a resolution of about 1,000 lines per inch (some go as high as 5,000 lines per inch) and an accuracy of 0.01 to 0.02 inches.

One company offers a nice, compact 5-x-5-inch graphics tablet that purports to be able to replace your mouse or trackball. It can be used as a system pointer, for creating graphics, and for tracing and directly inputting a drawing into your PC. It has a 2,000-lines-per-inch resolution and an accuracy of 0.01 inches.

Larger format sizes range from 12×18 inches to more than 44×60 inches, however their cost goes up almost exponentially. As a point of reference, standard blueprint E size drawings are 36×48 inches and D size drawings are 24×36 inches. Accuracies in the larger format sizes range from an incredible 0.002 to 0.005 inches.

⇨ Graphic tablet installation

Installation procedures for the graphic tablet are similar to that required for a mouse. A suitable space must be located near the display so that both the graphic tablet and the display can be easily observed. It may be convenient to place the graphic tablet in front of the display and the keyboard to one side when most of the inputs are going to be provided by the tablet. Most of the needed controls are on the tablet so it can serve as a primary input device for graphic intensive applications. The graphic tablet should plug into a serial port at the rear of your PC.

Installation software accompanying the graphic tablet should automatically load the proper files to inform your PC of its existence and should also provide the required software driver for your specific graphic tablet. You will probably also be required to inform your specific programs (CAD, etc.) that use the graphic tablet of its existence and select the proper drivers.

 # Peripheral sharing switches

"Smart switches" are available which allow 4 to 8 computers to share a common printer. One model is for parallel operation, another model is for a serial mode of operation. Optional memory boards are available to serve as printer buffers.

If more than one person is sharing a peripheral, an electronic sharing serial switch is available to permit this mode. This switch enables up to four computers to share a modem (or a bi-directional serial device such as printer or plotter). Three modes of operation are provided: modem (with selectable timeouts of 10, 25, 60, and 150 seconds), auto switch, and a manual switching mode.

Several other peripheral sharing devices are available, including a switch to connect a phone, an answering machine and a fax machine, a computer modem or any other ring-activated datacom device through one phone line.

 # Installation of peripheral sharing switches

Installation procedures vary widely among various types of peripheral sharing switches. In general, a central switching unit has to be installed and cables have to be run to each unit that is to be controlled. Assuming the switches are remotely controlled, the software accompanying the hardware must be installed in each unit which accomplishes the controlling. For specific installation procedures, refer to the documentation supplied with the unit.

Add serial ports

Your PC usually comes with only two serial ports. If you have installed a mouse and an external modem, you've run out of serial ports. One serial port is needed for each one (unless they have their own

interface card). However, it's easy to add serial ports by installing another I/O board in one of your vacant plug-in slots.

You can obtain either a one or two serial port board for a modest sum. To install the serial port add-on board, follow the directions in chapter 3.

⇨ Installation of serial ports

Here are the recommended assignments for your serial ports (a.k.a. COMM):

COMM1   Modem (IRQ4)
COMM2   Mouse (IRQ3)
COMM3   Scanner (IRQ4)
COMM4   Plotter or whatever (IRQ3)

Two devices can share the same IRQ as long as they're not used at the same time. COMM3 and COMM4 work from IRQ 4 and 3 respectively, the same as COMM1 and COMM2, but at different memory addresses.

Installation consists of informing the software that uses each port of its existence. Each software program that utilizes a serial port allows you to specify which serial port it will use.

⇨ Add parallel port

Most CPUs are designed to have a single parallel port; some CPU setups would profit by the addition of another one. For example, if you have both a dot matrix and laser printer, a second parallel port will enable you to output to each one without the need to mechanically switch from one to the other. Mechanical A-B switches, however, are not a good idea for a laser printer. Hewlett-Packard's warranty, for example, does not cover damage caused by the use of an A-B because a jolt of juice could fry your laser printer's controller.

All you need to add another parallel port is an available slot. Adding a single parallel port is very inexpensive; the board costs only about fifteen dollars.

Parallel port installation

Follow the directions given in chapter 3 to install the parallel port card. The only potential problem you might encounter is an IRQ conflict. Your existing parallel port is LPT1 and should be used by your printer. Your added parallel port would be LPT2. Your new port should use IRQ5, which should be available. Just like parallel devices, even if IRQ5 is used by some other serial device, it can share the IRQ as long as both serial devices are not used at the same time. Here are the standard default IRQ assignments. Don't mess with them unless you know what you're doing.

LPT1   IRQ7
LPT2   IRQ5

One problem that you may encounter is that your software may not know how to address LPT2. A tiny software program, LPTPORT (available from on online databases), will help you solve this problem.

Larger power supply

For most PCs, the power supply provided with the unit is adequate initially. However, as you upgrade and add more and more cards, a faster CPU, more drives, etc., you may find your computer is in need of a power supply transplant. The XT power supply provides 150–200 watts; the early AT supplies provide about 200–230 watts. More modern computers provide 230 watts and up.

Here are some of the power consumers in your PC:

➤ Empty 80286 motherboard—50 watts
➤ Each floppy drive adds about 10 watts

> Add-on boards add about 8–12 watts

> Hard drive adds about 25 watts

> RAM adds about 2 watts per megabyte

As you can see, it quickly adds up. If you're limping along with a 200 watt or less supply, consider adding a greater capacity unit. Some of the symptoms of having too little power is if your computer starts to act up after being on for 30 minutes or so, that's when the system is heated up. Other clues that your power supply is failing occur when you boot up. If it won't boot, or if you hear the hard drive and your screen is blank, you are probably having a power supply problem.

 # Power supply installation

You'll have to open the case to access the power supply. The power supply is the biggest module in your PC and is installed in a removable metal case. It's usually mounted on the rear of your PC chassis.

Make notes of the destination of each cable (and the wire colors) as you disconnect each cable. (Color codes are fairly standard among power supply manufacturers.) Some of the connectors may have locks that you have to snap before removing. Also make note of and label any cables which are not used. These spares are part of your built-in upgrade potential.

After carefully removing all of the cables, remove the screws securing the power supply case to the PC chassis and save the screws. Lift the supply out carefully; it should come out cleanly. Make sure that no cables are entangled.

If you're building your own computer from scratch, the power supply is supplied with the case and already mounted. Refer to the documentation that came with your case and your motherboard to help connect your cables. Most of the cable connectors are unique and will only connect with their proper destination connector. With

some cables or wires, polarity is important, so be sure to observe the proper polarity when you're making the connections.

Before you install your new power supply in your chassis, be sure it is set up for your line voltage. Most supplies allow you to use 125 or 250 volts ac and 50 or 60 Hz as your primary power. If the switches are not set up for your power, make the necessary changes at this time.

Next comes the physical installation of the new supply in its designated position on your chassis. Most power supply manufacturers use standard mounting holes, so it should mount nicely. Some supplies may require you to add adapter brackets so the supply fits in the PC chassis.

Finally, connect up all the cables you disconnected and labeled earlier. Some connectors may have locks and require you to pinch them open before insertion. As you make each connection, double-check it with your notes. Again, don't force any plugs in. If you have trouble making a connection, be sure the pins on both the connector and plug are straight. Remember, the male connectors and female plugs were made for each other; most are keyed so they can't be improperly connected.

Double-check all of your connections, then button up your unit and turn it on. All should be well.

 # Surge suppressors

Two types of electrical disturbances can affect your PC: power surges and line noise. Surges are brief, power disturbances from natural or man-made sources. Lightning striking nearby can send power surges through the electrical system. If you have lightning near you, the only solution is to pull the power plug on your computer. If your electrical utility loses power, when it's turned back on it sends a surge through the system. Power surges are also caused by utility-line switching.

PCs are vulnerable to surges ranging from 800 to 6,000 volts. Most power supplies can handle surges below 800 volts unaided. Surges over about 6,000 volts arc over the wires and do not reach your PC, so the 800 to 6,000 range is the one that has to be protected against.

Noise is like radio or television static that occurs when an appliance is operated nearby. Noise is a constant, less powerful disturbance, unlike a surge. It may cause your system to reboot or create random disk errors.

The solution to these problems is a surge suppressor for your PC and all of its peripherals. Surge suppressors actually serve two purposes; they provide several output sockets so that you can individually power your peripherals on and off, and at the same time they provide surge protection for all peripherals connected to them.

Surges are absorbed by what is called a Metal Oxide Varistor (MOV), a voltage-sensitive switch that reacts when the voltage reaches a hazardous level. The MOV absorbs the surge and dissipates the excess energy as heat. Line noise caused by high frequency interference (much higher than 60 Hz) is filtered out by a pair of capacitors and a choke on the surge suppressor.

 Surge suppressor installation

Installation is routine; just turn all of your equipment off. Mount your surge suppressor near your PC, make sure the main power switch is off. One of my surge suppressors fits under my display and has a built-in voltmeter so I can make sure that my line voltage is proper. The one for my other computer fits on top of my PC.

Plug the surge suppressor into your wall socket, it's probably a three-prong plug. Finally plug your PC and peripherals in and power up your PC. Then power up your display and any other peripherals. I control the power to my peripherals from my surge suppressor because I'd rather wear out one of the surge suppressor switches than have to replace a switch inside one of my peripherals. Besides, a surge suppressor has lights or indicators to let you know if power is being applied to your various peripherals.

⇨ UPS (uninterruptible power system)

Two basic types of UPSs are available:

> ➤ Standby
> ➤ Online

The standby units are lower in cost because they normally deliver line power to the PC and monitor this power. When the voltage drops below a preset level (e.g., 105 volts), the standby instantly switches over to the batteries and converts the battery power to the proper ac voltage.

Online units, however, use their batteries continuously as a primary power source, converting the battery dc voltage into the proper ac voltage. At the same time, primary power is used to keep the batteries fully charged. When the input ac power drops below a preset value, no transfer time is necessary because the batteries are fully charged and can continue to supply power for a length of time determined by its volt-ampere (VA) capacity (usually several minutes).

If you are in a location that has frequent power outages or brownouts, if your house wiring is ancient and subject to frequent power loss, or if your ac power decreases because of line drop, consider installing an uninterruptible power system (UPS). A UPS (not to be confused with that other excellent UPS) is a system that monitors the ac input voltage to your system. If the ac voltage drops below an acceptable level, the UPS jumps in, and in less than a millisecond it begins to supply power for your system. A UPS also improves power quality during brownouts, surges, and spikes. The UPS usually has a battery (with a battery charger) that can supply power for from 5 to as long as 30 minutes to give you a chance to save your work before it is lost forever.

A power rating of 400–450 VA should be adequate for most PC systems.

➪ UPS installation

Purchase a UPS that has adequate capacity to drive not only your computer, but also your monitor. If you do lose power, the UPS supplies power long enough for you to preserve what you are working on and back out of the program you're using.

Installation consists of connecting the UPS in series with the ac power supplied to your PC and monitor. If any settings need to be made, refer to the documentation supplied with the UPS.

➪ Fans, heat sinks, and fan cards

As PCs run faster and faster, they get hotter and hotter. As more and more add-ons are installed in your tight chassis, more and more watts are being dissipated inside your PC. With all this new internal heat, your PC may be running too hot. Several solutions are available to help you run cooler. A cooler running temperature helps your CPU and chips run faster (your CPU slows down a few MHz when it heats up) and will extend the lives of all of your circuitry, even beyond the lifetime the IRS has assigned to your chips.

You can, for example, replace your old fan (usually located in the power supply at the rear of your unit) with a larger or auxiliary fan for a relatively low price. Or you could add a dedicated CPU cooler. Coolers range in design from passive heat sinks that mount on your CPU to a miniature fan/sink combination.

Another method of improving the inside ambient of your PC is to install a fan card. Basically the fan card has two muffin fans mounted on an interface card that plug into any full-length slot. (One version has only one fan, but the dual works better because one fan moves air upward, the other fan moves it down). A fan card obtains its low-current drain from the motherboard and directs its flow across your other add-on boards, the motherboard and the CPU. No configuration is needed, just plug it in. Tests show that it reduces the internal temperature by as much as 20 degrees.

297

 # Fan, heat sink, and fan card installation

There are too many versions of fan, heat sink, and fan card installations to attempt to cover them here, so I'll discuss them in general terms.

As far as adding a fan is concerned, there are several low-cost possibilities. The tower chassis usually has a spare grille and mounting provisions for adding a second fan. Some desktop installations require mounting the fan inside the chassis, either with a bracket or some other method to affix the fan. Other fan installations are accomplished by mounting the fan on the outside of the PC case. Whichever way you mount the fan, use insulating washers to cut down on the ambient noise.

The addition of a heat sink on a CPU consists of simply clamping the metal heat sink directly on top of the CPU (some heat sinks ride above and don't contact the CPU, not an ideal arrangement). If the CPU has a "Do not remove this label under penalty of . . .," you have to remove this label first and accept the consequences. You need metal-to-metal contact for the heat sink to be most effective.

Mounting a fan/heat sink unit on a CPU is more involved. You not only have to mount the tiny unit on the CPU, you also have to search for a source of dc power to connect to the cooling unit. You'll probably have to use a Y-splitter power cable to obtain the needed 12 volts dc.

The fan-card fits in a plug-in slot. It should be mounted in an end slot if possible so that its height does not block the use of an adjacent plug-in slot. Check to make sure it is circulating the air where it is needed. The fan obtains power from the plug-in slot.

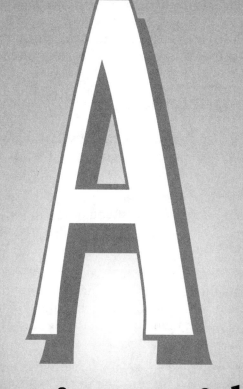

Buying guide

BEFORE you purchase components for your upgrades, review these guidelines covering where and how to purchase to make sure you receive the best values and highest quality for your money. Also, be sure to review the appropriate tradeoffs in the pertinent chapters before you obtain a quote and before you place your orders.

⇨ Where to purchase

When purchasing components, there are so many possible sources that it's difficult to make this decision. You have a number of possible sources:

> ➤ From a computer component supplier near you, one that can answer your questions, assist you, and support your decisions. If you don't live near a large town, this source may not be available for you.

> ➤ Mail Order. An excellent source because of the wide variety of components they supply from many different manufacturers and the lively competition they encounter. I've listed guidelines to follow in making mail-order purchases later in this Appendix.

> ➤ Computer swap meets near the larger cities, some have them every weekend. But be sure you're buying from a reliable source, the best sources are merchants who also have a store, or at least a regular place of business.

⇨ How to buy

My first recommendation is to buy all or most of your major components from a single supplier, even though some components may be a few dollars less expensive from a competitive supplier. One reason for this is because you are more likely to be assured that the components you purchase will be compatible with each other when purchased from a single source. The supplier should also assist you with this task. Ordering from a single source for mail order also makes sense when you consider that you have to pay a minimum shipping charge, no matter what you order, so the few dollars you

think you are saving are illusory if you have to pay for shipping charges from several different vendors.

Secondly, before you order any components, review the vendor list in appendix B. List the questions you want to have answered before you call or contact a vendor. One vendor may offer a motherboard at a much lower price, but doesn't inform you, for example, that it doesn't have a CPU installed, or that the monitor you're purchasing doesn't have the necessary cabling, etc. Another caution: if the price seems too good to be true, it probably is. The vendor may be unloading an outdated model, or a very inferior one. It's much safer to order from a vendor whose prices are near the average of all vendors.

Thirdly, pay by credit card. This gives you some leverage in case the components don't meet your specs. Legally, the credit-card company cannot refuse to pay the vendor, but they can be your ally, they can act as arbitrators to help settle any disagreement.

If you try to refuse to pay for the merchandise, the credit-card company will immediately suspend the payment, usually for a period of 30 to 90 days, while they contact the vendor with whom you have the dispute. From there on it gets kind of cloudy, depending on the situation. If you have the equipment and it's working, chances are you're going to have to pay for it. It's best to try to work any problems out between you and the vendor. If that fails, get the credit-card company to help.

Fourthly, check the terms of the purchase. Most vendors require an RMA (Returned Merchandise Authorization) which they have to approve prior to your returning the components. Some vendors also charge you a "restocking fee" for returned merchandise. This fee may be as much as 20 percent of the amount you paid for the components, and 20 percent of a $200 component is $40 out of your pocket. Also verify if the vendor offers a warranty policy, and for what period (ranges from 30 days to 1 year). Some vendors also provide a money back guarantee (ranges from 10 to 30 days). Overnight shipping is another option, but of course you pay extra for it. Fortunately, many of the more reliable vendors also provide technical support.

 # Special guidelines for mail order

First of all, check to see how long the vendor has been in business. If the vendor has been selling computers and components for a few years, chances are it's a reliable company.

Next, check the data I have included in appendix B to see what type of credit cards the vendor accepts, the vendor's warranty and return policies, their restocking fees, etc. If any of these items make you feel shaky, look for another vendor.

A reliable vendor will usually provide a modicum of technical assistance, such as helping you select compatible components, reminding you of the OBTWs (Oh, By The Way, I forgot to tell you that the CD-ROM drive does not include a driver card or software). Many vendors have excellent technical support personnel who will patiently answer both your dumb and brilliant questions.

Make sure you understand all the terms of the purchase; the cost, sales tax (if any), warranties, shipping date, and especially, return policies. Make notes of all of these items, write down the time, date, your purchase order number, and the name of the person who took your order.

If you buy from a vendor who sells both components and assembled systems, this type of vendor is more likely to have technical experts available for answering your technical questions. When you buy from this type of vendor, you're also assured of receiving the same quality parts they advertise. With vendors who only sell clones, you're taking a chance because some load their computers with inferior, low-cost components.

 # Some key definitions

Here are some key terms you're likely to encounter in your purchases. These terms are usually in small print at the bottom of the ad.

✳ **Acceptance**   This is the amount of time you have in which to decide if the component(s) is acceptable. Even though you prepay, that doesn't necessarily connote acceptance.

✳ **FOB (Free On Board)**   This term specifies whether the vendor's responsibility ends when the components are turned over to the carrier (FOB Shipping Point), or lasts until the components are delivered to you (FOB Place of Delivery).

✳ **Prices subject to change**   The vendor reserves the right to charge a different price than the advertised one. Here's a typical disclaimer:

"Prices and availability subject to change without notice."

Most vendors use this one, and for good reason. Component prices often vary from week to week (hopefully downward) because of supply, competition, and other factors. Vendors have to make educated guesses of what price to advertise their components because their ads won't be published until one to two months later. That's why you often see $CALL instead of a listed price in an ad. So, call and check for the current prices and make a note of them.

✳ **Specifications subject to change**   The vendor reserves the right to replace the component you ordered with one of equal or greater value. Here's a typical disclaimer: "Specifications subject to change without notice." Fortunately you don't see this one too often.

✳ **Restocking fees/refunds**   The restocking fee is the amount you are charged for the return of nondefective components (i.e., it works but it's not what you wanted). There is a reasonable rationale for this, too, since the component is no longer new. As far as refunds are concerned, here again are some typical disclaimers: "No refunds on opened software, monitors, printers, or memory." "All refund items must be returned within 14 days of invoice. There will be a restocking fee of 20% after the 7 day period and within 30 days of invoice."

✳ **RMA (Return Merchandise Authorization)**   Before you return your merchandise for refund or repair, you have to obtain an RMA or code number from the vendor authorizing the return. Virtually all vendors

require RMAs (a.k.a. RA or Return Authorization) that must be placed on the outside of the package you're returning.

Here are a few more general OBTWs:

➤ "Prices reflect a 3% cash discount." This means they jack up the price by 3% if you use a credit card.

➤ "Prices do not reflect any shipping charges. All shipping charges are nonrefundable."

➤ "Returns must be complete with all manuals, packaging, software, etc., with shipping prepaid and insured."

And some desirable OBTWs:

➤ "No credit card surcharges."

➤ "One year parts and labor warranties."

➤ "We don't charge your card until the order is shipped."

For mail order, confirm phone orders with a follow-up letter or fax. Save all of the original cartons and packing material the components were shipped in, just in case you have to send something back for return or repair.

When you receive your components, you'll usually receive warranty cards to fill out. Don't do it right away! If you fill them in and mail them, it technically makes your equipment used and unreturnable. The only legitimate reason for requiring warranty cards is to register your components for repairs. From a legal standpoint, a dated sales receipt with the components' name and serial number (if applicable) serves as proof of purchase. After you've used your components for a couple of months and are satisfied with them, fill out and mail the warranty cards.

Always check and see if the components you're ordering are in stock and ask when they will be shipped. If the vendor doesn't quote a shipping date, the vendor has to ship your order within 30 days. If unable to ship within this period, the vendor has to notify you of a new shipping date and give you two choices: a refund, or you can agree to the new shipping date.

Please don't let all of the above advice scare you away from dealing with in-store or mail-order vendors. I believe in erring on the side of caution. Most vendors must have and retain satisfied customers or they won't remain in business. Most of them are honest and do their best to please you because a satisfied customer is the best advertising any vendor can have.

Vendor checklist

For each vendor, obtain the following information before you place your order:

Name _____

Address _____

City _____

State _____ ZIP _____

Order Phone Number and hours of operation (order number should be toll-free _____

Technical Support Phone Number and hours of operation

_____

Warranty Policy (Period) _____

Money Back Guarantee (Days) _____

How do they ship Mail? UPS? Federal Express? _____

Is an RMA required? _____

Is overnight shipping available? What is extra charge?

_____

Is a restocking fee charged? _____ What percentage? _____

How do they handle repairs and replacements?

_____

_____

How long have you been in business? _____

Any other comments _____

_____

⇨ RAM checklist

Ask whether the SIMMs are manufactured with used or new chips. The used, of course, may have a shorter life. Try to obtain SIMMs that are surface-mounted rather than through-hole mounted because they use less power, generate less heat, and are more reliable. Check on the company's warranty on SIMMs, find out what it means.

Find out what the company's replacement policy is. Some provide overnight service, others wait until they receive your defective SIMMs.

Find out what kind of installation advice you can obtain from the company. Some companies send writeups on how to install, step-by-step, the larger ones may even send you a video covering installation. Larger companies also usually provide telephone support from people who can guide you through the installation process.

⇨ Motherboard checklist

1. Model No. _____

2. Cost _____

3. Delivery _____

4. Warranty _____

5. CPU Type (Be careful, some motherboards are sold without CPUs) _____

6. Math Coprocessor Socket or Math Coprocessor and type

   _____

7. Is a speaker Included? _____

8. Rechargeable Battery Included for BIOS? _____

9. Number of Plug-in Sockets—32 bit _____   16 bit _____

10. Type of I/O Interface—Are Interface circuits on motherboard?

Laser printer checklist

Here are some special questions to ask a laser printer vendor:

1. Model Number _____

2. Price _____

3. Delivery _____

4. Warranty _____

5. What fonts are included? (Should have at least three)

   _____

6. Are font cartridges or soft fonts available for this model?

   _____

7. What printers can it emulate, such as the IBM graphics printer needed for older software.

   _____

8. Printing speed? (Should be at least 4–6 ppm)

_____

9. How much RAM is included? (You need about 1MB for one page of graphics). How much more RAM can be added later as an upgrade?

_____

10. What is the cost of the toner cartridge?

_____

11. How many pages can be printed with a toner cartridge? (This recurring cost is very significant.)

_____

12. Is printer's warranty voided if a competitive toner is used?

_____

13. PCL5 compatible? _____

14. PostScript compatible or upgradeable?

_____

⇨ Tape backup checklist

1. Model No. _____

2. Cost _____

3. Delivery _____

4. Warranty _____

5. Formatted capacity _____

6. Formatted capacity with data compression

_____

7. Data transfer rate

_____

8. Read Compatibility

_____

9. Interface type (floppy drive or special board)

_____

10. If internal, what is height? (Half-height, one inch, is desirable)

_____

11. Type of cartridges used

_____

12. Is backup software included? _____ If so, whose?

_____

13. Tape capacity _____

⇨ CD-ROM checklist

1. Model No. _____

2. Cost _____

3. Delivery _____

4. Warranty _____

5. Access time _____

6. Software supplied? _____

7. Cables supplied? _____

8. Caddy or tray operation, which? _____

⇨ Hard drive checklist

1. Model No. _____

2. Cost _____

3. Delivery _____

4. Warranty _____

5. Access time _____

6. Formatted Capacity _____

7. Type of drive IDE, SCSI? _____

8. Manufacturer _____

9. Mounting Hardware and cables included? _____

10. Height of drive _____

11. Width of drive _____

⇨ Floppy drive checklist

1. Model No. _____

2. Cost _____

3. Delivery _____

4. Warranty _____

5. Capacity _____

6. Manufacturer _____

7. Mounting hardware and cables included? _____

8. Height of drive _____

9. Width of drive _____

Case and power supply checklist

1. Model No. _____

2. Cost _____

3. Delivery _____

4. Warranty _____

5. Size H × W × D _____

6. Output Power _____

7. Speaker Included _____

8. Number of Drive Bays _____

9. Lock on Front Panel _____

10. Indicators on Front Panel _____

11. Has power supply been tested and approved by either UL (Underwriters Laboratory) or CSA (Canadian Standards Association)?

_____

Vendors

THIS appendix lists several mail-order vendors that I have personally had satisfactory dealings with, and I have also indicated the conditions under which they function. The table below is only a small representative list; for a more complete listing of 300 vendors, check the latest issue of the fascinating Computer Shopper, the Sears catalog of the computer profession.

Most of the listed vendors offer overnight shipping at an increased cost. As you can see, warranty policy varies considerably; most are tied into the warranty supplied by the original manufacturer of the components. The money-back guarantee is for a specific period. "Restocking fee" is the fee a vendor charges when you return your unwanted equipment. This cost can be significant; if you have a restocking fee of twenty percent and purchase a $500 motherboard, that's $100 out of your pocket (or purse, as the case may be). Most vendors also require an RMA for returned equipment.

Best Computer Supplies
4980 Longely Lane
Suite 104
Reno NV 89502

Business hours:	M-F 6:00-6:00, Saturday 10:00-3:00 PST
Phone:	800-544-3470, 408-727-9048, Fax 408-727-9225
Tech support:	702-826-4393
Warranty:	Lifetime
Money back:	Lifetime
Restocking fee:	15%

Computer Gate International
2960 Gordon Ave.
Santa Clara CA 95051

Business hours:	M-F 7:00-5:00 PST
Phone:	408-730-0673, Fax 408-730-0735
Tech support:	408-730-0673
Warranty:	None
Money back:	14 days
Restocking fee:	None

Discount Micro
3430 E. 7800
Suite 107
Salt Lake City UT 84121

Business hours:	M-F 8:00-5:00, Saturday 10:00-3:00 MST
Phone:	800-574-3325, 801-562-4411, Fax 801-562-4456
Tech support:	714-827-7090
Warranty:	One year
Money back:	30 days
Restocking fee:	None

Jade Computers
4901 West Rosecrans Ave.
Hawthorne CA 90251-5046

Business hours:	M-F 7:30-6:00 PST
Phone:	800-421-5500, 310-973-7707, Fax 310-675-2522
Tech support:	800-421-5500
Warranty:	90 days
Money back:	30 days
Restocking fee:	None

MEI/Micro Center
1100 Steelwood Rd.
Columbus OH 43212

Business hours:	M-F 8:00-11:00, Saturday 9:00-7:00 EST
Phone:	800-634-3478, 614-481-4417, Fax 800-614-4867
Tech support:	800-634-3478
Warranty:	Lifetime
Money back:	30 days
Restocking fee:	None

Midwest Micro
6910 US Route 36 E.
Fletcher OH 45326

Business hours:	M-F 9:00-7:00, Saturday 10:00-4:00 EST
Phone:	800-972-8822, 800-328-8855, Fax 800-562-6622
Tech support:	800-243-0313
Warranty:	Varies
Money back:	Varies
Restocking fee:	Varies

Treasure Chest Peripherals
1310 Carroll St.
Kenner LA 70062

Business hours:	M-F 8:00-8:00, Saturday 10:00-4:00 CST
Phone:	800-677-9781, 504-468-2113, Fax 504-461-8095
Tech support:	504-468-2010
Warranty:	Manufacturer's
Money back:	30 days
Restocking fee:	None

Mostly shareware

THERE are some very attractive alternatives to buying costly commercial software. Some other avenues of obtaining free and low-cost software are:

➤ Public domain

➤ Freeware

➤ Shareware

⇨ Public domain software

Public domain (PD) software is a type of software to which the author has renounced all copyright rights. The author has, in effect, donated the software program to the general public to use, free of charge. You are free to do anything you want to with public domain software. You can:

➤ Give copies to your friends and co-workers,

➤ Use it in your home or office,

➤ Change it around any way you wish.

Public domain software is available from numerous bulletin boards, PD/shareware vendors, and telelibraries. Although this may seem to be an ideal source, only a limited number of software programs has been declared to be in the public domain. So, let's consider the next step up in quality and quantity: Freeware.

⇨ Freeware

Freeware is a class of free software in which the author permits anyone to use the program at no cost (you pay a nominal cost for the disks). However, the copyright for the software program is still maintained by the author, principally to retain control over it. You can use it at no cost, but you can't alter the software. There is a large volume of freeware available, much more than is available in the public domain. The next step up in quality and quantity from freeware is shareware.

 # Shareware

Shareware may be best described as "loaned" software. The shareware authors "loan" their software at no cost to you, so you can test and evaluate it for your applications. You can obtain shareware at no cost from bulletin boards, or certain telelibrary vendors, or by purchasing diskettes from shareware vendors (listed below) for the nominal handling cost of from one dollar to three or four dollars per diskette; the fee covers the cost of the diskette, duplication, administrative costs, mailing, etc.

If you determine that the shareware program meets your requirements and you decide to continue to use the program after your evaluation period has expired (typically one to two months), you are then requested to send a nominal "registration fee" to the shareware author. This registration fee can range from a few dollars, to over a hundred dollars for the more complex programs, still a terrific bargain when compared to comparable commercial programs.

This "try before you buy" concept gives you an excellent opportunity to thoroughly evaluate the shareware program in your own computer and test it by performing the specific applications you require of it. Once proven by your evaluation, your registered shareware programs should not end up in your closet as shelfware.

In addition to the software program(s), shareware diskette(s) usually have an ASCII manual stored on the disk, a manual you can print out on your printer. When you decide to keep using the software and register it with the author, you usually receive a printed and often fully illustrated manual, as well as periodic updates as the software is improved, plus additional benefits such as the opportunity to consult with the author. And, very importantly, you'll know that you will be encouraging other software authors to continue to make their creative endeavors available as shareware. Finally, you'll have a clear conscience that you are not pirating software that an author has devoted many, many creative hours developing.

Shareware and the ASP

The Association of Shareware Producers (ASP) is a trade group of professional programmers who have joined together to observe certain standards of programming and support. The primary goals of the ASP are to:

> ➢ Promote the Shareware idea.

> ➢ Establish standards of programming and support for programmers.

> ➢ Set standards for advertising and copyright compliance.

> ➢ Provide a means for Shareware authors to communicate with each other.

> ➢ Help settle any disputes that may arise between author, shareware vendors, and customers.

ASP requires that its members conform to the following standards:

> ➢ Acknowledge the license fees paid by users with a letter or other means.

> ➢ Provide guaranteed support to registered users.

> ➢ Not market trivial software programs.

> ➢ Not market crippled, time-limited, or usage-limited software as Shareware.

> ➢ Treat the customer in a professional manner.

ASP authors are generally designated in the Shareware vendors' catalog listings by the letters ASP after the author's or company's name.

How to obtain software

The major sources for obtaining PD, freeware, and shareware are:

> ➢ Friends and acquaintances

> ➢ Bulletin boards

> Telelibraries

> Commercial shareware vendors

> CD-ROMs

Friends and acquaintances (including computer clubs) are permitted to make copies of PD, freeware, and shareware and give them away. For freeware and shareware, the rules are slightly different. Anyone can give freeware and shareware away as long as the programs are copied in their entirety and not modified in any way.

Telelibraries and bulletin boards can also give away copies of programs under the same restrictions as mentioned in the previous paragraph. Telelibraries and bulletin boards are the best sources if you only need a program or two, or if you are in a hurry to obtain a specific program. Bulletin boards generally have a limited variety of programs; however telelibraries, such as CompuServe and America Online, have very large libraries of PD, freeware, and shareware.

You can obtain this software by downloading it with your modem communications program via the telephone lines. Even though your copy of the software is ostensibly "free," you still may have to pay to access the bulletin board or telelibrary and also pay for the telephone line time required to download the program. If a program takes 30 minutes or so to unload, and it costs fifteen cents a minute, the phone time alone is only $4.50. Still, it's quite a bargain if you're in a hurry.

The best sources of PD, freeware, and shareware, however, are the commercial shareware vendors, some of which are listed below. They have huge libraries of PD, freeware, and shareware; some of the largest have several thousand programs listed. The cost for their disks is nominal, ranging in price from one to three or four dollars. And many of these vendors often archive the programs so they can pack more software on a single disk, thus reducing the cost to you.

Bulletin boards

As mentioned above, one of the key sources for obtaining PD, freeware, and shareware is bulletin boards (BBs). Bulletin boards are

usually not-for-profit enterprises set up to serve two major functions for computer users:

➤ They work as a storage library for PD, freeware, and shareware for distribution to its subscribers.

➤ They are a means for computer users to communicate with each other to ask questions, offer advice, counsel, and receive the latest information on happenings in their fields of interest.

To obtain software from these sources, you need a modem for your computer, plus telecommunication software that allows you to automatically dial up a BBS and download software directly into your computer.

Thousands of bulletin boards are in operation; they are located all around the world. Check with your library or current periodicals for the name, location, telephone number, and the contents of their software libraries. One excellent source which lists many of the bulletin boards in the U.S. is the monthly periodical, Computer Shopper. Another source (although not as up to date) is the diskette titled "National BBS List," available from the Public Software Library and which lists over 7,000 BBSs across the United States.

Online databases

Another excellent source of obtaining PD, freeware, and shareware programs is "online databases," which I prefer to designate by a more appropriate name, "telelibraries" (that is, "libraries located at a distance"). You also need a modem and telecomm software to download PD, freeware, and shareware from telelibraries. Telelibraries are commercially managed enterprises that operate at a profit, so you'll be charged a nominal fee for your online time (and telephone line time) when you query and download software from these vendors. However, telelibraries have enormous and diverse libraries of PD, freeware, and shareware programs. If you contact them and download these programs during their off-hours (usually during night-time and on weekends), connect charges are minimized.

Among the most popular and large volume telelibraries that provide copies of PD, freeware, and shareware are:

➤ CompuServe

➤ GEnie

➤ Prodigy

➤ America Online

These telelibraries, and how to contact them, are covered in more detail in my (Uffdah, another commercial) book *Using Online Scientific & Engineering Databases* listed in the Bibliography.

 # CD-ROMs

Another excellent source of public domain, freeware, and shareware is CD-ROMs. This "library of the future" medium has an enormous storage capacity, at about 640MB and still growing. Several outstanding collections of free or low-cost software have been stored on CD-ROMs and are offered for a very low cost ($20 to $50). Considering the fact that several thousand programs can be stored on a single CD-ROM, the cost per program is less than one cent.

The outstanding software vendor, PC-SIG, for example, has an excellent collection on their CD-ROM titled "PC-SIG Library." The subject matter is divided into specific classes of programs, so it's easy to research and find just what you are looking for. PC-SIG also has a short description of each program to aid in your evaluation.

CD-ROM software is stored in an archived format. The CD-ROM disks usually have the unarchiving program also stored on the disk, so you can unarchive the program and download it to your floppy or hard disk for evaluation.

⇨ How to download from a bulletin board

To make sure that the software you download from a BB or telelibrary is one hundred percent correct, and to compensate for the fact that your telephone line may be noisy and garble the data, all software downloads should be transmitted to you utilizing what is called a "file transfer protocol." This protocol performs an error-checking procedure, which ensures that what you receive at your computer is identical to that which was transmitted by the BBS or telelibrary. Some of the most commonly used protocols are: XModem, YModem, and ZModem.

Most telecomm software programs can accomplish downloads using any of these protocols. Before you download, you have to select a file protocol transfer that you and the vendor have in common. These are often specified by the BBS or telelibrary. My personal preference, if I have a choice, is ZModem.

The specific downloading process may vary from one vendor to the another, but they usually use the same basic procedure. The general process (assuming you're logged on to the vendor) is:

1. Select the SIG (Special Interest Group) forum, or whatever library the vendor stores the specific software you're interested in, e.g.:

   `IBM SIG`

2. Select the protocol you have in common with the vendor. While error-checking protocols are not essential when downloading straight text, they must be used when you're downloading software programs because the loss or garbling of a single character could make the program inoperable. An example of such a protocol:

   `Zmodem`

3. Specify the directory in which you want to store the downloaded program in your own computer. You can use the vendor's file name or assign your own filename and directory.

   `C:\temp\Newfilename`

NOTE

Every computer should have a C:\temp, or similarly named directory for purposes such as this.

Alternatively, if it's a short program you can download it directly on your floppy drive.

4. Select the PD, freeware, or shareware program you want to download, then sit back and relax. The vendor informs you of the progress of the download, then lets you know when it's complete. Then you can log off.

Some telelibraries have simplified and largely automated their downloading procedures. CompuServe, for example, presents a series of easy-to-use menu choices for accomplishing this download. America OnLine has one of the best menus and easy-to-use procedures for downloading software, although their library isn't as extensive as some of the other telelibraries.

The programs listed below are shareware. Only a representative few of the many thousand available shareware programs are listed here. Check with the individual shareware vendors to obtain a copy of their catalog.

⇨ Typical shareware programs

Here is a brief listing of some typical shareware programs along with their descriptions.

❊ **4 Print**   Creates a variety of different print formats for documentation and text files. For example, you can use it to operate on a DOS file and print it as a book that can be stapled in the center. It can automatically make a DOS file into a landscape printed file, and print on the left and right sides of the page.

❊ **BackREM**   Reminds you when it's time to do a backup (every so many days), then does the backup. You can go ahead with the backup or postpone it.

❊ **BAKtrack**   Performs both partial and full backups. Maintains an index on your hard disk or backup diskettes. After making a full backup, daily

backups are fast and easy since BAKtrack keeps track of which files have been changed or added since the last backup, and backs up only those files.

✳ **Burn-In**   A program for conducting a burn-in for your PC. It runs complete and exhaustive tests, exercises and diagnoses your disk drives, CPU, display and drive, RAM, etc. It logs any errors.

✳ **DAAG (Disk At A Glance)**   Gives you a graphical picture of how your hard drives are being used. It uses a tree structure to illustrate all of your directories and subdirectories. A pie chart illustrates what percentage of the disk space each directory is using. This is very informative and lets you check to see if some of your files (your graphics or word processing files) are occupying too large a portion of your drives. If so, maybe you can offload some of the files you don't use too often onto floppy disks to make more room available on your hard disk.

✳ **Envision Publisher**   This outstanding full-featured desktop publishing program is comparable to PageMaker and Ventura Publisher, with professional features such as true WYSIWYG capability, a superb graphical user interface, and state-of-the-art fonts scalable from a tiny 4 points to a huge 108 point size. Envision Publisher provides an impressive array of drawing tools for lines, rectangles, circles, ellipses, polygons, curves and more.

You can import text and PCX files and utilize all page and document features such as style sheets, cut and paste, justification, master pages, full text block and column control, and more—the kind of features available only in professional packages costing hundreds of dollars. Comprehensive printer support works with virtually any laser, dot-matrix, inkjet, and PostScript printer. It supports Hercules, CGA, EGA, and VGA, and requires 450K, graphics, and a hard disk. Mouse support is provided, but not required.

✳ **ImagePrint**   Produces letter-quality printing on your 9- or 24-pin dot matrix printer. Prints the IBM extended character set—mathematical symbols, national characters, and graphics characters.

✳ **InfoPlus**   An excellent utility for finding information about your system. Eight screens of detailed data about every aspect of your computer, such as machine type, CMOS, CPU, RAM, serial/parallel ports, etc. This gives you an excellent education about your PC.

❋ **List**   Throw away your DOS "Type" command and replace it with this all-time favorite program that lists your files on the screen for reading, browsing, searching. Wild cards may be used. It also views compressed archive files. It's a must for every computer.

❋ **LQ Print Utility**   Provides near-letter-quality printing for Epson FX series 9-pin dot matrix printers. Font characters are 10×24 dots. Also includes BIGPRINT for printing banners.

❋ **PC Write**   A word processor with many features comparable to many commercial programs. Includes cut and paste, headers and footers, automatic page numbering, spell checking, multiple column layout, support of foreign language characters, plus much more.

❋ **Read My Disk**   Recovers ASCII data from a floppy or hard disk that has been severely damaged.

❋ **SafePack**   Optimizes your hard disk by defragmenting your files so each file occupies a single, contiguous block of disk space.

❋ **Slim**   Compresses files on disk to about half their original size and still allows them to be run, read, printed, etc.

❋ **What's In That Box?**   This program is highly recommended, it provides you a look inside a typical PC, shows where components are installed and explains what the various components accomplish. This one should be viewed on a color display.

⇨ Important shareware addresses

Here are some vendor addresses to ease your forays into the software market.

⇨ United States

Association of Shareware Professionals (ASP)
545 Grover Road
Muskegon, MI 49442
FAX 616-788-2765

CompuServe PPN: 70007,3536

Discount Micro
10881-B Portal
Los Alamitos, CA 90720
1-800-364-2725
(An excellent and huge selection of software.)

PC-SIG
1030-D East Duane Avenue
Sunnyvale, CA 94086
Orders 800-245-6717 Ask for Operator 2228
Information 408-730-9291
FAX orders 408-730-2107

PSL (Public Software Lab)
P.O. Box 35705
Houston, TX 77235-5705
Orders: 800-2424-PSL
Info/Help 713-524-6394
FAX orders 713-524-6398

Public Brand Software
P.O. Box 51315
Indianapolis, IN 46251
Orders 800-426-3475
Information 317-856-7571
FAX orders 317-856-2086
(An excellent selection of quality programs.)

Quantum Technologies
10985 Pinehigh Drive
Alpharetta, GA 30201
(404) 664-1097
(They bundle sets of archived shareware; the result is shareware for about a dollar a program.)

Reasonable Solutions
1221 Disk Drive
Medford, OR 97501-6639
Orders 800-876-3475
Information 503-776-5777
FAX orders 503-773-7803
(A very good, but limited, selection.)

The Software Labs
3767 Overland Avenue, Suite 112
Los Angeles, CA 90034
Orders 800-359-9998
Information 310-559-5456
FAX orders 310-559-3405
(A choice selection of software.)

Canada

Advance Computing
P.O. Box 2, Stn. M
Toronto, Ontario
M6S 4T2

Alternative Personal Software
269 Springside Drive Suite C-2
Hamilton, Ontario
L9B 1P8

Desktop Magic
931 Pensacola Way S.E.
Calgary, Alberta
T2A 2G8

ESCO Electronics
Box 2258
Pincher Creek, Alberta
T0K 1W0

Interface Software & Systems
P.O. Box 329
Cookston, Ontario
L0L 1L0

West Hill Sales
P.O. Box 304
West Hill, Ontario
M1E 4R8

The United Kingdom

College Shareware UK
Dept PCW12
The College Business Centre
Uttoxeter New Road
Derby DE3 3WZ

JD Computers Ltd Shareware
Cromer House
1 Caxton Way
Stevenage, Herts SG1 2DF

Needforward Ltd
52 Pennsylvania Avenue
Hesters Way
Cheltenham GL51 7JP

Premium Software
24 Station Road
Barton Halsall
Nr. Ormskirk
Lancs L39 7JN

SMS Shareware
19 Carshalton Road
Camberley
Surrey GU154AQ

Germany

Computer Solutions GmbH
Postfach 22 12 53
8000 München 22
Germany

Computer-Electronik-Erkins
Eythstr. 16-18
500 Köln 91
Germany

Kirschbaum Software GmbH
Kronau 15
8091 Emmering
Germany

Redysoft Software GmbH
Postfach 12 61
8150 Holzkirchen
Germany

Soft-Mail AG
Postfach 30
7701 Büsingen
Germany

Preventive maintenance

ALTHOUGH your PC was designed to have a long life, if you give it some preventive maintenance (some TLC from time to time) it will be more likely to function well on through its twilight years. Here are some simple things you can do to extend the lives of all of your major components.

❊ **CD-ROM discs**   Fingerprints are anathema to CD-ROM discs; a single print can wipe out thousands of bytes. Handle the discs carefully by their edges. Dirt and dust can also clobber the data, so keep your CD-ROM discs in a closed container, like the plastic carrier they came in or in a caddy. If you do accidentally leave your prints on the underside (I speak from experience), or if they have become contaminated, cleaning kits are available to remove the contaminants. The cleaning kit consists of a liquid that is to be deposited on four spots on the disc, plus individual pads for removing any dirt or debris that has accumulated.

❊ **Cleaning your PC's innards**   Dirt and dust are also going to collect inside your PC's chassis. Your fan is constantly pulling air in from the outside and passing this dust-laden air over your components. Some dust is bound to settle and stay inside. You should open your PC case every few months (or sooner if you're in a dusty atmosphere) and use a portable vacuum or a soft paintbrush to clean it out.

❊ **Dot matrix printer**   Although the dot matrix printer is one of the most reliable electro-mechanical devices you will have (it should last a few years with average use), it also needs a little TLC to extend its life as long as possible. For a smooth carriage ride, wipe the carriage off with a dry rag and apply a little 3-in-One oil or sewing machine oil (don't use WD-40 or TV tuner lubricant; they leave a residue that could wipe out your printer). With respect to tractor feed: paper is heavy, so don't ask your tractor feed to pull it all the way up from the floor. Put the paper-supply box on a shelf under your printer.

If you note that you are getting horizontal lines across your paper, try cleaning your print head. If your print head is especially dirty, remove it. It's not that difficult to do; just remove the two screws holding the print head in place and lift it up. Put some VCR head cleaning solution on a foam swab or a fine elastic sponge. Don't use a cotton swab, paper towel, or similar fibrous material because you could damage the printing wires. Rub the swab gently to dislodge surface

residue; place a drop of the solution on the pins and let the drop run down the pins' tubes to dissolve ink buildup. Finally, when the print head is dry, apply a drop of very light oil (the type used in watch repair) and let it run down the shafts of the pins to lubricate them.

Above all, don't forget to read your printer manual if you're puzzled about its operation. One self-test available on most printers is to hold in the LF (Line Feed) button while you turn power on to the printer. It will usually run a test program and print all of its printable characters available with different fonts.

✳ **Floppy disk drives**   Your floppy drives are also exposed to the atmosphere constantly and are susceptible not only to ambient dust and dirt, but also magnetic oxide from the disks which builds up on the heads (the magnetic heads must physically contact the disk medium in order to read and write information). You can purchase a disk cleaning kit from any computer store, or even from Sears or WalMart. A cleaning kit consists of a special cleaning disk and a fluid to apply to the disk. To use it, put a few drops of the fluid on the disk, put the disk in your drive, then access that drive. You'll get a "General Failure Reading Drive A: Abort, Retry, or Fail" message. Just keep hitting R for Retry until your disk has been exposed to the cleaning fluid for about 30 seconds or so. Then wait about 5 minutes before using the drive, to let the cleaning solution evaporate.

✳ **Laser printer**   If you get a low toner message, replace it immediately. Some printers actually count pages to let you know when it's time to change toner; others give you a low toner message. One emergency fix is to lightly tap the toner cartridge; you may squeeze a few hundred more pages out of it. If you get white or blank areas on your page, double-check the toner first.

If you see a dark line running along the length of the page, you might have a scratch on your drum. Unfortunately there isn't an easy solution to this problem; you need a new drum.

Use the copy paper recommended by the manufacturer. Don't use embossed stationery. Use only labels recommended for the printer. Don't use envelopes that contain clasps, rubber grommets, or string; they might scratch the drum. Use your laser printer as recommended and it will serve you well.

333

✳ **Mouse** Another component susceptible to room dust and dirt is the mouse. If you find your screen cursor jumping erratically when you move your mouse, it's time for a mouse cleansing. Twist the bottom mouse cover off and remove the rubber ball. Wipe the rubber ball off with denatured alcohol and do the same for the contacts inside. Let it dry for a couple of minutes; your mouse should then scurry around like a cartoon character.

Glossary

64-bit architecture A computer that handles chunks of data in 64-bit blocks. 32-bits are used in the 386/486.

abort The procedure for terminating a program when a mistake, malfunction, or error occurs.

abstract A brief summary of an article, book, report. Lists author, title, publisher, and date of publishing.

access time The average amount of time required to obtain a byte from memory or disk drive.

acoustic coupler A device for connecting a computer with a telephone for use with a modem for telecommunicating.

adapter An add-on card that is installed in an expansion slot.

a.k.a. "Also known as," denoting an alias or synonym.

aliasing Assigning a longer detailed command to a short set of keystrokes, similar to macro assigning a different letter (e.g., D:)

to create a partition on a physically existing disk (C:) so D: acts like a separate disk.

alphanumeric characters Character set containing letters, numbers and other special symbols, e.g., punctuation marks.

ambiguous filename Filename containing either the ? or * DOS wildcard character.

ampersand A symbol for the word "and" which looks like &.

analog voltage A continuous voltage that varies in amplitude, the magnitude of which is proportional to the effect that caused it.

AND A Boolean operator. A AND B provides an output only if both A and B are present.

application program Program written to enable the computer to perform useful work, such as a Word Processing Program.

archived files The process of using an algorithm to encode the pattern of frequently repeated letters, words, or pixels to compress data to occupy less space.

ascenders Lowercase characters that extend above the height of the x letter, such as b, f, and k.

ASCII American Standard Code for Information Interchange. A standard used for all communication to represent letters, numbers, and symbols as bit patterns. ASCII files can be read by practically all software.

aspect ratio The ratio of the height-to-width on a display screen or other device.

AT command set The Hayes command set, an industry standard for modem communication.

ATM Adobe Type Manager. A font utility used by Windows and OS/2 which produces WYSIWYG screen fonts and for non-PostScript printers, printer fonts. Competitive with True Type.

autodial A modem feature that lets the computer automatically dial a prerecorded phone number for connection to a host computer.

AUTOEXEC.BAT The configuration file which DOS executes every time it is booted up.

backing up Making copies of files for use in case original data is lost or damaged.

baud rate A technical term applied to the rate at which data is transmitted over telephone lines. In most cases, baud is almost the same as bits per second.

bay A slot of open space reserved for floppy, hard, and other types of drives.

Bernoulli drive The Bernoulli drive uses a cartridge that contains two flexible plastic disks coated with a magnetically sensitive alloy.

bezel A front panel covering for a blank drive bay.

binary A numbering system based on 2. Two numbers, 1 and 0, represent all possible mathematical values.

BIOS Basic Input/Output System. Instructions used by the computer to control fundamental operations, such as bootup.

bis French for revision, used with CCITT standards. Thus V.32bis is a revision of the V.32 standard.

bit Abbreviation for a binary digit, either a 1 or 0 character.

bit map The contents of a graphics data structure where a bit or byte represents each pixel.

bit rate Speed at which bits are transmitted over a communication link.

Boolean algebra Math for expressing logical relationships between truth values, using AND, OR, and NOT logical operators.

boot The process by which a computer turns itself on, literally lifting itself by its own bootstraps.

bps Bits per second. The speed at which data are transmitted.

BULL Bjelland's Upgrade Logistic Law. "As soon as it is plugged in, it's obsolete."

bulletin board A system consisting of a computer and modem with appropriate software which makes available messages over public phone lines at no charge.

bus mouse A type of mouse that requires a special plug-in card to be installed in your PC.

byte Smallest addressable unit of storage, usually eight bits long, an alphanumeric character is one byte.

cache A temporary storage place for data that is most likely to be repeatedly accessed.

cartridge font A hard font permanently recorded on ROM memory of a cartridge. The cartridge is inserted into the cartridge slot of a laser printer.

CCITT The French initials for the International Consultative Committee for Telephony and Telegraphy, an international body that governs international telecommunications data comm standards.

CGA Color Graphics Adapter. A low/medium resolution color graphics system for PCs.

chip An integrated circuit, such as that used for computer memory or a CPU.

click The process of pressing a mouse button once.

clip To chop a graphic to fit into a given window or viewport.

clock doubling When the CPU runs internally at twice the speed of the memory system/motherboard.

clock speed The rate at which the microprocessor in a computer operates.

cluster A group of continuous sectors on a disk; a sector is the smallest unit of allocation for files on a disk.

COM port A COMmunications port; an interface on the computer that is used for transferring information to another piece of equipment, such as a printer or modem. COM1 and COM2 are the most commonly used.

CONFIG.SYS The file which DOS executes every time to set up certain characteristics of your computer or to control additional devices connected to your computer.

controller A device, usually a plug-in card, which controls/drives a given peripheral.

coprocessor An additional microprocessor chip or circuit board, efficient at performing floating point calculations that supplements the regular CPU in a computer.

CPU Central Processor Unit. The main processor used in your PC.

CRT Cathode Ray Tube. The picture tube in your display or TV set.

cursor A short line or other symbol on your monitor that indicates where the next character will be input and displayed.

database A collection of interrelated data that can be accessed by computer.

database vendor A company or organization that markets online data bases.

data bit One of the seven (or eight) bits that makes up the code for an alphanumeric or nonprinting character.

data bus width The number of paths used to convey data inside a PC, they range from 8 to 16 to 32 and 64 (so far).

data compression A process that uses an algorithm to encode the pattern of frequently repeated letters, words or pixels to compress data to occupy less space.

daughterboard A printed circuit board that plugs into a motherboard.

DB-25 connector A 25-pin connector used for an RS-232-C serial interface.

de-archiving The reverse process of archiving, i.e., returning the archived data to its original form.

default A preset value used by a computer until it is specifically changed by the user.

descenders Lowercase characters which extend below the baseline, e.g., g, j, and p.

device A piece of hardware attached to a computer (usually a peripheral), such as a printer or a mouse.

device driver A special program that controls a hardware device or operation. Device drivers are usually loaded with a DEVICE=directive via the CONFIG.SYS file.

digitizer A device that converts analog data into digital data.

DIP switches DIP is an acronym for Dual Inline Package. DIP switches are small switches in a printed circuit board that allow setting certain hardware options.

directory A place on a disk where filenames are stored so DOS can find the files when needed.

disk cache See cache.

disk density Density indicates how closely magnetic information can be stored on a disk. The most common disk types are double- and high-density disks. Double-density disks store 360K (5¼" disk) or 720K (3½" disk) of data while high-density disks store up to 1.2MB (5¼") or 1.44MB (3½") of information.

display driver A program created to control a display.

dither Mixing a new hue by placing different-colored pixels next to one another.

DOS Disk Operating System. A specialized, disk-oriented program that provides an easy-to-use link between the user and the computer's disk drive.

dot matrix printer A printer in which each character is represented by a pattern of dots and imprinted on paper.

dot size A measure of the resolution of the smallest component of a displayed or printed element.

double click The process of rapidly pressing a mouse button twice.

downloading The process of retrieving information from a distant computer, loading, and storing it into your own. Opposite of uploading.

drag The process of pressing down a mouse button and while still holding down the mouse button, moving the mouse to highlight text or move objects.

DRAM Dynamic RAM. Typical form of RAM used in PCs.

DR DOS A competitive operating system to MS-DOS created and marketed by Digital Research.

DSDD Double Sided Double Density disks.

DSSD Double Sided Single Density disks.

duplex A communications system that can transmit in both directions.

EGA Enhanced Color Graphics Adapter. A medium resolution color system for PCs.

electronic mail a.k.a. E-Mail. A service that lets you send messages to other users on the same on-line system.

ellipsis In printing, a symbol (. . .) used to indicate that something has been left out of a phrase or sentence.

EMS Expanded Memory System. Additional RAM to provide more working space for applications programs.

ESDI Enhanced Small Device Interface. An interface standard developed by manufacturers for connecting a hard disk to a computer.

FAT File Allocation Table. FAT is a list maintained in DOS of all clusters on a disk. It includes their locations and records whether they are available, bad, or in use by a file. It also records the order in which clusters link to make a specific file.

fax machine Also facsimile machine. A device that scans documents, transmits them over phone lines and recreates them at the other end.

file A collection of related records treated as a basic unit of storage.

filename and filename extension The name assigned to a file; it can be 1 through 8 characters with an optional file extension of 1 through 3 letters. A period (.) separates the filename from the extension.

firmware Programs that are stored in a computer's read-only memory (ROM), such as BIOS.

floppy disk Thin, flexible, magnetic disk for storing digital data. Available in three sizes: 8, 5.25, and 3.5 inches.

floptical drive Floptical uses a hybrid of magnetic-floppy disk and optical disk techniques. It utilizes magnetic technology to store data and optical technology to locate it.

flush Even with margins. For example, for flush right all characters line up vertically at the right hand margin.

font A set of printable letters and characters with common typeface, size, weight, style, and orientation. Includes uppercase, lowercase, numerals, punctuation marks, etc.

font scaling The process by which an outline of a font is used to scale the font to a specific point size (e.g., 10 points).

footer Text automatically printed at the bottom of several pages.

formatting The process of preparing a disk so it can store data to a specific format.

freeware A special class of shareware in which the software is free, however the author has retained the copyright on the program.

full duplex Simultaneous, independent transmission of data in both directions on the same line.

full height Vertical space taken up by an internal device, such as a disk drive, usually 1½ inches.

gigabyte One thousand megabytes, 10^9 bytes.

GUI Graphical User Interface. The use of visual aids or icons, usually with pull-down menus, to control a computer and its programs.

half duplex The transmission of data in only one direction at a time on the same line.

half-height The height occupied by an internally mounted peripheral, such as a disk drive, usually 1 inch.

hard card A hard disk on a plug-in card.

hard copy Computer output printed on paper.

hard disk A rigid storage disk capable of storing much more data than floppies and which can be accessed in much less time.

hard font A type of printer font permanently written into ROM.

hardware The physical components or equipment that make up a computer system.

Hayes compatible Modems that use commands originated by Hayes Microcomputer Products. Hayes compatibility is not an absolute requirement but is a de facto industry standard.

head That part of a disk drive that records data on a medium and reads it back.

header Text automatically printed at the top of several pages.

header or heading Title or caption at the head of a chapter, section, column, list, table, or illustration.

hertz (Hz) Frequency in cycles per second.

high level format A formatting procedure invoked by the DOS FORMAT command. Creates the File Allocation Table and Root Directory on a hard or floppy disk.

host computer A computer that primarily provides services such as database access.

icon A graphic (picture) used to represent an object or idea.

IDE Integrated Digital Electronics. A type of disk drive in which the electronics are sealed in the same container as the electro-mechanical components.

inkjet printer An output device that prints by spraying a thin stream of ink onto the paper.

interface The point at which two systems interact, it can be a physical interface involving a connector or a logical interface involving software.

internal command A DOS command that is frequently used, so it usually is stored in RAM.

I/O Abbreviation for Input/Output.

jumper A short wire which shorts two contacts together.

K Abbreviation for Kilo or 1000 in decimal notation, i.e., 100K means 100,000.

kerning Adjusting the amount of space between characters to eliminate unsightly gaps so that a line of text looks better.

LAN Local Area Network. A communication system that connects several computers together so they may communicate with each other and share data and resources (such as a laser printer and a hard disk).

laser printer A high speed, nonimpact, quality printer in which a laser "writes" on a drum and prints alphanumerics, graphics, and special fonts.

leading Vertical space between lines of type, measured in points.

LED Light Emitting Diode. A solid state element that lights when voltage is applied, used as an indicator.

log off The process of terminating communication between a computer and a user.

log on The process of establishing and verifying the authority to communicate between a user and a computer.

low level format The basic formatting procedure that divides up tracks on the disk surface into sectors.

low profile The height occupied by an internally mounted peripheral, such as a disk drive, about one inch.

macro A special preprogrammed series of instructions initiated by activating specific key combinations.

magneto-optical Magneto-optical (a.k.a. Optical or MO) drives use a laser beam to write data to, and read it from, a plastic disk.

math coprocessor A group of circuits on a chip that speed-up handling of floating-point math operations.

megabyte (MB) A measure of computer memory, disk space, etc. Equal to 1,024K or about 175,000 words.

menu A list of available functions for selection by an operator.

MFM Modified Frequency Modulation. Recording technique formerly used for hard drives.

MNP Microcomm Networking Protocol. A series of methods of reliable error correction during transmission, especially for high-speed modems.

modem A contraction of Modulator/Demodulator. The interface box or card that converts a signal into two different frequencies so that it may be transmitted over telephone lines and which also performs the reverse function, converting the signal on the phone lines to ones which can be handled by a computer. The modem converts the computer's 1s and 0s into two musical tones that whistle down the telephone line and are turned back into 1s and 0s at the receiving end.

monochrome display A display that presents information in only one color. Monochrome displays generally have black backgrounds with white, amber, or green letters.

motherboard The main, large printed circuit board which serves as the mother, giving sustenance to all the other circuitry. It contains the CPU, the plug-ins, system RAM, etc.

MPC Multimedia PC. A standard for multimedia for the PC.

MS-DOS A DOS program created by Microsoft Corporation, includes both DOS 4.1 and DOS 5.

MTBF Mean Time Between Failures. A measure of the reliability and life time of a component or system.

multiscanning The ability to scan over a wide range of operating frequencies.

nanosecond (ns) One thousandth of a microsecond, 10^{-9} seconds.

NLQ Near Letter Quality. Pertains to output of some dot matrix printers where the quality approaches the quality of a daisy wheel or laser printer.

NT New Technology. A designation for the latest version of Microsoft's Windows GUI system.

online The state in which a computer is connected via modem to another computer.

online database A computer system that a user can dial into through the public telephone network with or without first paying a fee.

operating system A set of software programs that translates the user's commands and allows application and other programs to be entered with the computer's hardware. DOS (Disk Operating System) and Windows are operating systems.

optical mouse A mouse that uses light instead of the conventional ball-roller-point setup of the mechanical mouse.

OR A Boolean logical operator that indicates that the presence of either one or both terms provides an output. A OR B means that either or both A or B will provide an output. Also called "Inclusive OR." However, an "exclusive OR" gives an output only if A OR B, but not both, is present.

OS/2 An alternative operating system (to Windows).

overdrive A double chip series that doubles the speed of the internal operations of a CPU.

palette A fixed selection of colors available on a graphics screen.

parallel port A plug-in location used to connect parallel devices, such as printers.

parity A setting for an error-checking bit during transmission of data, can be odd or even.

password A special word or code that must be presented to a computer system to gain access to its resources.

PC Abbreviation for personal computer.

PC-DOS a.k.a. DOS 3.3, an operating system used on IBM computers.

PCL Printer Control Language. The software standard used by Hewlett-Packard printers. PCL5 includes support for scalable fonts.

PDL The generic abbreviation for Page Description Language or Page Definition Language.

PD Public Domain. Software in which the author has renounced all copyright rights.

pel Picture element. Generally the same as pixel, but may refer only to elements you can manipulate.

Pentium A high-speed Intel CPU chip.

peripheral An external device connected to a computer, such as a printer or modem.

pixel The smallest dot on a video screen, a contraction of "picture element." On a color monitor screen, each pixel is made up of one or more triads.

point size A standard unit of linear measurement, equal to $\frac{1}{12}$ of a PICA, or about $\frac{1}{72}$ of an inch.

port A jack where you can plug in cables to connect other computer equipment.

PostScript A device-independent language, meaning it can drive a 300 dpi laser printer as well as a 2,000 dpi typesetter.

PostScript font A font that is compatible with PostScript, a programming language developed by Adobe Systems.

ppm Pages Per Minute. An output rate of printers.

PROM Programmable Read-Only Memory. A memory chip that is preprogrammed with data.

prompt A symbol that appears on the video screen asking you to enter information, typically > or] is used.

protocol A set of rules for transmitting data between computers to detect and correct errors that occur during transmission.

RAM Random Access Memory. Storage in which data can be input and read out independent of its location in memory; that is, it can be randomly accessed. RAM is normally "volatile," that is, it loses memory when power is turned off.

raster The scan pattern created on a CRT as the beam sweeps horizontally and vertically across the face of the CRT.

rasterize To convert a mathematical function to a fixed pattern of pixels tailored to the resolution of a particular screen or output device.

resident font Font permanently written into ROM and stored in a printer.

resolution The number of elements (pixels on a CRT) that exist within a given dimension (often ppi, pixels per inch).

RISC Reduced Instruction Set Chip. A special type of microprocessor that speeds up processing by reducing the number of operations required of the chip.

ROM Read Only Memory. Static memory that cannot be changed by conventional procedures. Retains memory contents with power on or off.

root directory The main directory that DOS creates on a disk when the disk is formatted.

RS-232C The standard established by the Electronic Industries Association for serial transmission of data for telecommunications.

sans serif Without serifs, e.g., Helvetica. See serifs.

SCSI Small Computer System Interface. Pronounced scuzzy. A systems level interface used with many controllers to connect a computer to a hard drive. As many as seven devices can be daisy-chained to a single SCSI host adapter.

sector A section of track on a magnetic disk.

seek time The average time for the read/write heads of a memory drive device to move from one track to another track.

serial mouse A mouse which connects to a serial port (usually on the back of your PC).

serial port A plug-in location into which a serial operated device, such as a mouse, is plugged.

serif A tiny counterstroke that runs approximately perpendicular to the main stroke of a character, e.g., Times. Serifs help move the eye from letter to letter.

shareware A method of marketing software where customers purchase a copy of the program to test, then are requested to send in a registration fee if they decide to keep using the program.

SIMM Single Inline Memory Module. A specific packaging configuration of memory chips soldered onto a small plug-in board.

SIP or SIPP Single Inline Pin Package. A type of integrated circuit containing a single row of contact pins.

soft copy A copy of written material that is stored in digital form on a diskette or other storage media. A printer converts soft copy to hard copy.

soft fonts A font located on a floppy or hard disk. The font is loaded into a laser's RAM.

software Nonhardware component of computers, the "music" that makes computers play.

SSDD Single Sided Double Density.

SSSD Single Sided Single Density.

style Vertical slant of the font, e.g., normal (upright) or italic (oblique).

SVGA Super VGA. A very high resolution color display system.

system prompt The display on the screen which shows you that the operating system is ready to receive a command.

telecomm Telecommunications. Communications over a distance.

telelibrary A library located at a distance, such as an online database.

terminal A device that can send and receive information from a computer.

terminal emulation When a terminal is online to another system, the computer is in a terminal mode and emulates a specific terminal operation.

transfer rate The maximum rate at which information can be passed between a drive and the computer per second.

true color A color display mode that shows 16.7 million separate colors, more than are discernible by the human eye.

True Type A standard font used by a rapidly expanding library of scalable screen and printer fonts, used by Windows.

TSR Terminate and Stay Resident. A program that leaves some of its code in the computer's memory when you exit the program and return to the DOS command prompt. Makes it easy to re-activate the program when you are using a different program.

turbo A mode in PCs in which the computer performs faster than normal.

typeface A collection of fonts with a common appearance, but different point sizes, styles and weights, e.g., Courier.

Uffdah A unique word from the Norwegian language which serves in place of such overworked and trite expostulations as "You don't say!" "Well, I'll be!" "You'll never believe it!" Must be capitalized. It is also the name of the gentleman's farm the author lives on.

upgrade A word which brings joy to the heart of the author of this book. The process of installing new hardware or software in a PC.

uploading Sending information to a distant computer from your own. Opposite of downloading.

VDU Visual Display Unit. Monitor or TV display.

VGA Video Graphics Adapter. A high-resolution color system for PCs.

VRAM Video RAM. A type of RAM that is better suited for video applications.

virus A program whose sole nefarious purpose is to surreptitiously invade computers and modify the data stored on them, usually destructively.

weight The thickness of the characters.

Windows A specific icon-based graphical user interface, also used as a generic term for GUI systems.

WYSIWYG What You See Is What You Get, pronounced wizzywig. The characteristics of a display in which the presentation on the screen is the same as the presentation on paper when it is printed.

ZIF socket Zero Insertion Force socket that provides a built-in lever to ease the extraction and insertion of chips.

zoom Enlargement of portion of a display or image.

Bibliography

Bjelland, Harley; *Using Online Scientific and Engineering Databases*, McGraw Hill 1992.

Bjelland, Harley; *Online Systems: How to Access and Use Computer Data Bases: A Guide to Electronic Information Sources for Health Care Professionals*, Practice Management Information Corporation 1992.

LaPlante, Phil; *Easy PC Maintenance and Repair*, Windcrest/McGraw Hill 1992.

Pilgrim, Aubrey; *Build Your Own Low Cost PC and Save a Bundle*, Windcrest/McGraw Hill 1993.

Pilgrim, Aubrey; *Build Your Own 386/386SX Compatible and Save a Bundle*, Windcrest/McGraw Hill 1992.

Schueller, Ulrich and Veddeler, Hans-Georg; *Upgrading & Maintaining Your PC*, Abacus Books 1992

Index

About the author

Harley Bjelland is a full-time, freelance author who has had eleven books published so far and is constantly at work on others. He lives with his wife and helper Dorrie (a.k.a. Tokiko) on a 20-acre farm in the country outside of the small village of Erskine, Minnesota. A private lake borders their farm and they enjoy feeding and observing the many wild deer, pheasants, and birds of various hues and classes whom they have unofficially adopted.

After working as a degreed engineer for twenty-five years, Harley opted to work alone with only the honks of geese rather than the honks of cars to disturb his concentration. Working with two IBM compatibles and a Macintosh, he said he is having almost as much fun as he did when raising five kids through the turbulent seventies. Fortunately they all turned out well. One son is a judge, one son is an attorney, one daughter is a quality engineer, one is an accountant, and the youngest daughter is a computer software marketer. Uffdah! That was quite a ride through the seventies!

Harley's writing specialties are books about computers and writing. He feels that many basic principles of engineering, science, and math can be directly applied to writing, and reflects this in his books. He also believes that technical books are much too serious and need a dose of humor to liven them up. His hobbies are reading, ballroom dancing (with his wife, of course), and bicycling.